# Religious Education

The role of religious education in secondary schools is the subject of national and international debate. This book examines the current debates surrounding religious education and puts forward a new approach to teaching the subject that is non-faith based and focused on conceptual enquiry and the development of a clear pedagogy. The book is based on the Living Difference learning model developed in Hampshire and adopted in other parts of the UK, which is sparking international discussion and provides an effective approach to implementing the new secondary curriculum.

The chapters include examinations of:

- religious education and the curriculum;
- an interdisciplinary approach to religious education;
- the significance of pedagogy and learners' development;
- planning, progression, assessment and delivery;
- specific case studies and examples of good practice in schools;
- theoretical grounding and the future of religious education;
- the effects of globalisation, postmodernity and multiculturalism.

Providing a basis for developing thinking about religious education, its place in the curriculum and how it can be delivered effectively in schools, this book is essential reading for tutors, students and teachers.

**Clive Erricker** was until recently Hampshire County Inspector for Religious Education and History Strategy Manager. Prior to that he was a Lecturer in Religious Education at University College Chichester for over a decade. He began his career teaching English and religious education in secondary schools.

# Religious Education

A conceptual and interdisciplinary
approach for secondary level

**Clive Erricker**

 Routledge
Taylor & Francis Group

LONDON AND NEW YORK

First published 2010
by Routledge
2 Park Square, Milton Park, Abingdon, Oxon, OX14 4RN

Simultaneously published in the USA and Canada
by Routledge
270 Madison Avenue, New York, NY 10016

*Routledge is an imprint of the Taylor & Francis Group, an informa business*

Typeset in Bembo by Keystroke, Tettenhall, Wolverhampton
Printed and bound in Great Britain by MPG Books Group

*British Library Cataloguing in Publication Data*
A catalogue record for this book is available from the British Library

*Library of Congress Cataloging-in-Publication Data*
Erricker, Clive.
  Religious education : a conceptual and interdisciplinary approach for secondary level /
Clive Erricker. — 1st ed.
      p. cm.
  1. Religious education. I. Title.
  BL42.E76 2010
  200.71′2—dc22                                                    2009037339

ISBN10: 0–415–47873–1 (hbk)
ISBN10: 0–415–47874–X (pbk)
ISBN10: 0–203–85554–X (ebk)

ISBN13: 978–0–415–47873–1 (hbk)

To Jane, for any number of reasons

# Contents

# Figures

# Preface

This book is the product of over thirty years of being involved in education and religious education in different roles, as a classroom teacher, manager, lecturer and inspector/adviser. During that time the predominant model for RE has been a world religions approach initially influenced by Ninian Smart and related to the religious studies approach that emerged in higher education during the 1960s. However, despite the research, theory and projects which have been undertaken in the ensuing period up to the present, the way the subject has been taught in the secondary classroom has changed little during this time. What are the reasons for this?

This book analyses why this should be the case. It proposes that RE as a study of world religions has lacked a sufficient pedagogy, it has not been sufficiently concerned with changes in learning and teaching and educational theory in general, no sufficient connection has been made between research and theory in RE and classroom practice, it has failed to establish itself as a discipline and it has failed to establish sufficient principles upon which to base the connection between the development of students and the subject matter of religion.

As a result, at the heart of this study is the attempt to rectify these deficiencies in the classroom. This depends on establishing a methodological approach to conceptual development and the implementation of interdisciplinarity. In regard to both of these I have sought to ensure clear practical examples are provided based on what teachers have achieved within Hampshire schools. In 2004 Hampshire launched a new Agreed Syllabus, *Living Difference*, on the basis of which we sought to address the insufficiencies referred to above. In the ensuing years the Living Difference project has been one in which we have tried to develop and refine the delivery of religious education, its pedagogy, with these in mind. Part 2 of this book, 'Living Difference: an approach through conceptual enquiry', is a record of that and the progress made.

Part 1 of the book, 'Contextualising religious education', provides the background and analysis of religion, education and religious education in relation to changes over time; particularly it seeks to show how these need to be understood in the context of a changing world. It presents a number of current approaches to RE that offer different theoretical insights and some attempts to put these into practice.

Part 3 of the book, 'The future for education and religious education', builds on this background and argues for the contribution of RE to worldviews analysis (more than just an understanding of religious traditions), which focuses on the way in which worldviews impact on the world (their practical effects) and the need for students to engage with that. It also sets out ways in which RE can be an important contributor to interdisciplinary education.

Interdisciplinary is used in two distinct ways in this book. First, it refers to how religious studies as an academic subject draws on a number of different disciplines. It is an inter-disciplinary endeavour. Therefore, I argue, religious education, in order to be considered a discipline, needs to be interdisciplinary in the sense that it draws on different disciplines for its academic purpose. The second way in which interdisciplinary is used is to present ways in which RE can combine with other disciplines (for example art, science, history, etc.) to create more effective student development. This is exemplified in Chapter 9 and to some degree in Chapter 8.

For too long RE has sought to establish its curriculum credentials by arguing that it is a unique subject because it deals with a special aspect of life – the positive representation of religion. At the same time it has sought to argue its relevance to student development through the values religions promote and the cultivation of empathy. Whilst religions can be positive forces they can also be the opposite. Whilst we can find important values statements and teachings in religious sources, scriptures and religious practices are not always concerned with that. I hope this book will provide a practical basis, as well as a theoretical and pedagogic justification, on which teachers can approach the subject differently and make it wholly relevant to the development of young people, as its foremost aim.

Clive Erricker
Quiberon, 1 September 2009

# Acknowledgements

Acknowledgements are due to:

- Hampshire County Council, Hampshire SACRE and Hampshire teachers, especially those whose work I have cited or quoted in this book and those who contributed to the work of the county and regional secondary development groups. Any works included that were previously published by Hampshire County Council are under its copyright and are included with its permission, by licensed agreement.

- Further work produced by Rebecca Costambeys and Penny Morgan, Hampshire's Secondary RE ASTs, referenced in this book. Also to other members of the Hampshire RE County Development Group, regional RE development groups, and to the Hampshire History Steering Group, who informed the history references in this text.

- Katherine Wedell for permission to include parts of her report in Chapter 4.

- Lat Blaylock for permission to include aspects of his published work on Aung San Suu Kyi in Chapter 6.

- The Dean and Chapter of Chichester Cathedral and Judges Postcards Ltd, Hastings (www.judges.co.uk), to reproduce by kind permission 'The face of Christ' (detail) (Figure 7.1) and 'The raising of Lazarus' (Figure 7.2).

- My particular thanks to Judith Lowndes my primary RE colleague in Hampshire, Lydia Revett, the Hampshire RE Centre Manager, and Linda and Katherine, my support officers, for their professionalism, enthusiasm, humour and support.

- Thanks too to Geoff Teece of the University of Birmingham for his enthusiasm for this project.

# Contextualising religious education

## 1

# Religion and education in the modern world

## Introduction

The purpose of this chapter is to provide a summary of some of the major contextualising features that surround and impose themselves on the teaching of religious education today. In the sections that follow I have tried to provide a progressive 'map' of those features giving some historical information, some contemporary commentary and some informed opinions and judgements to help us make sense of the situation we are in if we concern ourselves with teaching RE. The aim, by the end of this chapter, is to reflect on what the present purpose of the subject should be, before embarking, in Chapter 2, on a more focused study of religious education and then, in Chapter 3, on some of the influential approaches that have been and are being undertaken. In brief we need to find our own starting point.

## The historical context and the present situation

Since the European Enlightenment there has always been the 'religious question' in that, as the Western nations developed and secularised, at the same time, religion persisted despite the sometimes secular constitutions put in place. By this I mean that the course of history, unlike before that time, was not dominated either by religious questions or religious groups. Consider the demise of metaphysics in philosophy, the rise of scientific method as the means to knowledge, the disappearance of any form of religious cosmology and the significant impact of the theory of evolution (and the recent controversies over creationism and intelligent design). To be sure, however, religion has persisted. It has a significant influence within the democracy of the United States and is still institutionally influential in Europe; for example through the Church of England and the Lutheran and Calvinist legacies in the north and the Roman Catholic persistence in the south. The latter also still has an international appeal. But, in particular, the 'religious question' has been more one of its accommodation than its previous dominance: a shift from power to varying degrees of influence. Blasphemy, whilst still on the statute books in the UK, was not taken so seriously. When Monty Python's *Life of Brian* was accused of just this offence it was, for the majority of the population, a source of amusement.

All that has changed. With the end of the Cold War, the demise of the Soviet structure, the bringing down of both the Iron Curtain and the Berlin Wall, the deposition of the Shah with the Iranian Revolution and subsequent events in the Middle East, Iraq and Afghanistan, globalisation has brought religion firmly back on the agenda. This is not just due to the rise of militant, fundamentalist Islam. As the Communist threat disappeared, so free-market economics boomed. The bringing down of barriers to freedom and democracy also resulted in the erasure of barriers to capitalism and the possibility of economic exploitation, of wealth and markets in new countries. As a result politics in the West has moved to the right, and this has had a concomitant effect on religion; its influential movements are now right wing. One example is the rise of the evangelical Christian influence in the United States. Their pro-life and anti-abortion stance has had a significant influence on the debate in this area, as has the influence of the Catholic Church. Similarly homosexual issues have come to the fore in the Episcopalian world, with the election of a homosexual bishop in New Hampshire and the subsequent protests by the African wing of that fraternity and the ceding of diocesan groups in the US to take up African pastoral leadership as a result – a phenomenon beyond conception only ten years ago. The gender issue, the right of women to be leaders in the church, has been attacked with renewed vigour.

Further afield, blasphemy as a serious indictment returned to our shores with the fatwah on Salman Rushdie. This was not condemned by other religious groups; nor indeed was the extraordinarily fierce Muslim reaction to the Danish cartoons or the violence of Sikhs at the showing of a Birmingham play, involving rape in a Gurdwara, by a female Sikh playwright, which caused the play to be closed. Honour killings regularly appear in our newspapers – the latest, at the time of writing, being the case of 17-year-old Basra student Rand Abdel-Qader in Iraq, who spoke with and came to know an English soldier, became infatuated with him and, as a result, was killed by her father, Abder-Qader Ali, with the help of her brothers. In an article in the *Observer* newspaper her father was interviewed and said, 'Death was the least she deserved . . . I don't regret it . . . and know what she did was unacceptable to any Muslim that honours his religion' (Sarhan and Davies 2008: 8). On the same page the paper carries a rider, in an accompanying article, that says honour killings are not sanctioned by Islam and they were born out of tribal culture. We shall come back to this tricky religious-cultural conundrum later. Suffice it to say, at this point, that the father cited Islam as an authoritative reason for his action, that he received support from police and friends and that the accompanying article is not polemically opposed in its approach, consistent with responses to the former events cited. What exactly is going on that we wish to refrain at all costs from criticising religion per se, except when we can siphon off 'extremists' or 'tribal groups' who can be said not to represent the true face of their religion but the face of 'terrorism' or 'tribal culture' instead? Contrastingly, back in 1996, the religious studies scholar John Bowker had stated, somewhat prophetically at the time, that:

> For years I have been pointing out that religions are likely to destroy human life as we know it now on this planet. Religions contribute to virtually all the intransigent and seemingly insoluble conflicts in the world.

> (Bowker 1996: 3)

It was on this basis that Bowker thought religions should be taught in religious education. He received little or no support from the RE community although his views were in some respects to be echoed by the scientist Richard Dawkins later.

This is introducing us to the dilemmas of postmodernity: a time in which modernity (the idea of progress) wrestles with the continued presence of the pre-modern (for example tribal cultures and fundamentalisms) and postmodernist criticisms (critics of the project of modernity itself with its over-arching grand narrative).

There is an historical dimension to all this and we need to recall it in order to understand the place of religion, and, often, the protection of it in the way it is represented in society (through the media and religious bodies) and in education, in the recent past and the present. In the period from the Second World War until the 1990s the United Kingdom went through a period of change that was significantly influenced by three factors: immigration from former colonies for those with UK passports; a substantial increase in the number of students who went on to higher education; and a progressive liberalism, most prevalent in the middle decades of that age and declining toward the end. During this period the policy of multiculturalism became a defining factor.

## Migration and multiculturalism

Migration to the United Kingdom is nothing new. In particular the area around what was the London docks, Whitechapel and Brick Lane has seen several waves of immigrants, Jews, Huguenots and Bangladeshis prominent among them, and areas like Southall have experienced a demographic change that totally altered it from white working class, in the main, to becoming a veritable 'little India'. To experience this to the full, go there at the time of the Sikh celebration of Baisakhi, when rented BMWs are driven up and down the main streets and the noise of the horns fills the night air as young men seek recognition from Indian girls walking the pavements (accompanied by older female members of the families in many cases, it must be said). Other urban manufacturing areas similarly acquired new ethnic populations in the Midlands and North West especially. Typically migrant communities initially seek to preserve what they have brought with them: from cultural habits and states of mind, to language and the recreation of a tribal geography that reflects the past situation. The multiculturalist policy of this period sought to embrace a sense of diversity in society and in schools as a new form of cultural wealth. The anti-racist policy of the time set out to highlight discrimination, oppose the 'racist' discourse and champion the cause of minorities. These policies were very different in type. Religious education tended to house itself within the former. This was partly because 'anti-racist' educators were concerned about 'racism' not religion. It was also because religious education needed to project a message that made it more prominent, useful and yet less controversial in the curriculum. For 'anti-racist' educators there was a progressive political battle to be fought and religion was not a progressive force.

RE had already embarked upon its most notable curriculum change. In 1944 (the Butler Act) religious education was still avowedly confessional. It was presumed that it was the vehicle for teaching Christianity to the progeny of a Christian population. This was also reflected in higher education in which religion was taught on theological degrees centred on Christianity. It was not until 1964 that the first Religious Studies degree, in its own right, was started at Lancaster University, the initiator being Ninian Smart, the first professor in the subject heading the first department of that name. The liberal tendency of that time brought about an interest in other worldviews and travel to other cultures, the hippy trail of the late 1960s and early 1970s. The mirage that we were shaking off the past and creating a new and quite different 'brotherly' or 'sisterly' future was beguiling and abounded in a new burgeoning student generation, partly precipitated by the reforms of the Wilson government and the initiation of the Open University. Religious studies found its niche within this. This mood was not about discovering new doctrines but one of replacing old doctrines with a doctrineless future. Of itself this had nothing to do with the parallel phenomenon of post-colonial immigration. It had, perhaps, more to do with the évènements of Paris in 1968. But the two events served each other well as far as the study of world religions in schools, as it came to be known, was concerned and, like all ill-fitting conflations of purpose, it resulted in confused policy and practice. (Were we teaching the religious views of an increasingly multicultural society or were we introducing children to a new, and potentially limitless, world of ideas? As we shall see later, these are not the same thing.) For example, the emerging teacher graduates did not reflect the new ethnic and religious population of England and Wales in their number, but often sought to represent them in the curriculum. But it did put world religions on the map. With graduates emerging from increasing numbers of Religious Studies degrees and with pupils in urban schools from immigrant families whose religion was other than Christian (Muslim, Hindu or Sikh most typically), the curriculum swung toward the teaching of religions rather than just Christianity. This was not uniform of course; the shire counties moved more slowly on the whole than urban populations and church schools more slowly still. Jack Priestley (2006: 1001–1017) points to the first break in the mould being the Birmingham Agreed Syllabus in 1975, which included five religions and created controversy. It followed on from the criticisms in the Ramsey Report, *The Fourth R* (Ramsey 1970). Priestley quotes Adrian Bell as saying that the latter 'constituted a "minor revolution" for RE within the curriculum, one that was based upon what the report called "educational criteria" rather than on any position of unique privilege' (Priestley 2006: 1012; Bell 1985: 190). Priestley adds that it was another decade or two before the more rural areas 'started to feel that multiculturalism was their problem too' (Priestley 2006: 1015). The significant thing about this progressively sweeping change was that it took no notice of the law in place at that time. It wasn't until the Education Reform Act of 1988 that the law acknowledged the need to teach the principal faiths in Great Britain, but with Christianity restored to a place of most significance.

That RE had turned into a different animal, in terms of the revision of syllabuses and the representation of religions, there was no doubt. Its connection to immigration is also clear from the case of the Birmingham syllabus, as is its connection to multiculturalism: the ideas of tolerance, acceptance and even respect for the beliefs and cultures of others (we shall return to the idea of 'others' again). This happened well in advance of any comparative issues elsewhere in Europe: for example, the Turkish guestworkers in Germany and the Parisian turmoils at the turn of the twentieth century and into the early twenty-first.

For some teachers of religious education, however, it was not the idea of multiculturalism that inspired them so much as the desire to infuse pupils with the emancipatory delights of delving into these worldviews and exploring such diverse ideas. It was a freedom of the mind from both secularity and institutional religion; they weren't necessarily teaching the religion on the ground but exploring different ways of understanding the world in their heads. This tension between different utilities of the subject, and the tension between Christianity as religious and cultural heritage, and the overall purpose of learning other faiths and how broad that curriculum should be, remained and remains still. Whilst the purpose of the subject had changed from a confessional one to something else more 'educational', there remained a sense of not knowing exactly what that educational justification was. There was a sense that a big battle had been won, so there wasn't a sense that further battles had to be fought at that time. From 1975 until now RE has largely been understood in the same terms by the broad populous of the RE world. Significant undercurrents emanating from university departments have sought to move it on and these will be returned to in the chapter on pedagogy, but the consensus that it was about the representation of religions has largely remained, within a framework of multi-culturalism. And yet that framework and the religions themselves are now under pressure to change from without (government policy on modernisation and integration) and under pressure of fragmentation from within (in RE terms, who or what groups are being represented within a religion; in terms of the religion itself, which groups are representing that religion and to whom).

The commitment to multiculturalism is a broad-based one that goes across the mainstream political spectrum. Witness the political suicide note of Enoch Powell in his 'Rivers of Blood' speech which warned against allowing immigration to Britain. This was before RE woke up to the need to teach beyond the Christian hinterland. By virtue of that speech, honest and authentic and prophetic in tone as it may have been, he denied himself any chance of high office in the Tory party. If we examine why, we have to consider the question of political expediency and policy. What Powell said was a gift to the racist right and the spectre of fascism (not so far in the past historically). In a much smaller way the present Archbishop of Canterbury did something similar when he said consideration of shari'ah law should be on the agenda within the British legal system in 2008. It was later acknowledged that the intelligence and reasoning of his intellectual argument was simply not considered by the response from the popular press. Right or wrong, in either case the consensus needs to be carried and controlled amongst the people; cohesion must be supported. This helps to explain, of course, the quite different reaction to wearing symbolic religious objects and dress in secularist France: ban it publically. Different histories and different constitutions and different discourse. France is a country where rights are more fundamentally embedded but not in relation to religion: historically a threat to the state post revolution. In Britain multiculturalism has long been the position du jour and religion has been protected by the state. In both countries, however, there is an overarching issue that needs to be attended to in present times, that of identity. This is most obviously presented in Pierre Nora's monumental work *Les Lieux de mémoire* (Nora 1984–1992), which is assessed in Tony Judt's *Reappraisals: Reflections on the Forgotten Twentieth Century* (Judt 2008: 196–218). Nora is referring to what creates the collective memory of national identity: Frenchness, and, we could say by transference, Britishness. There is a new debate on these matters, given the changes that have ensued over the last half-century and more particularly since the twenty-first century began, the movement to the right politically, the influence of globalisation in its many respects, which we can now investigate (especially post 9/11), concerning God, religion and democracy on the imprint of identity. This will influence how we approach education and religious education in particular.

## God, religion and democracy

A particular feature of the tensions between religion and democratic societies has been reflection on whether religion is a positive or negative influence. This has come to the fore since the events concerning militant Islam: New York, Madrid, London, Iraq and Afghanistan in particular. Commenting on monotheism, the religious heritage of the West, Regis Debray remarked:

> Concerning monotheism, everything has been said – and its opposite. That it is a humanism and a form of barbarism. A liberation and a plague. The cure for our malaise and a substitute neurosis. A kind of operatic duet, with alternating voices has been composed on this theme. I choose not to get involved in that particular confrontation . . . Let it be noted that the thesis and the antithesis can simultaneously be true: the divine pharmacy, like every other, has its ambivalence. *Pharmakos*, as is well known, means both elixir and poison. No need to break swords, once again, over a familiar theme.
>
> (Debray 2004: 4)

Debray, former colleague of Che Guevara (though also a critic of his fatal Bolivian expedition) and writer of the report on religion and culture in French schools (Debray 2002), is here expressing his view on the debate on religion that broke out in the early years of the twenty-first century in Europe. Pharmakon is a concept derived from Plato and revisited by the philosopher Derrida in 'Plato's Pharmacy' (Derrida 1981). The point being made, in postmodern fashion, is that what can be a power for good can also be a cause of evil: elixir and poison. It is a point that can be regarded as self-evident or preposterous dependent on your view of truth, amongst other things. Such a point of view will, necessarily, lead to heated debate; thus, in the context of whether belief in God is good for democracy, we do still 'break swords' and exchange opinions.

However, Debray introduces us to the complexity of the subject we teach, its contradictions and its ironies. We ignore these at our peril if we seek to be sufficient teachers and want our students to be sufficient learners. Too often, teachers inherit a received wisdom about the principles that lie behind teaching religion and this wisdom is always value laden, with a tendency to lopsidedness, in the direction of affirming religion's value rather than being also its critic. This does a disservice to our students which results in them treating the subject with either disinterest or, worse, disdain. I sympathise with them. The complexity of the subject runs deep. For example, at the time of writing the Babylon exhibition at the British Museum tells us much about the achievements of that civilisation and yet if you read the Jewish chronicles this is entirely absent: it is a place of exile and pagan belief. As the psalm says:

> By the rivers of Babylon, there we sat down
> and there we wept when we remembered Zion.
>     (Psalm 137, verse 1, *The New English Bible*)

Additionally, Nebuchadnezzar was painted in such a negative light because he oppressed the children of God, and the Tower of Babel speaks for itself as the icon of depravity.

The point is this, that from one perspective we can celebrate an ancient civilisation; from another we can observe the downfall of a tyrant at the hands of a righteous God. Even the capital 'G' reveals the preference. You cannot view history simply through the historical tribal perceptions of a particular group, in this case Jews. Yet, you can't believe in the Judeo-Christian God without accepting the divine's involvement in the world for the sake of, ultimately, its salvation. You cannot be a believer without that completely altering your judgements on the way the world is, was, should be and will be, on the basis that authorship and destiny lies elsewhere than just in our hands. In short you read history differently and, necessarily, in a partisan fashion. So how are you going to teach this subject? How would the historian? How would the scientist? The story of Jesus (as the Christ?) raises the same issues of interpretation, significance and judgement. Added to this we know that believers do not all believe in the same way. The reading of a text in an historical, geographical and cultural context 3,000, 2,000 or 1,000 years ago provides a different type of reading than one we find it possible to make today. Or, contrastingly, for some – fundamentalists and literalists certainly, but others too – the reading of a text that is regarded as sacred, because authored by God, cannot be changed over time, or even (in Islam) by translation from its original language. And its message remains the same regardless of history. Inevitably, believers disagree amongst themselves, believers of different faiths disagree with others, and those of no religious faith disagree again. The layers of disagreement are complex. We haven't yet taken account of the contemporary reader, the students in the teacher's class, and their enculturations. Nor have we taken account of the complexity of this globally, let alone locally. At the heart of all this are ideas of truth, existential ideas of meaning and purpose that humans hold and hermeneutics (theories of interpretation). If this sounds all too much then be prepared for a surprise in the classroom. Students will soon ask the unanswerable questions. Also, how you take this complexity on board, in the role of teacher, will determine what questions you think are askable. The more superficial your reasoning in relation to the complexity of the subject the fewer questions you will allow your students to ask, since you will narrow the parameters, and make shallower the depth of enquiry you are prepared to allow. There is nothing more off-putting for a student than to come up with a genuine question only to be told it is not a permissible question because it is outside the boundaries of enquiry you are willing to allow. At its worst the subject stops allowing enquiry at all and consists of the teacher telling 'facts' to avoid controversy. That is not education. The most common ways of doing religious education badly are to sanitise it, fudge it, moralise it.

The existentialist philosopher John-Paul Sartre commented that 'Events take place in one direction, and we tell about them in the opposite direction' (Sartre 1971: 57). This is certainly true of religions. A text is not created simply by writing an account of what happened and a canon is not the result of simply putting such texts in chronological order. Debray speaks of this as putting memory before history, by which he means creating a composite myth of identity rather than compiling an historical record. The monotheism of the Jews was predated by a henotheism in which Yahweh, the 'jealous' God, was chosen in preference over others. Monotheism, the idea that there is only one God, the others being false gods, emerges only after the Babylonian exile (Debray 2004: 26–28). But this is not the message of the canon, subsequently composed and compiled. This is why, Debray continues, 'every episode of Scripture (whose composition is spread over seven or eight centuries) speaks the language of the century in which it was written, not that of the time in which it is alleged to have taken place' (Debray 2004: 29). This is the territory of myth in which a communal identity over time and a progression of that identity are constructed. The power of this is self-evident when one turns to the Holocaust event and the rhetoric involved in the founding of the state of Israel. But this is not history. If, therefore, we are aware of how historically false such literature is, why do we not reject its powerful mythical constructions, especially when they are defended as 'true', 'sacred' and so forth?

Amongst other things we have to return to the human desire for meaning and purpose. It is a contradiction to say that we evolved as a species through the chance mutations of the evolutionary process, which has no respect for such desires, and yet we find ourselves needing to reflect on such significant existential questions. In part, at least, religions provide answers to these, therefore they have a significant function. Whether or not that function is ultimately meaningless is another question but we can recognise the significance of the phenomenon: their other functions aside, they are means of salvation. And depending which end of the equation you start from – an existential or a scientific one (or for some whether you are able to mix the two) – they become logical or illogical as a result. Squaring this particularly problematic circle is, in itself, the problem that creates the complexity. The issues concerning evolution and creationism and abortion and euthanasia are cases in point.

The question of whether modern democracies need God revealed some diverse responses in an *Observer* newspaper article. In the *Observer* newspaper, Review section, on 30 September 2007, we read, on page 9, the heading 'Is God democratic?' Various replies follow this:

> What a question . . . Of course God is not democratic; if he is, exactly how long is a heavenly term of office? (Mark Thomas)

> Since this question is so meaningless to me, I'll pretend that what you asked was, "Is there a place for God in a democracy?" One of the cornerstones of the democratic process is that discussion should be rational and that the bases upon which decisions are reached should be accessible to everyone. Religious beliefs do not fall into that category. (Brian Eno)

> If God stands for tolerance, compassion, the equality of all mankind and moral accountability, then this is all in keeping with the democratic ideal. (Riz Ahmed)

> God is above democracy. From a Muslim point of view, it is imperative that we take God out of politics. (Ed Husain)

> All deeply held faith has the capacity to be anti-democratic, because it places the supposed laws of God against the real laws of free men and women. (Nick Cohen)

> (*Observer*, 30 September 2007, Review: 9)

In the same newspaper on the same day (in the television guide preview of a BBC2 programme to be shown on 1 October: *Inside a Shari'ah Court: This World*) we read that 'More than 40% of Britain's Muslims want Shari'ah law implemented in the UK' rather than democratic rule, and that 'Shari'ah law is already practiced informally . . . to resolve Islamic divorce, inheritance and family disputes' (*Observer*, 30 September 2007, Television Guide: 6).

Out of the above exchange of views, and the reported observation on shari'ah law in Britain, come tensions that some would wish to confront and others to contain: that of religious influence in a democratic state. Different questions could follow. We might ask 'Does God serve democracy?' or 'Does democracy serve God?' The distinction between the questions is quite fundamental because it entails which takes precedence: democracy or God? One can view the above responses with these differing questions in mind and arrive at some nuanced conclusions in relation to how each responds. In general respects I would suggest that the democracy-first responses are more dogmatic and the others somewhat apologetic in this respect (see responses of Ahmed and Husain above). In turn, I suggest this tells us something about how religious adherents who wish to affirm democracy view their place in a democratic environment.

We might ask a different question again: 'Whose God is good for whom, if any?' This, again, is a question of a more nuanced instrumental kind. Here the emphasis is placed on distinguishing different sorts of Gods or differing interpretations of God that believers espouse. In other words, to put it bluntly, it depends on how fundamentalist the interpretation of God is.

Philip Pullman offers a perspective on this that enlarges the God question to an ideological one in the context of affirming the imperative of democracy:

> The real difference between theocracies and democracies is that the former don't know how to read.
> (Pullman 2004: 156)

Pullman's point is not what it might first seem. Theocracy does not imply God as such, but ideological regimes that exercise totalitarian control and thus prevent differing democratic 'readings' of the world and society. They are characterised by a scripture whose word is inerrant, prophets and doctors of the Church who interpret the holy book and pronounce on its meaning, the concept of heresy, a secret police force with the powers of an inquisition, a teleological view of history toward millennial fulfilment, a fear and hatred of external unbelievers, a fear and hatred of internal demons and witches (Pullman 2004: 157).

This characterisation, Pullman argues, is as consistent with a regime such as the Stalinist Soviet Union as it is with Khomeini's Iran. 'It isn't belief in God that causes the problem . . . the trouble with the way theocracies read is that they have a narrow idea of what literature is' (Pullman 2004: 158–159). Or, to put it another way, in their desire to control truth they are antipathetic and hostile to the world of ideas. Theocracies, to use Pullman's term, refuse to acknowledge the pharmakonic qualities of world and language.

However, God has a long history of proximity to theocratic activity dressed up in the rhetoric of antidemocratic truth. From the taking of the Promised Land to the silencing of Galileo and the denial of gay rights; in one form or another, fatwahs abound and enter the collective memory, either nourishing or fragmenting it. The liberal believers' antidote to this, acting from within, is to call upon the wisdom and sant traditions to rectify affairs. But, from the authors of Ecclesiastes and the Song of Songs, and from Rumi and Guru Nanak to contemporary liberation and non-realist theologies, this is a history of reaction to institutionalised authority rather than the reverse. It is not surprising, then, that for unbelievers there is a wariness concerning God's involvement in social affairs. Democracies fear the totalitarian instincts of movements susceptible to the ideological manipulation of social policy, structures and practices.

## Secularity

Secularity is not just a fact in the popular imagination of the European world; it is a mood or disposition. Terence Copley (Copley 2005), for one, has railed against it and its influence on RE (we shall return to Copley later, in Chapter 3). Arguments to the contrary, such as, for example, citing the number of religious faiths prevalent in Britain, need to take account of the 2001 census, in which no religious faith adherence, Christianity aside, was registered in more than single-figure percentage points. Christianity, it is true, registered 71 per cent, but, given falling church attendances and the general lack of interest in religious affairs in the country, it is hard to take such a percentage figure seriously as a register of committed adherents and believers. It is, we might say, a default position based on cultural heritage and the lack of inclination for people to describe themselves as atheist by conviction or even agnostic. However, we should not underestimate the power of cultural adherence; as Constantine and Eusebius showed, it can fashion an empire and inspire a sense of identity between nationhood or state and religious motivation. The Church of England might be seen as the natural heir to that.

However, the phenomenon of secularisation has been well documented sociologically as a public event, even if writers like David Hay can point to correspondence that suggests individuals do recall and have recorded experiences of a private nature that could be labelled religious or at least spiritual. Indeed he conjectures that the public mood of secularity may be a reason why they have not been more vociferous in making their experiences public (Hay 1987).

Secularity has emboldened critics of religion, as have the attacks made by Muslim fundamentalists on democratic countries. Most obviously, Richard Dawkins has spoken out in this respect in *The God Delusion* (Dawkins 2006) and Christopher Hitchens in *God Is Not Great* (Hitchens 2007). Dawkins remarks, quoting Robert M. Pirsig in *Zen and the Art of Motorcycle Maintenance*:

> When one person suffers from a delusion it is called insanity. When many people suffer from a delusion it is called Religion.
>
> (Dawkins 2006: 5)

However, we must question what is meant here by 'delusion'. For Dawkins a delusion is based on a lack of scientific evidence for an understanding of reality, which leads to a false 'reality' being constructed on other grounds that conflict with scientific understandings. In itself, this explanation could serve as the premise for the tensions between science and religion and secularity and religion. The point is that 'delusion' becomes a scientifically framed condition. From an Islamic perspective, by contrast, 'delusion' amounts to the equivalent of 'shirk', a forgetting of one's true nature as a creature of Allah. So one must be careful about the use of terms and the way definitions apply. The thrust of Dawkins' argument relies upon science's claims, not just in terms of 'facts' it presents but in terms of what follows from cumulative evidence and the implications for a worldview that follow. Most significantly, for Dawkins, the most important feature of scientific claims against religion is based on the scientific theory of evolution and the evidence that supports it. An aspect of this lies in the geologist Lyell's presentation of the age of the earth based on his research in the nineteenth century. The conflict with creationist claims in this respect could not be greater. With regard to the question of who is right there really isn't a feasible argument from a creationist perspective to put against Lyell's scientific research, especially when that is contextualised within further scientific research into the age of the universe. Therefore there seems little doubt that creationist dating based on biblical sources is as delusory as belief that the earth is flat. But that is not the entire point. We might characterise the contours of this debate as follows:

- Creationists of the literal and fundamentalist variety are not the only representatives of religion.

- Science, if it discounts other questions to do with a species obsessed with meaning and purpose, is legitimising its territory beyond its own remit.

- Religion, as a construct largely invented by the West in the nineteenth century, does not consist of 'delusions' of the same kind and for the same reasons across its variety. Consider the teachings of the Buddha and other sages, for example, who do not concern themselves with the same questions, in many cases, as monotheists (albeit Dawkins is concerned only with monotheism in his book).

- Delusion, from a scientific perspective, can only be claimed where there is direct conflict with scientific evidence of a reliable kind. Thus, it can be said, certain 'religious' questions still exist which do not contravene scientific injunction.

- Ideologies other than religions exist which cannot claim scientific bases. Does this make them delusory also – for example Marxism – or do they stand or fall by their achievements?

- If the test of a movement or ideology were its successfulness in making people happy or prosperous, then to what extent would a scientific judgement of 'delusion' be an appropriate one?

- Finally, if science offers us the extent of the answers we can regard as reliable and that leaves us, through theories such as natural selection, with unsatisfactory ones such as randomness and contingency, what are we to do with the rest of our questions? In other words, do we tend to be more concerned with satisfying our questions than with accommodating ourselves to unsatisfactory scientific answers?

Taking account of all of these points does not leave us with any conclusions but may help to explain why religion has persistence in the face of science and why 'delusion' is easily translated into 'truth' for those who seek a different principle and method to affirm our 'reality' from those offered by modern science.

It is worth noticing also that insanity is only acted upon when an individual acts in contravention of a social and moral code. That is when they get institutionalised as unfit to be in society; the same could be said to apply to those motivated by religion or any other ideology. 'Delusion' can be a therapeutically helpful state in a world of uncertainty, and the more uncertainty pertains maybe the greater the value of the 'delusion'. It can be a source of hope and comfort within hopeless circumstances.

What really disturbs Dawkins is the hegemony that religion still has in various areas of life. Its persistence still gives it power, or at least influence. For example, he comments on children and indoctrination:

> If you feel trapped in the religion of your upbringing, it would be worth asking yourself how this came about. The answer is usually some form of childhood indoctrination. If you are religious at all it is overwhelmingly probable that your religion is that of your parents. If you were born in Arkansas and you think Christianity is true and Islam false, knowing full well that you would think the opposite if you had been born in Afghanistan, you are the victim of childhood indoctrination. *Mulatis mutandis* if you were born in Afghanistan.
>
> (Dawkins 2006: 3)

> I want everybody to flinch whenever we hear a phrase such as 'Catholic child' or 'Muslim child'. Speak of 'a child of Catholic parents' if you like . . . but children are too young to know where they stand on such issues.
>
> (Dawkins 2006: 3)

It is true that Dawkins overstates his case by his generalisations and righteous anger. To be brought up within a prevalent faith is an indoctrination of sorts but the issue lies in the type of upbringing rather than its context, religious or not. Indoctrination abounds wherever you are. Pedagogical messages exist in all media from family conversation through to television advertisements and roadside hoardings, especially in societies where a free-market ideology is rampant. Indoctrination of a forceful kind is as prevalent in countries with atheist ideologies as it is in religious ones – consider China under Mao. Indeed any sense of leadership with vision is perforce indoctrinatory by virtue of being such; this is certainly true of schools that were founded by visionary educationalists. What I see Dawkins railing against is what comes to the fore in the second quotation. Children need to be educated to make up their own mind and develop their own beliefs and values. Thus, indoctrination is that state of affairs within which this is not allowed to happen. Pace Pullman, democracies should be societies in which children are given access to the world of ideas and not brought up to have closed minds – but this can apply in societies where there is or is not religious influence. What Dawkins has in mind is typified by the experience described by Hirsi Ali concerning her upbringing, which resulted in an arranged marriage organised by her father to a 'clan' member living in Canada. To avoid this she left her flight to Canada and sought asylum in Holland, where she made a new life, but estranged from her family. There are two statements she makes that are highly significant in the context of this debate:

> I knew that another kind of life was possible. I had read about it, and now I could see it, smell it in the air around me: the kind of life I had always wanted, with a real education, a real job, a real

marriage. I wanted to make my own decisions. I wanted to become a person, an individual, with a life of my own.

(Ali 2007: 187)

And later she remarks:

By declaring our Prophet infallible and not permitting ourselves to question him, we Muslims had set up a static tyranny. The Prophet Muhammad attempted to legislate every aspect of life. By adhering to his rules of what is permitted and what is forbidden, we Muslims suppressed the freedom to think for ourselves and to act as we chose. We froze the moral outlook of billions of people into the mind-set of the Arab desert in the seventh century. We were not just servants of Allah, we were slaves.

(Ali 2007: 271–272)

Hirsi Ali had found a new world in the West, leading to her rejecting the values of her upbringing on the basis of the new values she had found, which were liberating for her.

Her opinions reflect the values and aspirations of her new context, one that had come through and established itself on the basis of the European Enlightenment. Does that make her judgement correct? Maybe yes and maybe no, but what it enabled her to do was identify, in intellectual terms, what was not felt to be appropriate in her previous socialisation within Islam in Somalia, Kenya and Saudi Arabia, where her previous experiences occurred. To what extent can we generalise her comments?

One thing is clear: her disaffection with her experience of upbringing disposed her to embrace a new philosophy that empowered her. Critics of both her and Dawkins portray them as Enlightenment fundamentalists. What is the significance of this judgement? Its significance lies, at least in part, in its relation to the idea of tolerance. If we are willing to tolerate views which show a great deal of disparity, then, one could argue, that will create a better democratic environment. Nevertheless, this does mitigate against the Enlightenment project's idea that humankind can best create a human society by throwing off its older, unscientific, superstitions (religion of course coming into this category). Thus we have a profound tension. When religion is tolerant it tends to be left alone; when it becomes militant and fundamentalist the democratic cracks show. Problems are exacerbated when religions promote stasis on the basis of truth (found in scripture), since this is contrary to Enlightenment notions of progress. Pragmatically, however, attempts to promote secularity on the basis of Enlightenment ideas have always been countered by a significantly influential religious minority. When religion and culture has not been through the European Enlightenment experience or has reacted against it, problems arise. Thus Hirsi Ali speaks out in a Dutch immigrant situation of which this feature forms a part in relation to Islam. Immigrants to the West from non-European countries do not have the same cultural and religious history of ideas. We also find it with Catholic doctrine, an obvious opponent of Enlightenment philosophy. Interestingly, opposition also manifests itself in the United States from Protestant religious groups with a fundamentalist character. Since you cannot take a democracy forward without winning votes, eventually pragmatism and tolerance become major factors in the face of the persistence of religion. However, should the Enlightenment project founder entirely it is difficult to see how democracy could persist. There lies the conundrum and the reason why it is important to note the voices of those like Dawkins and Hirsi Ali.

## Western education

Western educational systems are implicitly secular, in some cases more overtly so than in others. The existence of the type of religious education in the English and Welsh system is unusual. Although religious education exists in other systems it tends to be related to religious nurture. In Germany, for example, it will be Lutheran or Catholic. In Australia curricula will be devised by the faiths themselves and taught by adherents of the faith. In England and Wales, in mainstream or state schools without a religious foundation this will not be so. To point out something of the practical implication of this, I was involved in joint teaching of an RE module by video conferencing with Hanover University in Germany. In one session it was explained to us that no religious symbols could be displayed or used in a classroom. However, there was a cross exhibited on the wall. In asking about this we were told that Christian symbols were permissible, and usual. In my class of students one woman was a Muslim who wore a hijab. She faced the camera and we asked whether she could teach RE dressed as she was. The answer was no. Thus, we can see something of the underlying issues that still pertain to the teaching of RE in different countries and how those issues are quite distinct from the teaching of other subjects.

The idea of secularity underpins approaches to subjects such as science and history, by default. Scientific or historical method and evidence are based on empirical research. There can be no place for religious forms of epistemology. Other subjects, similarly, have no recourse to the designs, claims and outcomes that could be associated with religious doctrine, as an aspect of pedagogical intent or expectation. This is so even if you are engaged with events or literature within which religious motivation plays a part: the Crusades or Milton's poetry, for example. In religious education, even in a non-indoctrinatory system, this does not apply in the same way. Taking an historical view of the development of education in the West provides us with an understanding of why RE so often finds itself out of step with the rest of the curriculum:

> In the early 19th Century the religious-classical tradition was confronted with a scientific challenge . . . Enthusiasts for educational reform, accepting the millennial promises of science, saw it as the means of effecting progress in education in two ways: by basing the curriculum on the sciences, and by a reconceptualization of teaching as a scientific activity.
>
> (Bowen 1981: 328)

In this period three different approaches to education existed. Supporters of natural theology, which believed science would confirm theological belief in the earth as an expression of divine order; opponents who rejected theological ideas and were mechanistic and materialist in approach; and those who advocated an organic understanding of the earth as a world divinely ordained, an emerging holistic approach that included Pestalozzi and Froebel were among these. But scientists were loath to allow theological speculation to interfere with empirical and sensory observation. The sense-empiricist approach was also pursued in educational learning theory by John Locke. It was scientific education that won out over time, though debated in many forms. The Pestallozi and Froebel influence remains in independent schools but has not penetrated the 'common' school or the arrival of mass education. As a result it is not surprising that religious education is seen as not fitting this educational venture, even if, in the model operating now in England and Wales (since the 1970s), it does not seek to nurture in a religion. The legacy of difference and the desire to embed education as scientific and based on empirical investigation do not lend themselves to absorbing religion in a way meaningful to such an enterprise. Therefore, however much we might complain at misunderstanding education in religion, it is a perceived misfit in this pedagogical design. I shall return later to the pedagogical insufficiencies of the subject, which have not helped matters, due to the subject having a strong tradition of instructional catechesis.

## Faith schools

Aligned to what has been noted above we have faith schools, and these are now burgeoning. Helen Johnson writes:

> Less than ten years ago, it was possible to remark on the *lack* of opposition to faith schools (or, as they tended to be called then, church schools). Today, faith schools attract an immense amount of attention . . . In England, some of this opposition is both very vocal and intense, . . . What has happened in this intervening period?
>
> Declared government education policy supporting a faith presence in education, parental perception and choice, seemingly contradictory trends including secularisation and cataclysmic events . . . have contributed to a much changed context in which these schools operate . . . It is despite and perhaps because of these factors (and others) that such schools are not merely surviving on the margins but are oversubscribed.

> (Johnson 2006: 1)

Johnson might have added mention of the proliferation of schools of other faiths than Christianity. Jewish schools have existed for some time but Muslim, Hindu and Sikh schools are now also in evidence. In part, of course, this is due to communities in a multicultural society, with a multiculturalist policy, seeking representation on the back of the tradition of church schools in English society. But faith is also entrepreneurial in other ways. Some of the academies now established are funded by Christian organisations. Also, traditionally faith schools in the form of Church of England and Catholic are perceived to be more concerned with values such that there is a middle-class interest in them on the perceived basis that they are superior in this respect. But this says a lot about perceptions of, and, perhaps, leadership and vision in, state schools, where this might be an absent feature or at least a not well-informed or well-directed feature. The phenomenon is complex. Certainly, with all faith schools there is a sense in which they represent a closer tie with the idea of maintaining a specific identity. Perhaps this is more so culturally and in relation to community and religious identity with Jewish, Hindu and Muslim schools, where there is an obvious minority identity issue. However, faith schools vary in many respects amongst themselves.

Critics of faith schools tend to be such because they think that these schools do not belong to the Enlightenment and scientific legacy, referred to on p. 3 and pp. 15–16. For example, take this attack by Roger Marples:

One of the major concerns shared by those of us with strong reservations about faith schools is that they may not attach sufficient importance to children's autonomy.

(Marples 2006: 22)

The autonomy or own agency of young people is a principle concern because, it is feared, faith schools will wish to prevent or curtail this in accordance with the dogmas that underpin religious belief systems. This in turn, as Marples points out, affects the capacity for independent thought and their potential for growth as individuals: 'Those who would frustrate, either intentionally or unwittingly, a child's capacity for independent thought, are denying the child a right to flourish' (Marples 2006: 23).

The matter of intention on the part of the educators, Marples makes clear, is not the main issue, but rather what is imbibed in an unquestioning faith school environment:

If children do acquire religious beliefs unquestioningly, out of fear or undue respect of parents and teachers, then they may be said to have been indoctrinated whether or not there was any intention . . . and it is unrealistic to suppose that all faith schools would attach priority to ensuring that pupils are encouraged to *critically* reflect on their religious beliefs.

(Marples 2006: 25)

He also quotes Mark Halstead's requirement that the curriculum should include 'education for democratic citizenship' (Marples 2006: 28; Halstead 1995) as an essential criterion for judging faith schools and for doubting their justification.

This echoes the voices of Dawkins and Hirsi Ali. Whilst Marples' concern needs to be put to the test with reliable evidence across the board, it is interesting to note that my own study of a Buddhist primary school in Brighton (the only one in Europe) conveyed evidence to the contrary, emphasising just those qualities that Marples prizes, but in an environment of care and nurture (Erricker 2009). However, this cannot be evidenced as typical of faith schools but is evidence that a faith school, albeit of a Buddhist variety, can be in tune with Enlightenment ideas *and yet* also promote spiritual values, especially the idea of compassion.

A recent report on faith schools produced by Rob Berkeley with Savita Vij for the Runnymede Trust (Berkeley with Vij 2008) provides some key recommendations on the basis of ways in which faith schools can contribute positively to the English education system and 'improve their capacity to fulfil the role of promoting cohesion' (Berkeley with Vij 2008: 2). They are (including some broader advice on RE in and beyond faith schools):

- End selection on the basis of faith (faith schools should be for the benefit of all to avoid social exclusivity).

- Children should have a greater say in how they are educated (Children's rights are as important as parent's rights. Far more could be done to enable young people's voice and participation, thereby demonstrating their commitment to democratic dialogue).

- RE should be part of the core national curriculum (following a common RE curriculum. In schools without a religious character, provision for learning about religion is often poor. In faith schools, provision for learning about religions beyond those of the sponsoring faith is also inadequate).

- Faith schools should also serve the disadvantaged (faith schools educate a disproportionately small number of young people at the lowest end of the socio–economic scale).

- Faith schools must value all young people (Important facets of people's identities operate beyond what they are able to express through their faith . . . it is not enough to privilege one marker of identity over others . . . gender, ethnicity, age, ability or sexual orientation) . . . Disappointingly, given their emphasis on values and moral education, faith schools have not developed a distinctive approach to learning about diversity.

(Berkeley with Vij 2008: 4–6)

The report concludes its recommendations by stating: 'If these recommendations are acted upon, faith should continue to play an important role in our education system. Yet, as currently constituted, they (faith schools) display an insular and too often absolutist approach to faith which excludes rather than includes' (Berkeley with Vij 2008: 6).

The report points out that faith schooling constitutes one-third of the schooling system. This is significant in terms of the socialisation and education absorbed by young people and their consequent attitudes, values and horizons. The recommendations of the report would require a radical reorientation of the vision of faith schools, and whether this can be done is questionable. In her book on Church and state partnership in education *Shifting Alliances: Church and State in English Education* Priscilla Chadwick quotes Bishop David Young on what he saw, in 1994, as the challenge of such a partnership:

> [It] is to articulate a vision for our nation in a fast-changing world . . . which embraces the pluralism of multi-culture and multi-faith, which builds on values shared, which gives energy and purpose to our economic and social life . . . a new vision must be discerned.

(Chadwick 1997: 147)

Clearly, as yet, it has not. In part this may be because faith schools think they can do a different job by arming their children against secularism. Terence Copley's view is that state schooling and RE need to take religious spiritualities more seriously, as creeds and doctrines grow out of spiritual experience and not the reverse. As a result 'religions have more to teach a society sometimes labeled post-Christian or post-religious, than they (secularists) thought' (Copley 2000: 142). But it is difficult to see how the idea of spirituality can be shared across faith and non-faith schools if the former are inclined not to wish to share their spiritual secrets.

## Spirituality

There have been a plethora of publications on spirituality in education since it was mentioned in the 1988 Education Reform Act as one area of development underpinning the whole curriculum. There is a sense in which it provides a focus for the sort of malaise underpinning the question of educational vision, in faith and state schools. Above we addressed the emergence of different types of pedagogy and the influence of science emerging at the beginning of the nineteenth century. Enlightenment ideas did not mention spirituality as a driving force of the project. Religions can see spirituality as their preserve within and against a secular world and faith schools can reinforce that. RE has recognised the value of spirituality and spiritual development being aligned with its function in the curriculum, and many of the publications produced have sought to make RE and spiritual development synonymous. And yet, just as faith schools have not established a vision for how they serve a plural society, according to the Runnymede Report, so spirituality is not commonly a part of the educational lexicon of teachers in state schools, including RE teachers, and in faith schools it is usually intimately aligned to their denominational allegiance or religious foundation. Spiritual development implies a close relationship with the vision of a school and its approach to teaching and learning. This is invariably not the case in state schooling. If it is to be meaningful a new vision for state education must emerge and a clear understanding of the role of RE within that.

## Conclusion: time to nail our colours to the mast

If one has the desire to promote religious education within our schooling system, then it is necessary to be able to articulate a reasoned and informed purpose for the subject. This is the challenge. In this chapter we have covered a series of inter-related issues concerning the place of religion in modern society, with a focus on England and Wales, and noted some of the complexities arising from religion and religion in education being part of a largely secular yet 'multicultural' or 'multi-faith' grouping of people with a significant Christian cultural heritage. I hope it has also been clear that progressive 'globalisation' and migrant movement pose a significant challenge in a world fast-changing in the context of this situation and that the effects of the European Enlightenment are still very much with us. So what is the purpose of religious education today in the light of that? It is a useful exercise to try and articulate a clear response to this question, otherwise we shall be quite unsure as to what, how and why we do what we do in the classroom.

# 2

# An analysis of the historical and contemporary significance of religious education

## Introduction

The purpose of this chapter is to focus more specifically on provision for religious education through providing an historical and contemporary account of how provision for RE has evolved in England and Wales. This will make reference to the Education Acts involved, the role of Agreed Syllabuses and Standing Advisory Councils for Religious Education (SACREs) with regard to local determination and the burgeoning influence of government agencies from the 1990s onwards. It will conclude by discussing the cast of mind of RE teachers and the importance of taking account of the way in which pedagogy in society has influenced attitudes to religious education and the pedagogical issues that this has raised with respect to educational thinking and classroom practice.

## Historical and geographical distinctions in religious education provision

In order to understand the present approaches to RE and the present guidance given by the Qualifications, Curriculum and Development Agency (QCDA), which we shall turn to later, we have to provide the historical context in England and Wales and beyond. For example, why is it that France has no RE, German RE is devised according to whether the school is Lutheran or Catholic, Australia organises RE on the basis of being a Catholic school or not and it is taught by a member of the faith, and in the USA religious education in schools is not allowed by law? However, England and Wales teach a number of faiths prominent in the UK with a primacy put on the teaching of Christianity, in terms of curriculum time, but it is non-denominational and non-confessional, across all religions taught. At the same time France is a secular state with a high proportion of Roman Catholics, and still refers to Protestant churches as sects; the USA is significantly influenced by religious belief; and, arguably, despite the results of the 2001 census, the UK is one of the most secular Western democracies. What is clear from this is that we have complicated histories in relation to religion and that RE, as a result, is much influenced, as a curriculum subject within schools, by those histories. One vital aspect of this is how Western democracies have evolved since the European Enlightenment. For example, both France and the USA experienced revolutions in the late eighteenth century. It is noteworthy also that the European countries so far mentioned are all 'northern'. Spain, Portugal and Italy, for example, are all still Roman Catholic countries in historical legacy and have experienced different relations between Church and state. Russia experienced communist rule in the first half of the twentieth century, until the fall of the Berlin Wall heralded the collapse of communism and the end of the Cold War. Poland became communist, along with other satellite states of the USSR, after the Second World War but in these countries there has been a revival of traditional religious faith; Orthodox and Catholic, respectively. These experiences have had a major shaping influence on religious education. There is a credible argument that RE in England and Wales has been more liberal, broader and freer of religious or at least denominational influence than elsewhere. But this alerts us to the powerful underlying effect of religion shaping national educational projects and curricula both in Europe and across the world by its particulars of presence, absence and configuration, in relation to state policy and power.

## A brief history of religious education in England and Wales

Historically, RE in England and Wales has been Christian. Thomas Arnold, as headmaster of Rugby School, stated 'the great principle that Christianity should be the base of all public education in this country' (Barnard 1961: 78). He resigned from the Senate of the University of London 'when it was proposed to introduce a voluntary examination in theology' on the basis that this made it merely a branch of knowledge and not an essential part of the system (Barnard 1961: 78–79).

This gives some indication of how important Christianity was understood to be not only as a subject taught but also as underpinning the curriculum and school values and ethos at that time. When the Education Act of 1870 was passed the aim was that an adequate supply of schools for all children would be introduced (in elementary education) without the necessity of fee paying, thus for the education of the poor. By 1876 there were a million and a half new school places but two-thirds of these were provided by the churches rather than by the new school boards, which were set up by local authorities and were secular and non–denominational (Barnard 1961: 118–119). As a result we have the 'dual system' which remains in place today in the legacy of church schools and now faith schools.

## 1944 and 1988

By the time of the 1944 Education Act, with controlled voluntary schools under the local education authorities' (LEAs) support, it was 'laid down that in every county (state) and voluntary school religious instruction should be given, and that the school day should begin with an act of collective worship; though . . . the right of withdrawal on conscientious grounds was safeguarded' (Barnard 1961: 299).

Barnard adds that this was the 'first time in our educational history that religious instruction and school prayers have been specifically enforced by an Act of Parliament, and it affords striking evidence of our national unwillingness to add "secular" to the formula "universal, compulsory and gratuitous"' as a description of schooling (Barnard 1961: 299). In Clause 36 we then have mention of religious instruction in county schools needing to be in accordance with an Agreed Syllabus.

So, the persistence of religion, in the form of Christianity as religious instruction, is significantly evidenced in the clauses of the 1944 Act. There was opposition at that time and before it to this religious imposition but its legacy continues even now in the compulsory nature of both RE and collective worship, with the withdrawal clause and the Locally Agreed Syllabuses. These stipulations were reaffirmed in the 1988 Education Reform Act. As Terence Copley points out, it was in the House of Lords that the battle waged over the place of RE and collective worship and the question of entitlement (Copley 1997: 137–146). The voice opposing the Christian right was Graham Leonard, Bishop of London, himself a conservative thinker but against the more strident claims of others. He was specifically a supporter of Agreed Syllabuses produced by local authorities and opposed to the call for RE to be part of the national curriculum and, as he feared, centrally controlled. This position won the day. It is helpful to be aware of this battle in the Lords because otherwise a reaffirmation of the 1944 legislation might have come about, in that Christianity and the Christian basis of RE might have continued. But why continue with RE being a compulsory subject? Why reaffirm the manifest absurdity of collective worship? There was still a strong challenge to secularity in such bastions of tradition as the House of Lords and the Church of England and this influenced the contours of debate.

## Contours of debate

The more recent history of RE in England and Wales, since the 1970s, has been one in which Christian nurture has given way to the study of different world faiths, and the term religious instruction is no longer used. This reflected the movement of RE into an educational rationale consistent with other subjects in mainstream schools and against the idea that RE was principally an educational space in which Christian nurture could continue. This was a radical change and the effects of it have not been entirely resolved and responses to it have not entirely disappeared. There has been a typically British pragmatism at work in this transformation which has not been reflected to the same degree in the attitudes of other countries and this has been mirrored in some ways in differing approaches to multiculturalism during the same period. The positive in the approach in England and Wales has been its comparatively smooth transition; perhaps the negative is that the transition never seems to be fully achieved. There are reasons for this, different factors involved; there are currents beneath the surface that run deep and the battle above over the 1988 Education Reform Act is one manifestation of them.

One of these factors, as introduced in Chapter 1, is the increasing secularism of Western society generally and Britain in particular. Despite the 2001 census, mentioned previously, in which 71 per cent of respondents registered their Christian affiliation – which is not reflected in church attendance – the disparity is huge. A reasonable conclusion would be that there is a majority of cultural Christians who do not have any positive sense of faith, let alone a dogmatic certainty of belief, but still some sense of belonging. It is a default position available to those who implicitly recognise the historical legacy of Christianity, or some vague sense of Christian values and the comfort of nominal belief. However, it is not a basis on which to declaim the importance of the religion as a fundamental aspect of British identity. To evidence this one only has to teach RE in a school.

The antipathy of many pupils to RE is based on their sense that they do not want to be nurtured in religion, however erroneous might be their understanding of the aims of the subject, and that reflects their lack of identity as being religious. Whilst this might not be the same for some students registered as Muslim, Sikh or Hindu it cannot be taken for granted that coming from a family with those self-represented designations the pupils will be more than culturally 'religious' or that they want to know about religions other than their own. Cultural designations and religious designations can overlap but the one should not necessarily be taken for the other, nor should it lead to the expectation that religious education is to be valued.

A further complicating factor, again introduced in Chapter 1, is that while becoming more secular our society has also become more 'multicultural' as a result of immigration, which has occurred increasingly since the Second World War. For RE this was a significant factor that influenced its direction. The equation of multicultural with multi-religious is not a synonymous one, but was advantageous to the transformation of the subject. This is not to say that originally immigrant populations campaigned for a change in the subject; they did not to any significant degree. Their children being brought up in their traditional faith they regarded as their province of concern, not the state's duty. The secular nature of society generally was of much more importance. The voices of religiously immigrant populations were not a significant factor in the change in RE provision. Far more important was the change in the higher education provision being offered. Again, as stated in Chapter 1, in 1964 the first university Department of Religious Studies opened at Lancaster University; this discipline then flourished over the next thirty years until it came to be as, if not more, ubiquitous than the discipline of theology. Then, in the 1990s, it started to decline. The reasons for this mirror changes in government policy and the ways in which universities were forced to function as businesses. It is also the case that, unlike theology, religious studies has no comparable support from established institutions, i.e. churches, and since many, though not all, courses exist in smaller universities with religious foundations this is a complicating issue when theology may be the preferred discipline.

The contestation, and change, that occurred in the UK from the 1970s until the latter half of the 1990s was due to the reorientation of higher education provision toward the study of religions and the concomitant recognition that the demography of the population was changing such that other religious identities in the population had to be acknowledged, given that RE had already, for different historical reasons, become situated on the curriculum map. Universities were already educating their students in the study of religions, and a substantial number of these embraced teaching as a vocation. Their orientation was to teach different religions. Lobby groups emerged that encouraged the subject in this direction. The change in demographic reflected this need. The curriculum provision changed as a result, before the law caught up with the 1988 Education Reform Act and created a statute that reflected that change at least in terms of the content studied in the curriculum.

However, this change, as significant as it was, did not bring about a complete break from the past. Bishops still stood, and still do, in the House of Lords, and, to that political extent, Britain is still a country in many ways religiously dominated by Christianity. We might characterise the present situation thus: whilst religion is embraced by a minority, it still has significant political importance. As far as RE is concerned this has a dubious but undoubted influence. On the one hand it is protected by statute; on the other it is seen as educationally of no great significance and often, wilfully or not, misunderstood in terms of its purpose.

## Agreed Syllabuses

The legislation in both 1944 and 1988, with reference to RE, resulted in the enforcement of statutory local legislation, in the form of Agreed Syllabuses. In Chapter 1 comments on the Birmingham Agreed Syllabus of 1975 by Jack Priestley were included. The publication of these was and is the responsibility of local groups charged with the monitoring of RE and collective worship, SACREs under the auspices of the local (education) authority. The constitution of a SACRE is dominated by representation from local religious community representatives, with a bias toward the Church of England. Thus, agreeing the text of an Agreed Syllabus, a main feature of a SACRE's duties, is, in theory, dominated by the interests of religious groups. The danger is that this over-rides the educational interests at stake. Representatives may be more concerned with the representation of their religious group (in the content of the syllabus) than with the educational value of the subject beyond that. This is not surprising given that such representatives are not chosen for their knowledge of education, in the first instance, nor are they necessarily concerned with pedagogical intentions, as their major interest. It will only be the supporting guidance of the local education officers (inspectors/advisers) and the astuteness of the councillors of the local government that will ensure that such a document is fit for educational purpose. It will not be surprising that consequent variation in product is a result and that teachers in schools feel remote from this policy enactment and yet have to abide by its regulation.

The introduction of the Qualifications and Curriculum Authority (QCA, now QCDA) at the same time as the establishing of a national curriculum became the enforcer of codes, but in RE its guidance was necessarily non-statutory. It operated in that domain by exerting influence, which it has done ever since through Non-Statutory Model Syllabuses and subsequently through a Non-Statutory National Framework, the demands of which are now reflected in most Locally Agreed Syllabuses, though erratically. However, this leaves the educational health of RE in a still less than satisfactory state. To exemplify:

■  As a result of the institution of SACREs there tends to be an emphasis on religious representation in the subject, rather than on educational sufficiency.

■  Similarly there is a tendency for RE to think of itself as somewhat distanced from new pedagogical initiatives affecting other subjects in education.

■ Also, debates in RE tend to be overly religiously oriented; thus, for example, as to what religions should or should not be included according to local determination.

■ Also, the variable strength, and budgetary capability, of specific local SACREs can be significant in determining the resultant quality of RE in schools.

■ Also, whilst SACREs uphold the statutory influence of RE in schools, their influence can be and most often is marginal in terms of influence on classroom practice.

■ Last, the influence of the QCDA on RE has become dominant, in its influence on Locally Agreed Syllabuses, but not educationally significant in promoting effective pedagogy due to the limits of its brief, which is policy but not practice oriented. The QCDA has no remit to make pronouncements on pedagogy or on the sufficiency or excellence of Locally Agreed Syllabuses because of the statutory arrangements in place.

In his analysis of the history of Agreed Syllabuses (Priestley 2006), mentioned in Chapter 1, Jack Priestley refers to 'The Spens Report' (Spens 1938) and its statement that 'no boy or girl can be counted properly educated unless he or she has been made aware of the fact of the existence of a religious interpretation of life' (Priestley 2006: 1004; Spens 1938: 208). What Spens said then in the singular, if now translated into the plural, acts as an appropriate basis on which to construct religious education. However, along with changes in content to RE, attention needed and still needs to be paid to educational distinctions centred on terms such as instruction, learning and development. In this respect John Dewey's approach based on child-centredness became influential. The tension over plurality disappeared in 1975. After that time all Agreed Syllabuses, following the Birmingham syllabus of that date, referred to faiths in the plural (Priestley 2006: 1012). The tension over instruction versus child-centredness has moved in favour of the latter approach but in a confused way despite the length of time since the West Riding Agreed Syllabus of 1966 advocated it (Priestley 2006: 1010, 1015). Religious education still has significant pedagogical difficulties here, to which we shall return in the chapters that follow.

Today we find ourselves in an interesting situation. Priestley again: 'There can be little doubt that the days of locally agreed syllabuses of Religious Education are now numbered' (Priestley 2006: 1015). As a result he asks, 'How, for example, can innovation take place?' He cites Copley on the need to address locality when considering the content of RE in relation to local culture. 'What about Glastonbury?' asks Copley, the point being that different localities spawn different religious characteristics and multicultural differences due to demography (Priestley 2006: 1015; Copley 2005: 94–96). Priestley is distrustful of the ability of national agencies such as the QCDA to both innovate and accommodate diversity. Historically, that distrust has some commendation. However, the QCDA has already moved to seek the inclusion of Humanism within RE and its new secondary and primary curriculum documents have innovated in their focus on the development of the learner with its three aims: successful learners, confident individuals, responsible citizens. I suggest that Priestley's judgements on the value of Agreed Syllabuses are somewhat overestimated, but that we might still need to be suspicious of the vagaries of policy of government agencies.

We have to investigate what might have been lost by RE being treated as a special case, with its own local determination. The variable qualities of the syllabuses are not disputed, thus whilst Priestley can extol the ones that were innovative, many were not. One of the consequences of this has been that innovation in one local area has not been seized upon as valuable to the educational advancement of another. There can be a local rationale to this since the syllabuses were entrusted with ensuring that the content was appropriate to the religious population it served.

Nevertheless, such a stance is erroneous when we consider the wider educational significance such a document needs to serve. Content is but one aspect of its instrumentality. Representation of its religious communities in an accurate fashion is certainly important but this cannot be allowed to be the sole rationale of its function. To the extent that it became so, RE became separated off from educational innovation and trends generally. Whilst national documentation for other subjects addressed more than content it was still possible for the local Agreed Syllabuses for RE to concern themselves primarily with what should be taught. Calling the local RE documents 'syllabuses' signifies that their function is limited to statements of content. The fact that no other curriculum subject retains the word 'syllabus', all having adapted to using the more multiply-layered word 'curriculum', signifies another way in which RE seems to follow rules that are not fully educational. The variation in what was provided was determined by factors such as the local authorities' concern with the subject, or otherwise, and the amount of resources put into supporting it. This tended to decrease with the arrival of Ofsted and the QCA and the establishing of unitary councils in cities, separated off and differently resourced from the larger county councils, of which they were previously a part. All these factors contributed to the decline in the advisory support for subjects generally and for RE in particular during the 1990s and after, along with the marginalisation of local authorities and the reduction in their budgets for education instigated earlier in the Thatcher era. As a result some local authorities produced very little in the way of guidance for RE within Agreed Syllabuses and increasingly relied on the QCA, as was, Non-Statutory National Framework (NSNF) for RE (QCA 2004) as a substitute for its own efforts. Since the NSNF was not designed to offer any significant pedagogical guidance itself, the vacuum in this respect, one that already existed, was not filled.

At the same time, those local advisers in place, who took pride in their local document, saw this new Framework as a national threat to their local determination. The emergent picture had, and to date still has, the following characteristics:

■ variability in Agreed Syllabuses and supporting material;

■ variability in resource regarding advisors and their variability in expertise;

■ isolation of RE from generic progress in pedagogy;

■ distance between theorists in universities, advisers in local authorities and practitioners on the ground;

■ disciplinarity: whilst RE support is very enthusiastic about the subject, as are its teachers, the notion of it being a discipline, such as history, is weak. Conceiving of RE as a 'subject' but not a 'discipline' has led to an emphasis on knowledge acquisition rather than the development of skills or a focus on concepts. Some have suggested that RE is a coalition of disciplines, held together by concerns that are not always educational and by a disproportionate focus on content at the expense of skills, attitudes and concepts.

## The centralised agencies: the Qualifications, Curriculum and Development Agency (QCDA) and the Office for Standards in Education (Ofsted)

Between 2007 and 2009 QCDA (previously QCA) revised first the secondary, then the primary curriculum, in each case including programmes for RE, based on the national framework, on a non-statutory basis to guide local Agreed Syllabus conferences. In 2008 and 2009 QCDA advised SACREs that Locally Agreed Syllabuses due for review just prior to or during this period might benefit from waiting for the outcome of the curriculum review and align their statutory guidance for RE accordingly. The intended result was to create a consistent standard for RE, one that made use of the same planning paradigms as the rest of the curriculum, that would be widely taken up in local syllabuses. Of course, such a recommendation can equally be seen as a threat to local determination in the long run; if there is such consistency amongst Locally Agreed Syllabuses what argument is there for keeping determination local? Priestley's expectation of Agreed Syllabus demise might thus come to pass. Nevertheless, it can be argued, this is of the local authorities' own making. It seems indefensible to produce statutory guidance locally that is of variable educational quality when a national alternative is possible that could incorporate the best of what has been achieved. Also, it can be argued that it is the case that the QCDA is now providing the lead in terms of the construction of a curriculum that is 'learner' centred, concept led and skills oriented. Realistically it has to be acknowledged that some small authorities would be only too happy to simply adopt the present national framework, as one to my knowledge was all too prepared to do, in order to save time and money. The question that remains is whether the central RE documents can continue to evolve significantly to provide better guidance, particularly on pedagogical issues, and can, in doing so, take onboard best practice both from Locally Agreed Syllabuses and the wider educational, and specifically pedagogic, models available to it.

The new secondary curriculum was devised on the basis of the QCA Big Picture (QCA 2006) which reoriented the aims of education on the basis of the Every Child Matters agenda introduced in 2003 (DCSF 2003):

- Enjoy and Achieve
- Stay Safe
- Be Healthy
- Participate
- Be Economically Active.

The key to understanding the Big Picture diagram (QCA 2006) lies in the column in which the aims are expressed. For a curriculum subject to contribute to the overall development of children it needs to demonstrate its effectiveness in contributing to producing:

- successful learners, who enjoy learning, make progress and achieve;
- confident individuals, who are able to live safe, healthy and fulfilling lives;
- responsible citizens, who make a positive contribution to society.

The curriculum is understood as more than what is offered in schools as subject learning. The curriculum includes all those experiences and opportunities available to children. Thus, there needs to be a marriage between the experiences and acumen that children bring to the classroom and schooling and what goes on within subjects and schooling. The nature of the design of the Big Picture diagram reflects this intention. It is horizontally organised, not vertically. This is disorienting to the thinking about the curriculum that preceded it. Traditionally one would expect to see a collection of vertical lines representing subjects as the spine of the curriculum. That spine has disappeared. Psychologically and professionally, this means it is no longer possible to just think within one's subject in isolation, with subject specific aims that accord with that. The requirement was to determine how subjects could justify their contribution to the development of children in the school together. In turn, this required schools to have an umbrella set of aims, vision, ethos, structures and processes that ensured this more holistic model could operate effectively and be evidenced to do so in terms of the way children reflected on their own development, aspired to develop themselves and valued the contribution of and relevance of the learning that took place in schools and subjects. A further expectation that followed was that subjects worked together so that a pattern emerged across curricular learning that made sense to children in terms of how subjects were connected and contributed to their development. Learning had to be meaningful and seen as such by secondary school students.

In a presentation at the 7th International Conference on Children's Spirituality at Winchester University in July 2006 Mark Chater, the QCA subject leader for RE, commented upon the Big Picture by identifying specific advantages it offered:

- a less congested curriculum offering more time for cross-curricular collaboration;
- a more diverse curriculum which behaves as if people mattered;
- an owned curriculum meaning more to teachers and learners;
- a coherent curriculum that triggers change in workplaces and societies.

The intended result would be:

- a flexible, dynamic and diverse curriculum;
- a meaningful pedagogy;
- an end to subject silos.

(Chater 2006)

This message, repeated elsewhere by QCA/QCDA representatives, might have come as a shock to secondary school subject specialists, whose main concern is often that their subject might lose its intrinsic importance (for example to understand history or religion) because it might have to contribute to extrinsic, broader aims.

Within subjects the new curriculum identifies specific concepts, skills and processes that drive the subject and move it away from knowledge acquisition for its own sake. This orientation toward concepts is the driving force in disrupting an otherwise inchoate series of units of work that often has no principle behind progression apart from the idea of what it is thought ought to be covered.

For secondary and primary RE the designated key concepts (actually called 'essential knowledge' in the primary documentation) are:

1  Beliefs, teachings and sources

2  Practices and ways of life

3  Expressing meaning

4  Identity, diversity and belonging

5  Meaning, purpose and truth

6  Values and commitments.

(QCDA 2007 and 2009)

The problem with these concepts is that they look like themes or areas of learning. In themselves they cover what RE has traditionally been since the 1970s, the study of world religions but taking account of these 'lateral' factors. The question remains how these concepts or themes can translate the subject into something more meaningful, relevant and skills oriented to enhance students' development with the overarching three aims of the secondary curriculum kept in mind and with an orientation toward working in concert with other subjects to achieve those aims. It is not that this new orientation does not make sense, but how is it going to be achieved? It is like putting together a jigsaw, but not as the one who seeks to construct the readymade picture but as the person who has to devise it. Competence in jigsaw making will be necessary in all Agreed Syllabus conferences. This is a big ask for the RE community. The reason why lies with the state of pedagogical health of the subject. This was commented on by Ofsted, as we shall see.

In 2007 Ofsted produced a Long Report on the health of RE: *Making Sense of Religion* (Ofsted 2007). In its Executive Summary the following critical points were made:

■  Many Locally Agreed Syllabuses for RE still do not define progression in the subject clearly enough and therefore do not provide a secure basis for teaching and learning, curriculum planning and assessment.

■  Because assessment is often weak, subject leaders do not have enough reliable evidence about pupils' progress and are not able to analyse strengths and priorities for improvement.

■  The use of two attainment targets (widely adopted in Agreed Syllabuses) creates difficulties for planning and assessment.

■ Many Agreed Syllabuses . . . are not having a significant effect on improving standards and the quality of provision. Nearly half of the secondary schools visited in 2006/7 had not implemented their most recently published Agreed Syllabus effectively.

■ Many local authorities do not ensure that SACREs have sufficient capacity to fulfil these responsibilities (to provide support for RE and community cohesion) effectively.

■ The curriculum and teaching in RE do not place sufficient emphasis on exploring the changing political and social significance of religion in the modern world.

(Ofsted 2007: 5–8)

Additionally, it quoted the recent *Diversity and Citizenship Curriculum Review*, stating:

RE teachers face this challenge constantly. It is often simpler for them to fall back on the mechanics of religion instead of tackling the reality of being religious . . . It is an area that needs considerable work if we are to meet our objectives of developing active, articulate, critical learners who understand the value of difference and unity and have the ability to participate and engage in current debates.

(Ofsted 2007a: 12)

In addition, again, in relation to diversity, it makes four key points for improvement:

1 RE cannot ignore diversity within each religion.

2 RE cannot ignore controversy. We should dispense with the notion that we should encourage pupils to think uncritically of religion as a 'good thing'.

3 RE cannot ignore the social reality of religion . . . It now needs to embrace the study of religion and society.

4 RE cannot ignore its role in fostering community cohesion and in educating for diversity . . . Pupils have opinions, attitudes, feelings, prejudices and stereotypes. Developing respect for the commitments of others while retaining the right to question, criticise and evaluate different viewpoints is not just an academic exercise . . . RE should engage with pupils' feelings and emotions, as well as their intellect.

(Ofsted 2007a: 41)

Whilst also praising some aspects of RE provision, Ofsted's Long Report expressed strong concerns about the severe systemic weaknesses in RE. Subsequent inspection evidence has reinforced the overall picture. The Long Report of 2007 ended by recommending that, since the local determination of RE produces hit-and-miss results in the quality of planning, teaching and assessment, the SACRE system should either be made to work more effectively or be reviewed. This argument is damning but justified. The reasons why I say this are discussed in the section below.

Before moving on to that section, which highlights evidence of practice from my own experience in Hampshire, it is worth recording further evidence that corroborates the Ofsted findings found in Julian Stern's book *Teaching Religious Education* (Stern 2006), which has a chapter on 'Investigating text and context'. On page 8 he cites a study carried out by the

Association of Religious Education Inspectors and Advisers (AREIAC), which can be found on their website (www.areiac.org.uk). It compares the use of texts in history and RE. The findings are damning in that historians use texts to develop skills and use them in a challenging way, whereas RE teachers are identified as using them simplistically with a low level skill expectation. Given the centrality of texts to both subjects these findings highlight in greater detail the judgement made by Ofsted on progression in RE and the suggestion that RE has been far too focused on content. I return, in more detail, to this finding in Chapter 5 when considering progression and skills development further.

## The cast of mind of religious education teachers

I took up the post of County Inspector for RE in January 2003, previously having been a Reader in RE at what is now Chichester University, where I conducted my previous research. Part of that research had involved a project (the Children and Worldviews Project) on younger children's responses to significant events in their lives and the way those events impacted on the meaning they constructed. Some findings from this project were published in *The Education of the Whole Child* (Erricker *et al.* 1997). What this research pointed to was the ability of young children to reflect deeply and articulate well their reflections on these experiences and form their beliefs and values on the basis of that reflection. Some findings from this project are discussed in more detail in Chapter 4. I carried this evidence of younger students' capabilities into my new role. Here I shall reflect on my experience of observing lessons and scrutinising planning in secondary schools, where students were older than the ones interviewed in my previous research.

To put my observations in context, Hampshire has always had a strong reputation for RE. Its Agreed Syllabus at the time of the 1988 Education Reform Act was mentioned by Bishop Graham Leonard in the Lords' debates as an example of why Locally Agreed Syllabuses were important in progressing the subject. As Copley noted it had been adopted by twenty-two other LEAs (Copley 1997: 139). When I came into post the Hampshire Agreed Syllabus, at that time, was also recognised as a document that advanced good practice in the subject. It had been devised by an inspector who subsequently was responsible for drafting the above Ofsted report. There was a handbook also, which contained imaginative activities and stimulating units of work.

I had six months in which to determine the health of RE in Hampshire prior to the review of the Agreed Syllabus in September 2003. What struck me was the way in which many teachers were focused on teaching rather than learning. I can divide the types of teaching I saw largely into four:

1  teaching facts and giving information;

2  using RE to convey moral messages;

3  using interesting activities and resources to stimulate engagement;

4  using experiential activities.

I can offer examples of each of these.

In lessons where facts and information were dominant there was also a tendency towards over-control in the management of classroom participation. Teachers would instruct either through writing on a board or using textbook information, and students' roles were reduced to recall of what had been presented to them or comprehension of texts. Where baseline assessments were in place for new Year 7 students they were to write down basic information about their knowledge of religions so that teachers could tick or cross them and the result would be translated into an attainment level upon entry. In one school I arrived to support a teacher in his planning and delivery of a lesson and he intended to ask students to copy symbols of major religions into their books and write beneath what the symbol was and what religion it belonged to. This was a lesson on symbolism. Here we have much low level learning about religion and no learning from religion, in QCDA attainment target parlance. Put another way, it is low level cognitive engagement and no affective engagement.

In lessons where moral messages were the main point I witnessed one lesson where stimulating video footage was used in a debate on a mother not being able to forgive others for the murder of her child. The point being made was that not forgiving was harmful to the person as well as being conflictual socially and for others. At the end of the lesson the teacher made the point, not in a dictatorial way, that we all needed to forgive. In another piece of planning the Native American way of life was studied in order to understand that their values of being in tune with creation, thanking God when buffalo were killed and not wanting to own the land were values we should aspire to return to. Chief Seattle's speech was used to help persuade to this point of view. What struck me about these lessons was that the underlying objective was to change student's values and inspire them to higher ones. However, I was not at all sure how we could become like Native Americans in our lifestyle or forgive as a matter of course after dramatic loss. There was a lack of realism in these lessons and a lack of open dialogue with students as to their views. Here we have attempts at learning from religion but in a didactic way. There can be affective engagement but cognitive skills are not appropriately addressed and the substance of religions can be marginalised.

In lessons where interesting activities and resources were used to stimulate engagement there was a variety of practice. Again with symbolism in mind, there was often recourse to football badges etc. to interest boys. But there was no discernible link to religion other than that there were secular symbols too to connect with the religious ones. In two lessons, for Year 7 and Year 8 at the same school, I witnessed, in the first lesson, a way in which the idea of light was used to move to the understanding of the Pascal candle and Jesus as the light of the world. The problem lay in the fact that students never engaged with the figurative understanding of 'light' involved but they participated well in an activity on which image was the best one: the Christmas tree, the Pascal candle and the Christingle were involved. Almost unanimously they chose the Christingle because, as it turned out, they had done it in Year 6 in primary school. The rest of the lesson went swimmingly as they recalled their prior knowledge and impressed the teacher. In the Year 8 lesson a stimulating group exercise had been devised. Students in groups were presented with a collection of texts on a particular aspect of Sikhism. One group was studying texts on God. The task was to decide which texts to use and compose a paragraph on what Sikhs believed about God. The leader of the group would then read out their paragraph. When the leader of the God group did this I was impressed and asked him how he and the group had come to the decision on what to put in the paragraph and what to discard. He explained that some texts they left out if they didn't understand them. I asked him for an example and he showed me a statement by Guru Nanak 'God you are the river in which we swim'. The students enjoyed the exercise, they were involved, they achieved and the teacher praised them. But they still didn't grapple with religious metaphor as a result. Here learning about religion is prized over learning from religion despite the fact that symbolic and metaphoric texts are used. The principle achievement lies in the engagement of students not in the advancement of their skills.

Some teachers were aware of the experiential activities devised by Hammond and Hay and colleagues in *New Methods in RE Teaching* (Hammond *et al*. 1990) and those devised by Phillips in her Theatre of Learning approach (Phillips 2004), and they incorporated the risk and openness involved into the teaching and learning with their students. These lessons were high on participation and involvement and focused on student reflection. Clearly the foremost aim was that students should enjoy the lessons and feel they were worthwhile. They could also take away their reflections as a form of spiritual development. The problem lay in the fact that they were using stimulating activities that simulated religious practice in terms of ritual, symbolism and metaphor without actually entering in to religion in any other way. This ended up as borrowing from religious practice to enhance personal or spiritual development but there was no intention to engage with religions per se. It was an end in itself: a form of experiential nurture. Here affective engagement is high but cognitive engagement lower. It is focused on a particular form of learning from religion rather than learning about religions. To put it another way, it was about replacing religions with student engagement in activities that simulated religious activity but in the context of their own lifeworlds.

In my commentary above I do not wish to criticise teachers but simply to record an observation and classification of the practice I observed. The variation in this might well be considered to be a systemic failure. It was a means of determining what needed to be borne in mind when seeking to review the statutory guidance in place. What was clear was that there was no common purpose as to the function of RE in the curriculum and this was due to there being a disparity of approach in relation to what to teach, how to teach it and why it should be taught. Importantly, there was also a lack of emphasis on the systematic development of learning and the skills to be developed through engagement with the subject. Progression and assessment were largely alien concepts. Either they were connected to testing knowledge where learning about religion was prevalent or they were irrelevant, where learning from was emphasised in differing ways.

One of the most noticeable things was the shyness in dealing with the substance of religion as a phenomenon in a direct and meaningful way. Religious presence and practice as they happened in the world and social affairs were seen as difficult things to enable students to engage with. There was also, as a result, no attempt to be critical of religion. Possibly this was because it was thought students would be critical enough, in a negative way, if you presented them with it.

The underlying impression was that, despite being in many cases enthusiastic about their subject, teachers had no pedagogic rationale on which to base their practice. The writings of

Hay, Hammond *et al.* and Phillips aside, where an experiential approach was advocated focused on students rather than religions, I witnessed no influence from the theorists who had published in the field. There was a significant lack of communication across this divide. The result of this was that it was difficult to know where teachers were getting guidance from. The attainment targets of the Agreed Syllabus in place were used but that did not determine the approach. The handbook provided texts and activities that were used but largely because they engaged students; this did not mean they fitted an overall purpose in terms of the ongoing progression of learning and skills. Other resources and materials that had been published nationally, by teacher magazines like *RE Today*, were in evidence but not fitted to an overall scheme of work. Further resources, artefacts and posters were in evidence but again as stimuli rather than integrated into a rationale for the subject. It was as if nothing had changed between the 1970s and 2003. But why was change needed? Nothing had happened to promote change in the teachers' world. The content of the curriculum had largely remained the same and engaging students with the subject was the main aspiration; whatever approach worked for you and your students was the approach to use. More skilful and more risk-taking teachers succeeded better than others; there was nothing new in that.

In conclusion I asked myself the question: in the context of these disparate approaches to the subject what were my educational principles for deciding what was a good RE lesson and why? There was no obvious answer because no common principles applied. There was an elephant in the room and no one was talking about it.

My conclusion was that the problem was systemic. If change was needed, which in my view it clearly was, then this could only be done by introducing it at a systematic pedagogic level. The way this was done in Hampshire is addressed in Part 2 of this book.

The subject of Chapter 3 is pedagogy in religious education and recent approaches by theorists and researchers that have been presented. This will allow us to grasp different ways in which RE has been addressed in recent years and ways in which thinking about the subject has changed. Before we move on to analyse these it is important to address the larger idea of pedagogy as it pertains to society generally and how that impacts on education.

## Pedagogy in society and education

What do we mean by pedagogy?

We can begin to answer this question by thinking of the way in which we have been influenced by the society and culture in which we have been brought up and how that also applies to the students we teach. We need to do this because although pedagogy in its institutionalised educational sense commonly refers to the theory and practice of teaching and learning we must first take account of the socio-cultural context within which that occurs. This larger context is the one that shapes our way of thinking, our values, goals and interests, and therefore has a direct influence on the way we approach education, the curriculum and teaching and learning in schools. In the larger sense of pervasive messages in society that have a specific ideological base that is meant to determine a specific mentality of citizens, we can cite the obvious examples of Nazi fascism and Stalinist communism. However it is also true within other 'theocracies' (see Philip Pullman's comments in Chapter 1) and free-market democracies. The messages we receive from politicians, through the media and advertising, construct the framework in which we think and to which we respond. Again, following Pullman, the purpose of education could be said to be to learn the art of reading such that we can deconstruct these messages and recognise and respond to these messages in a way that we think appropriate. In religious education, for example, Terence Copley has attacked the pervasive secularism and materialism of Western society, and called for the need to recognise the alternative presented by theology. Even if God does not go wholly missing, his point is that RE is reduced to working within the dominant pedagogy and reducing the theological to the moral (Copley 2005). It is in this sense that we can apply what Bourdieu and Passeron refer to as the 'cultural arbitrary', in that it is not a necessary or a given and could be otherwise. There is no given natural order to society; it is created, it evolves and changes and there are agents of change. They write: 'All pedagogic action is, objectively, symbolic violence insofar as it is the imposition of a cultural arbitrary by an arbitrary power' (Bourdieu and Passeron 1990: 5) which, as a result, intends 'perpetuating the principles of the internalised arbitrary' (Bourdieu and Passeron 1990: 31). By this they mean that change is brought about by specific agents intent on such change and this becomes a cultural imposition by those agents which creates the cultural norms then under-stood to be normative.

In some cases the change is sudden and revolutionary, for example in Iran with the Iranian Revolution, which affected every aspect of life, including the way in which women were to dress, with the introduction of rules (fatwahs) on hijab. In Turkey we can witness another interesting situation where a secular state has been challenged by a religiously oriented Muslim movement, and again the question of the wearing of the headscarf has become a dominant issue in reverse: should it be banned in public, as indeed it has been in secular France but not in Britain? These are pedagogical issues. This leads us to ask who creates the dominant pedagogy, how and why? What leads such pedagogies to become controversial rather than agreed? These are indeed the subject matter of religious education. This also helps to explain why RE often receives a negative response from students, such as being irrelevant to them because they are not religious. Although they would not express it in this way, they are viewing religion, and by implication RE, as an alien ideological imposition. However, this can equally apply to education generally and schooling. It is possible to illustrate this idea with some simple examples that, as teachers, we are well aware of; they are of different kinds which illustrate the pervasive impact of a socio-cultural environment on the delivery of education. We may call each of these examples different aspects of pedagogical dissonance.

1 If you work in a 'deprived' school, one with a catchment area of low socio-economic class, you will be aware of the difficulties you can face in creating interest in lessons in whatever subject, but this can be particularly the case in RE. In Hampshire, for example, there is a low percentage of such schools compared to elsewhere. Nevertheless, in my role as an inspector/adviser these schools figure prominently in my deployment. Pedagogically the problem is this: children from families who are in the catchment areas of these schools lack aspiration and many of them are antagonistic to schooling. In terms of community cohesion these areas are fragmented, lack economic capital and educational capital (I shall return to the issue of

capital later), but education is not, therefore, prized. Thus, the message conveyed to children in these schools, by parents, is often that education does not matter. Also, that which is prized by these students is contained within narrow local horizons, on the one hand, thus notions of identity are geographically and ethnically restricted, and they tend to be influenced more by aspiring to material values because of their lack of material advantage. As a result, the need to deploy engaging teaching and learning strategies to interest them in lessons is at a premium. A lack in this respect results in unruly behaviour and possible chaos. Getting a critical mass of these students on your side is essential. If you use a didactic, instructional method of learning it will not work, especially in RE, which is seen as an authoritarian, indoctrinatory instrument by many students and parents alike.

For these students and often their parents we are witnessing an attitude which is well described by Bourdieu and Passeron when they speak of pedagogy as 'symbolic violence insofar as it is the imposition of a cultural arbitrary by an arbitrary power' (Bourdieu and Passeron 1990: 5) which, as a result intends 'perpetuating the principles of the internalised arbitrary' (Bourdieu and Passeron 1990: 31). What this means in practise is that students regard education in general and RE in particular as an arbitrary imposition upon them which does not relate to their own perceptions of aspiration, identity or worldview, and they will react by seeking to ensure that we fail in seeking to ensure that they acquire that which we wish them to learn and, as a result, internalise or accept the values that the learning is based on. For example, teaching these young people to empathise with others as a main aim of RE will be rejected, and especially so, for example, if it means asking them to empathise with members of another community that, within their own socio-cultural horizons, is of no significance or negatively conceived. In schools of this kind with catchments that are white, rather than being ethnically diverse, this will be especially true if you present them with non-white Muslim images and materials. This is not to say you cannot achieve some success in this respect (and I shall exemplify how this might be done later), but that pedagogically the relationship between their culture and that which you are introducing is distanced and the two are likely to be understood, as a result, as both irrelevant to each other and the latter as being imposed arbitrarily, for no good reason.

2   Contrastingly, you may teach in a school with students whose parents belong to a higher socio-economic class and who have much higher aspirations. They may have clear expectations of the sorts of careers they wish to enter based on social status and economic privilege (earning power). These students may come from very different ethnic and religious backgrounds, or not, but have quite similar aspirations. In this situation the students and parents may have clear educational goals of achievement, related to examination attainment, but are likely to rate the value of some subjects much higher than others. RE is unlikely to rank highly in this respect unless individual parents see it as important in some broader educational way, which might encompass spiritual and values dimensions of development, but this is unlikely to be the view of the majority. In this situation, pedagogically speaking, the subject is likely to be viewed as an add-on to the curriculum, which some pupils might opt for in Key Stage 4 as a GCSE subject if it is sufficiently popular because of the teacher(s) involved. Nevertheless the pedagogic dissonance is still present: RE does not sufficiently

relate to the aspirations and primary instrumental goals that students and parents recognise as important in the context of schooling and beyond. Again, but in a different way, it is an arbitrary. The pedagogical intent of the subject does not fit centrally with the pedagogy espoused by the parents. In my experience there are many schools which come into this category in Hampshire and elsewhere, located in more affluent areas.

3  A third example can apply to special needs students, but in a different way. Special needs is of course a diverse category but if we take the example of students with severe needs, who can lack basic functions such as speech, it has to be asked why RE applies to them as a statutory entitlement. What, in practice, could this mean? As RE is defined in educational legislation and as it is taught in mainstream schools, it is irrelevant to their basic needs and development. The imposition in this case works the other way round: because the subject is there in statute it has to be applied and yet it is difficult to conceive of what value it could have. It is an arbitrary of no value to the development of the students themselves. It exists by virtue of an outdated historical legacy.

Returning to Bourdieu and Passeron, we may note that they use the terms pedagogic action, pedagogic authority and pedagogic work. Pedagogic action is the imposition and inculcation of social norms which are 'the precondition for the establishment of a relation of pedagogic communication' (Bourdieu and Passeron 1990: 6) which 'corresponds to the objective interests . . . of the dominant groups or classes, both by its mode of imposition and by its delimitation of what and on whom, it imposes' (Bourdieu and Passeron 1990: 7).

Pedagogic authority is the authority that lies with the dominant group that exercises pedagogic action. It is the authority that claims its objective truth in asserting its pedagogic authority. In other words, it uses objectivity to assert its hegemony and maintain it as uncontestable. This results in 'the necessary (inevitable) representation of this arbitrary action as necessary ("natural")' (Bourdieu and Passeron 1990: 13).

Pedagogic action entails pedagogic work, 'a process of inculcation which must be long enough to produce a durable training, i.e. a habitus, the product of internalization of the principles of a cultural arbitrary capable of perpetuating itself' (Bourdieu and Passeron 1990: 31).

Bourdieu and Passeron then enunciate the difference between an implicit pedagogy and an explicit one. An implicit pedagogy is 'the unconscious inculcation of principles which manifest themselves only in their practical state, within the practice that is imposed. An explicit pedagogy is a result of this 'producing a habitus by the inculcation, methodically organised as such, of articulated and even formalised principles' (Bourdieu and Passeron 1990: 47).

You don't have to be a conspiracy theorist to understand the import of this analysis. It applies to Pullman's comments and Marples' criticism of faith schools and Dawkins' criticism of religions and religious education, in Chapter 1. The significant issue is to uncover how a dominant authority through implicit pedagogic action (in the social and political domain) can influence the principles and interactions that take place explicitly in classrooms and schools.

The role of the teacher is crucial in this process. The teacher must be aware (though so often they are not) of his or her critically evaluative role in determining how young people should learn and what they should learn. John Dewey's comments are salient in this respect:

> The teacher is not in the school to impose certain ideas or to form certain habits in the child, but is there as a member of the community to select the influences which shall affect the child and to assist him in properly responding to these influences . . . the teacher's business is simply to determine, on the basis of larger experience and riper wisdom, how the discipline of life shall come to the child.
>
> (Dewey 1902: 22)

However, even beyond Dewey's comments there is another level of critical reflection relating to how the teacher reflects on the political influences that attend his or her curriculum and pedagogic approach.

In religious education the political influences on representation in the curriculum are significant and these, in turn, affect the pedagogic activity (or pedagogic work, in Bourdieu and Passeron's terminology). For some time the uncritical representation of religions has dominated the way religious education has been delivered (both at a national level and locally, through the representation of religions on local SACREs); to a large degree pedagogical issues have been secondary if not ignored. Vivienne Baumfield makes this same point (Baumfield 2007: 125). This does not mean that there is no pedagogic work being done; rather it means that there is no appreciation of the pedagogic work that needs to be done to counter a prevailing tendency toward, at best, inculcation of descriptive understanding that represents religions positively and, at worst, implicit or explicit instruction. There needs to be a determination to create a 'critical leverage to step outside the field . . . of (knowledge) producers' (LiPuma 1993: 23), to ensure that religious education is not the curriculum handmaiden of religions.

Other writers who have been influential in addressing pedagogy include Paolo Freire and Henry Giroux. Freire wrote:

> I have encountered, both in training courses which analyse the role of 'conscientization' and in actual experimentation with a genuinely liberating education, the 'fear of freedom' . . . Not infrequently, training course participants call attention to 'the danger of "conscientization"' in a way which reveals their own fear of freedom. Critical consciousness, they say, is anarchic; others add that critical consciousness may lead to disorder. But some confess: Why deny it? I was afraid of freedom. I am no longer afraid!
>
> (Freire 1980: 15)

Freire's point is made in the context of his approach and context (Brazil), in which he sought to expose the injustice of an unequal social order that dehumanises both the oppressed and oppressor. Those being exploited he seeks to 'conscientize' such that they understand the nature of their society and its impact on them and respond by changing it. Within that approach to pedagogy the ideas of critical consciousness and fear of freedom are significant. But we could argue that within any democratic setting these ideas are significant. Surely all teachers should be seeking to enable their learners to be critical thinkers and, as a result, effective citizens concerned with social justice, and, in doing so, are likely to encounter the 'fear of freedom' that comes with taking seriously the rights, responsibilities and costs involved. In particular, this should apply to RE as a fundamental aim and a way in which it is pedagogically linked to the rest of the curriculum and a vision for education.

This larger contextual sense of pedagogy that we are exploring seeks to identify what messages are given and what forms of communication take place through which these messages are conveyed. This amounts to identifying the values statements that are made within societies and the values principles from which they derive. Here we are investigating a broad range of forms of communication from pub-talk and family and peer conversation to advertising to political pronouncements to media articles to educational 'frameworks for delivery', as they are often called. In effect, pedagogy refers to the discourse(s) within and across societies and their intention(s). The 'art of reading' and 'conscientization' can be said to be at the heart of any democratic educational programme.

It follows that individuals need to be able to read these pedagogical discourses in order to become well informed and enabled members of democratic societies. It also follows that in healthy democratic societies these discourses are likely to be varied, contestable and contesting. But literal reading, of itself, is not enough. Literal reading, as an educational aim, would consist of something akin to what is called (in lesson objectives, attainment targets, levels of attainment, etc.) knowledge and understanding. This demands limited levels of skill on behalf of the learner.

Beyond that notion of reading comes the art of interpreting and communicating an interpretation. This involves a more complex engagement with texts and contexts. For example, what are we to make of the Tower of Babel story (Genesis 11: 1–9), which we mentioned in Chapter 1? This invites all sorts of issues. Why is this story there? What do we think its purpose is? How would different people read it? What difference does it make that it is part of a sacred text, Torah or the Christian Old Testament? How was it meant to be read and how can we read it today? Can we respect readings of it other than our own? What are the larger implications of ways in which people read texts differently? Here we are not dealing with finding answers as to how learners *should* read the text but enquiring into a complexity that impacts upon our own society. We take learners as far as we can into this process, according to levels of ability, but we should not avoid this process altogether and just satisfy ourselves with low level skills related to knowledge and understanding.

Beyond this lies the art of persuasion, by which democracies arrive at the notion of consensus that makes them operable; when this breaks down the result is that conflict becomes more desirable than consensus. Persuasion (disregarding for the moment the basis upon which persuasion becomes effective) gives direction and purpose to the democratic process. The art of persuasion in the classroom is the basis on which students exemplify their capacity as critical thinkers.

This is addressed by Henry Giroux when he writes:

> Rather than invalidate the importance of schooling, public pedagogy extends the sites of pedagogy and, in doing so, broadens and deepens the meaning of cultural pedagogy. [It] underscores the central importance of formal spheres of learning that unlike their popular counterparts – driven largely by commercial interests that more often mis-educate the public – must provide citizens with those critical capacities, modes of literacies, knowledge and skills that enable them to both read the world critically and participate in shaping and governing it.
>
> (Giroux 2004: 21)

The implications of this relationship between public pedagogy and formal schooling are highly significant. For example, if teaching and learning bear no relationship to students' experiences in the wider world they become irrelevant and the students will have no sense of purpose within their learning or desire ownership of it. Also if, for example, in RE we decide not to introduce students to Islam because it has a controversial image within public pedagogy, then we do our students an educational disservice. We should be aiming to support students in making the connections between religion and public space, to show its relevance. This is necessary regardless of whether particular aspects of religion are controversial or not. Also, in order for students to make these connections we must focus on the development of their capacities and skills so that they can be critical in an informed way and desire to participate. Participation in lessons is an aspect of and practice for further participation in society.

My aim is to show how this broad reading of the character of pedagogy can act as the basis of the educational sense of what it means to speak about the theory and practice of teaching and learning. We should then arrive at what the process of the latter is, based on having regard to it in the larger context from which it is derived. This can be understood as a significant and meaningful way of addressing the three aims of the QCA curriculum: successful learners, confident individuals, responsible citizens (QCA 2006).

## The impact of public pedagogy on classroom pedagogy

Once we become aware of how public pedagogy impacts on pupils' (and parents') worldviews and values we start to get a much more inclusive and contextual understanding of classroom pedagogy and its role. This alerts us to the following:

- that students come to the classroom with views and values that are already shaped by their experience and the inevitable discourse that has formed them;

- that these views and values are likely to be shaped by varying influences, that students may more likely than not have reflected upon them and that they may be limited and even misinformed in their construction, but not necessarily;

- that our role as teachers will need to take account of these views as a necessary contribution to learning;

- that our subject will, as a result, be far more politicised than if we resort to a more instructional model of teaching;

- that student contributions in the classroom are highly significant and necessary and that we must skilfully negotiate the process of learning with this in mind;

- that when it comes to the subject of religions students should be invited to comment freely but responsibly in relation to religious pedagogies and their impact on the world;

- that RE, as our subject is called, can only function to its potential if worldviews beyond the religious are included;

- that the process of student intervention and informed conversation between students is the most significant activity to be promoted;

- that the material we present to students should not be regarded as simply subject content but be instrumental to a larger purpose in relation to their development;

- that our own interventions need to facilitate and progress learning, opening up further questions and promoting further and deeper interaction between students and between students and the material studied;

- that enquiry-oriented learning needs to be the basis of any effective progress in students' development: their capabilities, skills, knowledge and understanding and awareness.

## Conclusion: where do we stand now?

This chapter has considered a number of issues that have affected the provision for religious education to date. It should have stimulated your ideas as to how religious education can progress in the future and the important areas it has to address. In turn it has, hopefully, clarified your thinking and progressed it beyond your stance taken at the end of Chapter 1. It would be useful for you to determine what you think are the main issues to address at this stage and relate them to the discussion of pedagogy introduced above prior to moving on to the approaches analysed in Chapter 3.

# 3

# Pedagogy in approaches to the study of religion and religious education

## Introduction

This chapter analyses approaches to religious education currently developed by theorists and researchers in the subject, linking this to the academic study of religion. Five different approaches are the main focus of this chapter. The chapter will analyse these approaches, link that analysis to the pedagogical issues raised in Chapter 2 and ask the question as to what extent RE can regard itself as a discipline. It will then summarise the ground covered in Part 1 of this book, the first three chapters.

## Approaches to the study of religion

One of the significant characteristics of religious education is that it draws on the study of religion as a multi-disciplinary area of enquiry. This is not true of all curriculum subjects; for example, history constitutes a discipline in itself, as does science. Figure 3.1 shows a grid which has been constructed to show the disciplines that the study of religion draws upon and the ways in which those disciplines are influenced by different movements over time, resulting in new methods.

Think of this grid as a way of mapping approaches to the study of religion based on different disciplines (vertical axis) affected by different movements (horizontal axis). When we put a vertical and horizontal heading together we arrive at a particular type of method, for example feminist psychology, postmodernist (or non-realist) theology, existentialist theology (as in Paul Tillich, for example), Marxist sociology (by which I mean a Marxist oriented approach to the sociology of religions) – take, for example, the studies on *Mohammed* (1971) and *Islam and Capitalism* (1974) by Maxime Rodinson. In this chapter we shall consider different contemporary approaches to RE, the approaches to the study of religion from which they are derived and the pedagogical differences between them that have resulted.

| | Anthropological | Sociological | Historical | Theological | Philosophical | Psychological |
|---|---|---|---|---|---|---|
| Pre-modernist | | | | | | |
| Modernist | | | | | | |
| Postmodernist | | | | | | |
| Feminist | | | | | | |
| Marxist | | | | | | |
| Existentialist | | | | | | |
| Phenomenological | | | | | | |

**Figure 3.1** RS grid

## Pre-modernist, modernist and postmodernist approaches

These terms are somewhat different to the others in the horizontal axis and here I need to explain my use of them in the context of epistemology and pedagogy:

1 Pre-modernist: affirming that metaphysical and revelatory sources are the basis for moral and social judgements and that religious and social networks are the means by which these are maintained and are the primary basis for identity construction.

  Pedagogically, modes are instructional or catechetical and responses required are most likely to involve a lower level of skills and critical thinking due to the hierarchical location of authority.

2 Modernist: affirming a universalist stance on moral issues and an understanding that religions can accommodate themselves to this, on the basis of critique and consensus; also, that European Enlightenment thought is both the basis on which this judgement is made and its means of arbitration; and that nationalistic ideas of citizenship are primary arbiters of identity construction that accommodate religious affiliation.

  Pedagogically the emphasis will be on the skills and attitudes required to produce consensus, allowing for democratic argument. As a result authority is diffused and outcomes are less predictable but still circumscribed. The idea of arriving at a framework of understanding that constitutes objective knowledge is valued.

3 Postmodernist: affirming that identity construction is fluid and open to change and ambiguity and that values positions are subjective and contestable; that there is no consensual, universal or transcendent principle that determines values, identity or knowledge.

  Pedagogically, the emphasis will be on the development of skills and attitudes required to debate and deconstruct knowledge positions and construct persuasive argument. Authority will be contestable and negotiable. Subjectivity will be valued. This means that engagement with ideas, events and texts is open to re-readings by individuals and groups on the basis of their instrumental or contextual value – there is no fixed reading.

These different positions influence both public space and the basis of educational activity. They interact with both those disciplines on the vertical axis and movements on the horizontal axis, but selectively. For example, it is possible for theology to be pre-modern, modernist and postmodern in method. Also, we can ask whether a particular feminist theology belongs to a postmodernist or modernist category. Some illustration of this classification will be given below on pp. 45–68 and later in the book.

In the following sections I analyse how approaches to religious education have been influenced by approaches within the study of religions.

## Phenomenological approaches to religious education

The phenomenological approaches referred to below are modernist in design in that they sought to accentuate what religions have in common, often, as in Smart's case below (pp. 45–46), by providing a typology of dimensions of religion, a sort of family resemblance (see Smart 1971). Thus, one could say, there were universal characteristics.

## Ninian Smart

Ninian Smart was the proponent of a phenomenological approach to the study of religions that had a direct influence on the method then used in RE as it changed from a Christian-based subject to the study of world religions in the 1970s. Phenomenology best fits within a philosophical category, though we have to understand this in a broad way because we can also speak of a phenomenological approach to social anthropology and other disciplines. This will become clear when we study Robert Jackson's adaptation of Smart's approach (pp. 46–51). We need to bear in mind, however, that the approaches used are not always simply binary. Smart was influenced by the philosopher Husserl in the construction of his method, especially in relation to the terms eidetic vision and *epoche*. He was also an admirer of Van der Leeuw and his more aesthetically oriented approach to phenomenology. The origin of the term, or at least the point at which it gained its importance, can be located in Hegel's *Phenomenology of Spirit* (1807 [1977]). But its meaning varies with different writers. Whilst *epoche* involves the restraint of judgement, or 'bracketing out', eidetic vision is the resultant capacity to see what is really, 'objectively' there, as a result. This is epistemologically problematic since it presumes that when viewing cultural and religious phenomena subjectivity can be suspended. This in turn would mean we are able to throw off the constraints of our own enculturation. There is also a sense in this phenomenological approach that we are able to intuit an understanding of the phenomenon at some essential level. Smart's way of simplifying this philosophical conundrum was to focus on understanding a religion from the viewpoint of the believer. This had a major influence on religious education in England and Wales in the 1970s as this premise for a phenomenological approach became axiomatic. This approach was also influenced by the values position that Smart held and later expressed explicitly in his desideratum:

A multicultural or pluralistic philosophy of religion is a desideratum, and it is amazing how culture-bound so many Western philosophers have been: an unconscious (to be kind) imperialism . . . We have surely passed beyond a stage in human life when national values stand supreme, after all the horrors national wars have caused during this passing century. Nationalism sometimes makes good politics: but its dangers are well advertised. We need to see religions in the same sort of context: just as democracy is a way to eliminate violence in the choice of policies: so a kind of spiritual democracy should eliminate inter-religious and inter-ideological violence . . . we need an overarching worldview for all human beings.

(Smart 1998: xii–xiii)

Smart's utopian vision, in such contrast to Bowker's, cited in Chapter 1, should not disguise his analysis of religious phenomena and the need to make clear distinctions between religions. However many phenomenologists of religion took a more naïve approach by simply trying to describe the phenomena. This then tended to ignore the hermeneutical problems involved, and many teachers replicated this in the classroom by taking a descriptive approach to the literal activities of religion, reducing religious education to a factual exercise and therefore demanding little of the learner. Much of the richness of Smart's approach was lost in translation from the study of religions to RE. It was almost as if the 'exotic' would be fascinating in itself. As RE progressed into the 1990s and government agencies gained a more centralised influence over Locally Agreed Syllabuses by introducing the Non-Statutory Model Syllabuses in 1994 and later the non-statutory framework for religious education in 2004, so the two attainment targets for both documents, learning about and learning from religion, took hold and a consequence of this was that the descriptive 'learning about' became much more prevalent than the ambiguous 'learning from' in classroom practice. The attainment targets were taken from the pedagogy of Michael Grimmitt (1987) but used in a way not intended by him and which he later criticised with some pedagogical fury (Grimmitt 2000).

## Robert Jackson

Jackson (1997) refined the phenomenological approach in RE by introducing a socio-anthropological dimension taken from the work of anthropologist Clifford Geertz and others. Geertz speaks about distance near and distance far conceptual constructs that underpinned the worldviews of different groups and their sense of identity. To take an example, the idea of a primary individual identity, prevalent in Western societies, was alien to some tribal groups investigated by Geertz. Thus he came to recognise that some conceptual constructs of identity and of the world were not easily translatable into Western constructs. It was not just the conceptual constructs themselves that were alien but the whole 'grammar' of the culture. For Jackson this meant that what was necessary was to arrive at a 'grammatical' reading of a culture to understand it and that this was what a phenomenological approach should entail. This he termed an interpretive approach.

Geertz explains, as conveyed by Jackson, that '[t]he art of anthropological analysis is to grasp concepts that are for another people "experience near" well enough to place them " . . . in illuminating connection with experience-distant concepts theorists have fashioned to capture the general features of social life"' (Jackson 1997: 35; Geertz 1983: 58.). Jackson quotes the example of Geertz, referring to the Javanese people he studied, in which the concepts of *batin*, *lair* and *alus* were significant. Whereas *batin* refers to subjective feelings, at root identical across all individuals, *lair* refers to outward actions in the social domain. *Alus* connotes refined, civilised and smooth and is the regulator of both *batin* and *lair*. Geertz then provides a narrative, the experience of a young man whose wife has died, greeting everyone by acting according to the protocols of *alus* and the effects of that on his inner feelings and the discipline exercised over them (*batin*) and his public behaviour (*lair*). Coming to an understanding of this pattern of conceptual inter-relationship or cultural 'grammar' that determines both behaviour and self-understanding prevents 'the inadvertent projection of one's own concepts and ways of using them on to a different set of concepts with a different grammar' (Jackson 1997: 35–37; Geertz 1983: 61–70). It is akin, Geertz suggests, to interpreting a poem (Geertz 1983: 70). It is also Geertz's answer to his key question as to 'how each set of concepts should be deployed in order " . . . to produce an interpretation of the way a people live which is neither imprisoned within their mental horizons . . . nor systematically deaf to the distinctive tonalities of their existence' (Jackson 1997: 24–35; Geertz 1983: 57).

If I understand Geertz's approach, and Jackson's explication of it, correctly, here we have the basis of a pedagogic model based on conceptuality illustrated with regard to narrative that influences the way in which we engage students with conceptually distinctive cultural and religious systems that are 'distance far' or at least to a certain extent dissimilar to their own. The hermeneutic circle in these terms is determined by this engagement with 'distance far' concepts and bringing them into an encounter with our own 'distance near' ones, the result being to be open to, grapple with and reflect upon different cultural grammars without reducing another's to our own or dismissing it as alien and therefore of no interest or simply impenetrable, peculiar and irrational. Both Geertz and Jackson also use the term 'translation' with respect to this, the point being, it seems to me, that what must be avoided is the tendency to translate out another's grammar into the conceptual confines of our own. The rigour of such a conceptually based pedagogic model, which involves both rational and affective engagement, is laudable, clear and eminently suited to religious material, both at a conceptual and narrative level.

Whilst this was influential in moving religious education forward in theory, it again suffered, as Smart's approach did, from being reduced to a more descriptive exercise in practice when applied to the RE textbooks produced based on the study of different religious groups in the Midlands.

Jackson commented on the process of producing the textbooks and the 'constraints' experienced, which resulted in the difficulty of explaining the method to the publisher, and the difficulty of trying to set up the process of communication between the material and the students in class within this format, the teachers not necessarily using the books as intended (Jackson 2000: 141–142).

In his later book (Jackson 2004) Jackson further discusses his interpretive method and also discusses other pedagogical approaches that he regards as complementary. He points out that interpretive approaches are approaches to 'understanding the ways of life of others' and complement 'other aspects of religious education, such as the application of philosophical techniques or thinking skills to RE or the use of arts' and 'has sometimes been combined with other methods' (Jackson 2004: 87). In his chapter on interpretive approaches to religious education (Jackson 2004: 87–108) Jackson's focus is to show the relationship between interpretive approaches and religious education pedagogy generally.

In summarising the interpretive approach introduced in his earlier work (Jackson 1997), he draws attention to the pedagogic importance of reflexivity, 'the relationship between the experience of students and the experience of those whose way of life they are seeking to interpret'. He identifies three aspects:

■ learners re-assessing their understanding of their *own* way of life (being 'edified' through reflecting on another's way of life);

■ making a constructive critique of the material studied at a distance;

■ developing a running critique of the interpretive process.

(Jackson 2004: 88)

He goes on to discuss the pedagogic implications of these aspects of reflexivity by identifying 'an approach to teaching that encourages reflection and constructive criticism and which sets out to equip pupils to make their own judgements about religious claims' (Jackson 2004: 88–89). He adds that 'the pedagogy for this approach to religious education also requires methods that allow students to gain insight from their peers and to be able to examine the different ideas of truth held within the classroom' (Jackson 2004: 89). In this way learning will become dialectical and genuinely conversational across diversity.

The studies provided in Jackson's chapter by teachers working with interpretive approaches highlight ways in which they have employed them within their differing educational contexts. Anne Krisman's report (Jackson 2004: 99–101) is on adapting the interpretive approach to RE in a special school in Greater London. Her focus was on personal stories that would resonate more effectively with her pupils' sensitivity to feelings. Two stories used related to Guru Nanak and Lalo, the carpenter, from the Sikh tradition, and the story of Kisagotami and the Buddha, in the Buddhist tradition. She adapted the telling of the stories to incorporate the evocative affective language used by her pupils in order to resonate with them. In this way they came to gain a deeper understanding, for example of the wider meaning of the story of Kisagotami in addressing the acceptance of death and suffering.

Jackson refers to this process, in general terms, as building conceptual bridges, as presented in the Warwick RE Project materials. Here it is understood as building a connection between the pupils' 'own spiritual vocabulary' and 'the characters introduced' (Jackson 2004: 100). Krisman employed the technique of a 'Wall of Wisdom' where pupils' comments were displayed in speech bubbles, giving their work status and recognition. 'The display of these often profound comments and questions, says Krisman, 'encourages pupils to see themselves as part of a construction of understanding in RE' (Jackson 2004: 100–101; Jackson 1997: 19).

In the other three examples that Jackson cites, of which I shall report on two (Jackson 2004; O'Grady 2003; Eriksson 2000), a similar intent, despite differing strategies, emerges. Because of Grady's desire to increase student motivation of a Year 8 (12–13-year-old) class in a mainly white urban comprehensive, he encouraged their own questions about the Islamic material presented and linked the idea of Islamic dress to their own interest in fashion. This involved action research with the pupils as participants who kept diaries, evaluated work in progress and responded to questions in semi-structured interviews. From this exercise, and the findings gathered from pupils, O'Grady redesigned his unit of work on Islam for the future. Eriksson's Swedish school-based research was focused on values. The pupils were mainly white, middle class and native Swedish. He wanted to 'determine the central values of life held by the pupils he studied' (Jackson 2004: 101). This encouraged democratic participation with plenty of pupil–pupil as well as pupil–teacher interaction. The year's research started with a written task answering questions as follows: 'When I think about death, I think . . . When I think about the meaning of life, I think . . . When I think about God I think . . . An analysis of a final essay on the topic 'What is most important to you in your life?' was the main data used for his findings. The relevance to pedagogy in RE lies in Eriksson's suggestions for the practitioner, which include:

- recognising the importance of encouraging pupils to reflect;
- using knowledge about pupils' needs, cognitive skills, experiences and thoughts in planning lessons;
- including work that encourages pupils (especially boys) to write in order to explain and defend their ideas;
- including pupils' written reflections or 'inner dialogue' in teaching material;
- using pupils' own problems as a starting point for lessons.

(Jackson 2004: 102–103)

In Jackson's summary discussion of the above examples he comments:

> Each of the case studies sees religious education as a hermeneutical process . . . Each has a different emphasis. If we think of learning in religious education as an unbroken hermeneutic circle, then the case studies begin at different points on its circumference . . . The interpretive approaches outlined here are intended to provide opportunities for different religious and cultural positions to be understood in a methodologically sound and self-critical way . . . [they] show that teaching and learning can begin at any point on the hermeneutic circle, with a critical overview of a representation of a religious tradition, with a study of an individual person or case study, with pupils' experiences or interactions in the school or with a concern or question from students.

(Jackson 2004: 105–108)

In his review of dialogic approaches, which he has also promoted, Jackson emphasises the value of those that

> recognise the agency of children and young people, treating them as co-learners, co-designers of curriculum and even as co-researchers. In this regard . . . dialogical approaches have much in common with interpretive approaches . . . but emphasize the child both as actor and processor of ideas from others engaged in dialogue. There are also certain features that overlap with the personal narrative approach [Erricker and Erricker 2000] although the approaches discussed in the present chapter are not grounded in an anti-realist epistemology.

(Jackson 2004: 109–110)

The dialogic approaches Jackson reports on have the following characteristics:

- pupils examining their local culture and moving outward, in historical time or toward a more globalised context, as in the work of Heid Leganger-Krogstad in Norway;

- intercultural/interreligious learning aiming at pupils engaging in communication within a multicultural context, as in the work of Wolfram Weisse in Hamburg;

- research on the religio-cultural and theological influence of children upon one another within a multicultural primary school class and their formation of new ideas through encounter, as in the work of Julia Ipgrave in Leicester.

(Jackson 2004: 111–121)

However, in reading Jackson's reports of the classroom practice and research placed under the interpretive and dialogic headings, mentioned on pp. 46–50 above, the conceptual rigour of Geertz's principles is not apparent to the same degree. Is this inevitable in the same sense as Ninian Smart's phenomenological model tended, in many cases within the classroom, to be reduced to mere description, and lack the hermeneutical and thus pedagogical complexity of engagement? The report on Krisman's work with special school pupils using personal stories works in a rich way at the narrative level and her strategy of working between the evocative affective language of her pupils and the story of Kisagotami to bridge narratives and make the latter meaningful is clearly effective on a narrative plane of resonance. It does not necessarily engage the pupils with the conceptual dissimilarities at work based on the Buddha's concept of dukkha. Similar questions could be asked of the other examples Jackson gives. They operate at a strategic level of engagement with a concern to enrich and extend pupils' horizons but not necessarily to challenge their conceptual constructions. If this is the case, then the richness, rigour and ultimate sense of conceptual grammar that were the basis of Geertz's hermeneutic cycle have been reduced to something more concerned with reflecting on one's own narrative and expanding it to consider those of others. Eriksson's suggestions for the practitioner on p. 49 seem to have more of this flavour to them. It could be argued that this is inevitable and appropriate when moving from academic research to classroom practice, especially given the need to engage students, and special needs students in Krisman's case, with wider horizons than their own personal ones. If so we have to acknowledge the importance of that change of emphasis and shift in depth of engagement. But if the hermeneutic circle is a matter of engaging with religious material to encourage reflexivity, without operating at a conceptual level, then something vital may be lost in terms of depth of engagement and the skills required beyond empathy. Effective strategies for engagement, at specific points in the learning process, are quite different from having an overall systematic pedagogic strategy (or methodology) that underpins the pedagogic process as a whole. The former have to be embedded in the latter to create a coherent and systematic rationale for learning.

There is always a tendency to understand the other in terms of your own cultural 'grammar' and its conceptual base. That is an obvious starting point. But, for example, as mentioned above, to understand the Buddhist concept of dukkha by translating it into a Western conception of suffering renders its powerful diagnosis of the causes of suffering and the resultant prescribed method of cure anachronistic. In the West we do not regard suffering as a chronic condition but as something that happens from time to time and more to some than others. That is not the Buddhist point. Similarly, to translate the Muslim concept of jihad into the Western idea of struggle or striving will tend to work on only the superficial level of striving to achieve something, not the notion of life as a striving toward Allah – literally a spiritual vocation. What I call 'translating out', rather than the far more significant task of 'translating in', is a way of ignoring the 'grammar' within which the concept is embedded and can result in a more superficial comparative exercise based on similarity, with some apprehension of difference, rather than a more rigorous attempt to engage with a different worldview. Narrative can take us so far in engagement but it will not necessarily bring this point home. I do not contend that the above was the case with Jackson's examples, but that it is not sufficiently explicated.

Pedagogically, phenomenological approaches are primarily concerned with cognitive appreciation at the level of descriptive comprehension being linked to affective awareness, as in the quality of empathy or more significantly the appreciation of the cultural grammar of other groups.

## Experiential approaches to religious education

The experiential approaches referred to below are modernist in design, being universalist in their assumptions, and draw on the idea of a universal wisdom found within earlier religious texts and practices. But this also suggests a pre-modern understanding of 'universal wisdom'.

Experiential approaches to RE are usually understood as a type of phenomenological/ psychological method but they have strong existential overtones. They are concerned with the phenomenon of religion, but with an emphasis on the spiritual value of religious ideas and practices of a spiritual kind.

## Mircea Eliade

We can typify the method within the study of religions that characterises these approaches with reference to the work of Mircea Eliade and his volume on *The Sacred and the Profane* (Eliade 1959). This set out to show that the modern, secular world had led to a diminishment of human understanding of the world, humanity's relationship with the world and a consequent lack of understanding of each individual's understanding of him/herself and life's purpose. He did this by arguing that we had lost those rituals and, as a consequence, the mythic or spiritual understanding that performing them conveyed, which were present in archaic societies. His proposal could best be said to fall into a psychological approach to religion influenced by Jung and the theory of archetypes. Contentiously perhaps, we could say, on the lateral axis, this was also a pre-modernist approach in that his thesis is that we need to return to a pre-modern understanding of the world/human society and cosmology (at least figuratively and psychologically speaking). Thus, though arguing for something rather different, and pursuing a different, psychological method, his thesis can be compared to, for example, Catholic theologians who were concerned with the contemplative, such as Ignatius Loyola, who has been an influence on David Hay.

Eliade was much criticised by anthropologists, who claimed he had no anthropological evidence for his claims to these behaviours, there was no fieldwork. They were right of course but that wasn't the point from Eliade's perspective. To insist on empirical evidence is a very modernist form of argument, important to the status of anthropology as a social science. Eliade was simply pursuing the idea that we were alienated from the world and ourselves and, as a consequence of losing sight of the sacredness of things (both literally and figuratively), and suggesting how we could regain that. Such an idea does not even lie within the realms of modernist thinking so it is not surprising that his way of pursuing it was not modernist in method.

Eliade's approach (also mediated through writers like Joseph Campbell) is conducive to an idea of spirituality. Thus we find this type of method in the approach to religious education employed by David Hay, John Hammond, Sue Phillips and others at a practical level because of their concern that secular society has lost the spiritual dimension that religion provided and, as a result, religious literacy, for example the richness of such concepts as transcendence, atonement or grace. This is a point also made by Wright (pp. 54–59), but for different reasons. The articulation of this is most clearly expressed in the strategies for approaching religious education in Hammond *et al.*'s *New Methods in RE Teaching* (1990) and Sue Phillips' Theatre of Learning techniques (2004). In these the primary rationale is to enable pupils to get in touch with their spirituality. The vehicles for this can consist in religious material from the major religions, usually of a contemplative or ritual kind, or activities that are more broadly based in implicit religiously oriented material.

In both cases it is about affective learning, rather than cognitive learning, involving ritual, symbol, myth, rites of passage, meditation of different kinds and performance. The emphasis is on the kinaesthetic mode and also techniques within specific religions, Ignatian prayer or Buddhist meditation for example. A further point to draw out here is that such learning is the antithesis of catechetical or doctrinal instruction. As a result the orientation of the approach reflects a particular distinction in the history of religion itself: the difference between the sant/wisdom tradition and that of the institutional doctrinal tradition. Ron Geaves has pointed to religious education being too oriented to the latter (Geaves 1998).

The sant tradition in India recognised (and recognises) the importance of the holy person as the one to go to for spiritual guidance, as the repository of the spiritual due to his/her closer proximity to the divine. It was of less, if any, significance what 'religion' he belonged to and the message of the sants was often that to be concerned with this was an error. Take, for example Guru Nanak and, in a different sense, the Buddha. What was important was receiving the spiritual teachings, the wisdom and the blessing of being in the proximity of holiness or wisdom. In the non-Indian traditions we have the Wisdom Literature embedded in the Jewish and Christian scriptures: Ecclesiastes, the Psalms and the Song of Songs, for example. These are about the poetics of human experience not the doctrinal truths of a religious group. Experiential approaches in RE tend to reflect the concerns of the sant/wisdom traditions.

# David Hay

David Hay's approach to the pedagogy of religious education (Hay 2000) is rooted in a conviction that, following on from the biologist and zoologist Alister Hardy, religious experience is an essential aspect of organic evolution because of its survival value. He also posits, as a result, that it is a universal trait. His approach is also influenced by the empirical research he has conducted at the Religious Experience Research Unit in Oxford, through which he proposes that the experiential dimension of religious or spiritual experience is a facet of most people's lives even though they most often are not affiliated to a religion nor attend institutional religious observances. In a secular age he refers to this experiential connection with religion as salient but hidden: it is not reflected in public life. He saw this reflected in education generally and even in the attitudes of RE teachers who feared being seen as indoctrinating children into religion. This approach acts as a corrective to the religions-based emphasis prevalent in the 'learning about' and 'learning from' categories of the QCDA model and as a critique of the value of 'learning about' religions.

Hay's motivation in promoting experiential RE has been based on the paradox, within Britain, of there being only a minority of religiously practising people, giving rise to the impression of an overwhelmingly secular society, and yet one in which religion still has an 'immense political and social impact' (Hay 2000: 74). It could be added that this is also generally true globally and that Hay's research on religious experience actually uncovers a very significant, non-institutionalised connectedness with experiences of transcendence. For Hay the work of RE amounts to a de-indoctrination of pupils influenced by secular society by questioning 'hidden cultural assumptions that constrain our possibilities as human beings' (Hay 2000: 74). For this pupils need to be introduced to different ways of understanding reality that question self-evident cultural assumptions. The barrier to this is the hegemony of a one-dimensional culture that actually operates with a rigid sense of conformity in relation to the acceptability of specific interests and beliefs. The RE teacher is placed in a position of emancipating pupils from this narrow cultural constraint on their potential. To do this Hay advocated that teachers should not teach didactically but undertake to do the following:

- Introduce pupils to raising personal awareness and the 'point mode' or here and now of experience through exercises of prayer, meditation and contemplation and allow them to explore aspects of themselves through these. They focus on our embodied nature and empathising with the self-perceptions of others.

- Through exercises advocating using texts from different traditions which dwell on existential questions about the self and the universe. They are eclectic and 'wisdom' rather than dogmatically oriented in nature. They rely on figurative expression: metaphors and symbolism.

- Use exercises employing the imagination, often with guided fantasy narratives that evoke religious meaning but not necessarily by using religious texts.

Hay's work on awareness raising in the RE classroom, which resulted in *New Methods in RE Teaching: An Experiential Approach* (Hammond *et al.* 1990) in collaboration with other authors and schools involved in the project, has made a significant impact on classroom practice, with its readily employable activities addressing the pedagogical approach described above. Since 1990, this has been supplemented by Hay's work on relational consciousness. This is a term that emerged out of a focus on the spiritual life of children and a project he conducted with Rebecca Nye. It resulted in the volume *The Spirit of the Child* (Hay with Nye 1998). From this research with children Hay deduced that when children talked about spirituality their level of awareness and perceptiveness was higher than with conversation on other matters. Also, he remarks that, without exception, their conversations related to how they 'related to reality; either God, other people, themselves, or the material world' (Hay with Nye 1998: 83). Thus, Hay coins the term 'relational consciousness' and emphasises that addressing this is 'the first step in creating the conditions for an insight into the roots of religion. This, of course, will entail attention to the way in which teachers themselves relate to pupils in their classrooms and the basis on which such a pedagogy operates.

It can be argued that the work begun by Hammond *et al.* (1990) has been extended at classroom level by Sue Phillips. As an experienced teacher in a secondary school in Bognor, West Sussex, UK, she has developed an experiential approach because of the need to engage pupils in RE such that they find it meaningful to them. Out of this approach has developed her Theatre of Learning project and her publications that show how different religious traditions and spiritual development can be taught and learned by using experiential strategies for learning (http://www.sfe.co.uk/products/tocs/TOL_toc.pdf). Her approach is very popular amongst a number of Hampshire teachers and her influence extends to other areas of the UK and other countries as well. The type of 'relational consciousness' approach that Hay describes can be seen at work in both her approach to teaching and learning and in the type of conversations in which pupils are engaged in her lessons. She views religious education explicitly as a vehicle for developing young people's spirituality and generating empathy for others.

Pedagogically, experiential approaches are primarily concerned with affective rather than cognitive learning and are designed to promote spiritual development based on a universalist hypothesis that regards religions and religious practice as instrumental to that purpose. In effect experiential approaches work from the premise that secularity impoverishes the fulfilment of human potential.

## Theological approaches to religious education

## Andrew Wright

Andrew Wright's approach is modernist in design in that it is based on critique, objectivity and the idea that knowledge of the way things are is possible, if not yet known (critical realism). The caveat is that he wishes to show that transcendental sources of authority can be and should be considered, thus the idea of spirituality in his work. He is, therefore, also critical of outcomes of the Enlightenment project. In this we might recognise some anti-modernist sentiments in his, rather paradoxical, appeal to the correlation of modernity as the search for objective truth and transcendent reality as its apotheosis.

Wright's work revolves around his Spiritual Education Project, which seeks to:

- analyse and evaluate the nature of contemporary spiritual education in England and Wales;
- develop an alternative critical rationale;
- present proposals for a new critical pedagogy.

(Wright 2000: 170)

Wright's approach is theological (but in a philosophical sense). His critique focuses on the inadequacy of liberal religious education and its anthropological ideal of the autonomous individual. The result, he maintains, is that 'our identity is rooted in introspection, so our language operates as the secondary expression of primary experience' (Wright 2000: 171). The thrust of this observation, for Wright, is that we seek to make the world conform to our experience rather than recognising it as it is. Religious doctrines, as statements of cognitive truth claims, and thus religious truth, are bypassed in favour of stimulating children's apprehension of spiritual experiences as opposed to 'realistic religious truth' (Wight 2000: 172). In place of this state of affairs Wright wishes to substitute a 'critical theory of religious teaching' (Wright 2000: 172) by understanding language to be engaged with an external reality not a personal sense of spiritual awareness or feeling. In this comment we can observe the distance he creates between his own position and those who have pursued an experiential method. As a result he wishes pupils to explore conflicting worldviews (Wright 2000: 172), rather than being inducted into a 'single paradigm' of spiritual feeling that has no rational edge or relationship with the external world.

He states that his method, critical realism, is founded in the Enlightenment pursuit of reason as a vehicle to truth that is, as yet, beyond our apprehension but still a project worth pursuing as the only means to establish a 'contingent rationality [on the basis that] [t]his is the best sense we can make of reality at present, now let's see if we can achieve anything better' (Wright 2000: 173). In this way Wright seeks to avoid both confessionalism and the liberal idea, developed through phenomenological approaches, that religious teachings are commensurable aspects of the same truth or that spiritualities promoted through different traditions are universal and common to all humanity. Spirituality is intimately related to truth in that it 'is the developing relationship of the individual within community and tradition, to that which is – or is perceived to be – of ultimate concern, ultimate value and ultimate truth' (Wright 2000: 175).

Wright identifies that differing communities and traditions have gone about constructing these 'ultimates' in differing ways and with differing outcomes which manifest themselves through the teaching of the major religions. In the context of this pluralism a critical religious education must therefore:

- reflect the 'genuine diversity of religious and secular perspectives on religion' and the 'ambiguous, controversial, and conflicting nature of theological truth claims';
- encourage children to express their 'emergent religious beliefs and attitudes' so that this becomes 'a conscious and integral part of the learning process';

- 'insist on the primary importance of providing pupils with the skills, knowledge and wisdom' to 'explore both their own ideology and the various ideologies presented by religious and secular traditions';

- 'demand the cultivation of intelligent conversation between the two horizons' (the child's and the religious) 'as a means to further clarifying, enriching and developing the child's religious beliefs';

- attend to religious literacy which will promote 'the manner in which they [children] come to their own religious belief systems' and their 'ability to take part in an informed, critical, sensitive and ideologically aware conversation'.

(Wright 2000: 177–180)

The above constitute Wright's five pedagogical principles for critical religious education. But we may note his lack of discrimination between what constitutes a 'religious belief system' and what might constitute children's informed but not necessarily religious worldview.

In the Grimmitt volume Wright sets out his outline for a pedagogical procedure in three phases:

- Phase one: The Horizon of the Pupil, involving an introduction to the topic; an open exploration; an articulation of initial beliefs.

- Phase two: The Horizons of Religion, involving presenting a spectrum of conflicting beliefs; the location of pupils' positions within this spectrum.

- Phase three: The Engagement of Horizons, involving development of critical thinking skills; conversation across and between horizons; re-articulation of pupils' initial position.

(Wright 2000: 181)

Whilst we may note the systematic procedure that Wright adopts, it is open to criticism on the basis of his phrasing. 'Topic' is not a particularly useful term for the construction of an enquiry and 'concept' would give more rigour to the process.

It is worth dwelling, at this point, on Wright's distinction between political and comprehensive liberalism. The former refers to agreement on the four basic liberal virtues of respect, freedom, tolerance and equality as desirable character traits and worthwhile virtues that enable democratic polity; the latter refers to those virtues as an ideological position that all should affirm as '*constitutive* of the good life itself' (Wright 2007). The pedagogical point for Wright is this: political liberalism refers to the way in which a democratic process is conducted. The latter insists that such virtues should be ideologically normative. To take homosexuality as an example, as he does citing the case of Rocco Butiglione, Italian European Affairs Minister, one could be tolerant of homosexuality within a democratic environment whilst ideologically being of the view that it is morally wrong. This was Butiglione's view as a Roman Catholic. However, comprehensive liberalism insists that tolerance must be identified with acceptance of homosexuality without opposition. Wright points out that Butiglione was forced to withdraw his candidacy for the post of the European Union's new commissioner for Justice, Freedom and Security as a result of his position but that this was a result of the imposition of the idea of comprehensive liberalism not political liberalism, with which he concurred – he did not wish to impose his views on the political process (Wright 2007: 34). I think Wright might be being politically disingenuous in citing this example but all the same let's consider how the difference might play out in the classroom. I suggest that it is quite often the case that RE teachers operate according to the comprehensive ideological model rather than the political – and not always to the advantage of liberalism but often so. On the one hand RE teachers are often uncomfortable with criticism of religious teachings; on the other they are often inclined to ensure that what they choose to teach presents liberal virtues as uncontestable and, as a result, tend to present religions through the lens of teaching some virtues uncontroversial because of broad consensual appeal, for example anti-racism. But equally they may well avoid those that are in contestation – for example homosexuality. There is a confusion here – often not consciously acknowledged – that riddles the pedagogy of RE in its delivery and practice. The result can be the teaching of accepted liberal values rather than investigating religion and not presenting the controversial illiberal teachings within religion. Wright correctly points us in the direction of RE losing its critical edge. The question of what that leaves as uncontestable, and in the RE classroom not to be tolerated, is the further issue that needs to be investigated.

Wright is ambivalent here. Following Karl Popper's 'paradox of tolerance' he agrees that some things are not deserving of tolerance: 'racism, sexism, homophobia, slavery, genocide' (as, for example, in Holocaust denial as well). Thus, he concludes that 'there is a right not to tolerate the intolerant' (Wright 2007: 38). Thus, it follows that 'it is not sufficient to teach such abstract principles as freedom and tolerance, 'teachers must also help pupils make informed moral judgements about their potential use and misuse'. One way of expressing this is to speak of contextualising the way in which these principles or concepts are interpreted and acted upon in specific situations. We shall return to that in Chapter 4 but the idea that everything has to be analysed in 'context' would seem a useful way to take Wright's point forward pedagogically.

Wright's chapter on the pedagogy of learning elaborates on his approach in relation to developing a pedagogic theory (Wright 2007: 233–260). He points out that he has no intention here of relating this theory directly to classroom practice and refers to *Learning to Teach Religious Education in the Secondary School* (Wright and Brandom 2000) as the source for that. However, there is no obvious systematic relationship between what Wright writes in this chapter on pedagogic theory and the variety of classroom-based contributions to teaching and learning in the earlier (2000) publication.

Wright's pedagogy of learning is based on the variation theory of learning and phenomenography (2007: 237–260), which he regards as being inclusive of the current differing approaches to RE presented in Grimmitt's earlier volume (Grimmitt 2000).

The significant features of this approach are as outlined below.

## The variation theory of learning

1  We have to understand how pupils learn before thinking about how best to teach them.

2  We must establish an appropriate 'space of learning' or learning environment.

3  Variation is experienced when the learner comes to be able to see the world in a variety of new ways.

4  Some people have become better at experiencing the world, they experience it in a better way or have gained better knowledge, and the teacher's role is to help pupils learn in this sense of better experiencing and gaining better knowledge.

5  This can be illustrated with regard to RE by saying they will learn more about ultimate truth and develop competencies for truthful living.

6  This will involve discernment: recognition of the relationship between parts and wholes, thus, for example, understanding the complexity of Islam through its various differing expressions; variation: an understanding of contrasts and connections, for example how Muslim prayer is connected with the desire to submit to Allah and how that contrasts with living a life in which God has no role to play; simultaneity: focusing on different dimensions of variation simultaneously, for example by being aware of significant variations and how the overall 'picture' and its complexity are more richly perceived in that way.

In summary, the role of the teacher is to lead the learner toward a more complex, critical and less partial discernment of the whole but with the expectation that the teacher has a fuller grasp of ultimate truth and truthful living – perhaps a rather idealised expectation.

## Phenomenography

1  Phenomenography aims to identify the critical variation that exists within any given group's experience of a phenomenon. This means the teacher begins by identifying the prior understanding of learners as a starting point and organising leaning on that basis so that they are exposed to the significant variations in experience they currently lack.

2  The teacher maps the various ways in which learners experience the phenomenon of interest to discern the internal relationship between those who have an experience and that which they experience.

3  At the root of phenomenography lies an interest in describing the phenomena in the world as others see them and in revealing and describing the variation.

4  This critical variation amongst the learners and the critical variation that exists of the phenomenon being studied (as it is presented in literature, media, for example with Islam) are brought into conversation with one another. This is the site of learning. The teacher constructs the lesson around the most significant dimensions of variation.

The summaries I have given above are heavily but not exclusively based on Wright's text. It is surprising that Wright does not place more emphasis on conceptuality in the way in which he describes how his pedagogic theory can relate to the classroom because this would give rigour and clarity to his idea of 'significant dimensions of variation'. Also, we have to note that there are, as yet, no practical, classroom informed, examples, as there are with Jackson (see pp. 46–51) and Copley (see pp. 59–63), published by Wright's project, of how this approach would translate into teaching and learning at a practical level. As with Jackson, narrative is shown to be important and he also emphasises critical engagement, which seems to be the locus of spirituality – the forming of a cognitively coherent worldview rather than the affective development of learners.

## Terence Copley

Copley's approach provides the clearest traces of the pre-modern in that he wishes to emphasise the idea of God acting in the world as the distinctive, and lost, aspect of religious education.

In *Indoctrination, Education and God: The Struggle for the Mind* (Copley 2005), his concern is with the marching tide of secularism and the ebbing tide of Christianity in particular and religion in general. His attack is on the indoctrination into secularism and the belief that educational institutions are complicit in this without so much as a debate on the issue being mounted. It is, he perceives, an unacknowledged indoctrination in which we are indoctrinated out of religion as a pervasive cultural force. His charge in this respect is aimed specifically at the UK and more generally at Europe, since he identifies that it is not a global phenomenon. 'Across the surface of the planet religions are alive and well. They are extremely potent forces – not always for moral good – in the lives of women and men' (Copley 2005: xiii). Yet, he reminds us, according to the 2001 national census 71.6 per cent of people in the UK expressed adherence to Christianity. 'What is going on?' he asks (Copley 2005: xiv).

In discussing indoctrination Copley is persuasive. Given that indoctrination is a means by which '[e]very culture inducts its young into its beliefs and values and provides them with a worldview' (Copley 2005: 3), such induction or indoctrination is an inevitable activity. Enculturation and indoctrination appear to pass for the same thing. However, the nature of the beliefs purveyed is also of importance. Pullman's distinction between theocracies and democracies determines very different mindsets and dispositions which are encouraged to be less or more questioning, and therefore one might say that different enculturations might be observed to be more or less indoctrinatory in the sense of open to the questioning of their own authority. Copley's point, however, is that indoctrination by omission is possible (Copley 2005: 5), by which he means that if a child, at home or through the school curriculum, receives an enculturation in which religion and God are never mentioned, they may, by omission, 'view the entire question of God as unnecessary and irrelevant, even incomprehensible' (Copley 2005: 5). This is significant if we share the view he offers that this will tend to result in a closed mind and a lack of ability to critique or question the idea that God is irrelevant. So, Copley's point could be said to be that a democracy that closes itself to the idea of a God and brings up the young, by default, in that view is not being democratically reflective of its anti-democratic, albeit perhaps unconscious, behaviour.

It would follow that such a democracy has to pro-actively assert the need to attend to its omission in the same way it might do with gender or sexuality issues. However, due to secularisation, 'religious institutions and practices become peripheral or almost invisible in a society in which they were or were perceived to be central and pivotal' (Copley 2005: 7). It follows that this will happen to the extent that institutions in such a society, such as educational ones, regard themselves as secular (when previously, of course, they would have regarded themselves as religious). Of course, what is being debated here is the effect of the European Enlightenment and whether the course of secularisation, as a consequence, has resulted in anti-democratic activity. Is this a contradictory or an inevitable and consistent outcome of that project? Well, of course, this is contested and it is the contestation and its results that produce the outcome.

Copley refers to the ubiquitous supermarkets and the conspicuous concern with celebrity behaviour as two signifiers of not only the secularisation but the materialism and shallowness of the modern age (Copley 2005: 12). But is this a consequence of a lack of religion? It seems more complex than that; after all high ideals are not necessarily religious in nature and religion itself, in its history, is not significantly characterised by seeking to instil creative thinking in its adherents.

When he focuses on education and religious education his diatribe finds new foci: 'For instance, in Britain the schoolteacher is *not* a respected figure' (Copley 2005: 13). He also speaks of the 'dumbing-down' of degrees (Copley 2005: 18). The thrust of all this is that we have lost the higher purpose that both religion and education stand for and thus we live in a mundane social reality defined by the lower goals that eschew higher purpose, and this, it would seem he is claiming, follows from the lack of higher belief, or a society in which unbelief has triumphed over the 'claims of belief' (Copley 2005: 20).

Having outlined Copley's underlying purpose I wish to turn to its intended effect on the practice of religious education and the malfunctions he observes in this field. He embarks on this from page 111 through to page 150. The thrust of his argument is as follows:

1 RE was marginalised within the curriculum by not being a national curriculum subject. It also suffered by being transformed from one that changed from nurture in the Christian heritage to a 'neutral' or 'secular' focus on worldviews as an object of study. The sub-text was that RE was anti-indoctrinational. In becoming so RE sanitised the representation of religion, avoiding the significant issue of 'truth-claims', and failed to address the pre-dominance of Christianity as the historically and culturally predominant religion (here Copley cites the census figures of 2001, discussed on p. 21 and p. 23).

2 RE became 'multicultural', that is, it served multiculturalism. This avoided divisive issues in the pursuit of making it a vehicle towards a more tolerant society (Copley 2005: 116). He makes the point that *The Swan Report: Education for All* (Swan 1985) makes no mention of RE as a contributor to multiracial education and that its sights were set on racism, which was not primarily served, if at all, by religious confessionalism. RE, in the service of multiculturalism, was focused on the idea of the enrichment brought about by diversity of culture not on the distinctions created by religious distinctiveness.

3 RE was being absorbed by other areas of the curriculum that eradicated its religious character, primarily PSE and Citizenship. Partly as a result of this and partly through the tendencies within the subject itself, there was a tendency to focus on similarities across religions through themes, such as pilgrimage or sacred texts or using *Joseph and the Amazing Technicolour Dreamcoat* as a resource. Also, RE was reduced to moral tales: David and Goliath

was a tale that 'presented the theme of bullying' (Copley 2005: 124) and the Good Samaritan became the well-worn classic in exemplifying Jesus' message as a moral teacher (Copley 2005: 126); and Martin Luther King is a civil rights activist, without recourse to the importance of his Christian motivation and theological message (Copley 2005: 126–127).

4 Throughout all the above RE is in the service of secularism. Referring to John Hull, Copley makes the point that 'children never realize that the Bible is about the deliverance of the oppressed by God' (Copley 2005: 122).

Summarily, Copley's point is that RE has to be theological, it has to insist on central theological narratives that contrast it with secular Humanism in its different curriculum guises and it has to challenge the educational spirit of the age. God is central and God delivers. Copley is not wrong when he points this out. The question that remains is how do you incorporate this message into an overall curriculum which eschews the idea of theological influence?

Epistemologically Copley is at odds with the implicit assumptions of other curriculum subjects and with overall educational policy, a modernist construction emphasising cohesion and the compatibility of diversity. His position is shared by both Wright and Trevor Cooling (Cooling 1994), in so far as they also wish to raise the epistemological question to assert the marginalisation of theological perspectives. All three challenge the assumption that education can do without a 'god-orientated' perspective that significantly alters our hermeneutic or worldview. Many within other theistic faiths would certainly share this view; it is a problematic question for them also. The faith representation constituency of SACREs can often find themselves concerned with the problem of whether they can flex their collective muscles against non-religious worldviews being incorporated within RE. There is a very real sense in which the parameters of the subject are being contested: is it about worldviews or religions? There is nothing 'theological' about Humanism. This makes for strange bedfellows if the subject has a theological raison d'être but, of course, 'religions' such as Buddhism might well also fall outside the fold. The fundamental question is whether the subject is about God. Copley comes close to asserting that it is not just RE that has a problem but education and society generally.

His critique of the shallowness of much RE teaching is appropriate since, without any purposeful resolve, the subject does its best to avoid the fundamental issues that beset it and avoids such controversy. It becomes something descriptive, lacking conviction, resorting to justifications that are extrinsic rather than intrinsic to its purpose and, eventually, lacking both impact and status. It remains by virtue of its special status, awarded by historical significance and residual influence but little more. My encounters with RE teachers often tend to offer little in the way of conviction for the subject apart from individual passion for the importance of RE as a repository for different, non-materialistic, conceptions of human endeavour. These are not always aligned with Christian visions, or Muslim or Jewish, but with those of 'alternative civilisations' of an indigenous kind or with the wisdom that can be culled from the non-dogmatic assertions within the major faiths: sufis, sages and prophets who contest the spirit of our own age, not the distinctions between themselves. This, for many RE teachers, is the source of what they would regard as spirituality, distinctive to their subject. In this they are not wrong but the question is whether that should be the bedrock and educational justification for the subject being on the curriculum.

Copley's Biblos project provides teachers with textbooks based on his approach. The aim is to 'present biblical narrative in its cultural context', and encourage pupils to 'provide their own theological interpretations', so that 'we can pen the Bible for children' (Stern 2006: 11). The aim is to look for meaning in the text rather than, as Copley claims other approaches do, look for meaning in the reader (Stern 2006: 11), which is what Copley discerns in the approaches of Don Cupitt, Clive and Jane Erricker, and John Hull. Stern points out that there must always be 'an *engagement* between text and reader: nobody looks to the text or the reader alone' (Stern 2006: 11). However, Copley's point needs to be taken seriously. I spoke earlier of what I call 'translating out' and translating in' and stated that 'translating out' would mean that teachers can seek to make a concept, or a narrative, in Copley's approach, amenable to students' learning by equating it with their own prior understandings. This would be to miss the point of the exercise. Copley's point is, for example, that the text is then given a moral rather than theological message. In his pupil textbooks and secondary teacher's handbook, based on themes such as Encounter, Vulnerability and Destiny (Copley *et al.* 2003), the approach is exemplified. For example, in *Troubled People* (Walshe 2003), based on the theme of vulnerability, the Adam and Eve story is presented, some accompanying information is introduced, discussion questions are identified plus a task in which pupils list clues that indicate the way in which relationships changed as a result of Adam and Eve's act of disobedience. Then a Find Out section asks pupils to explore further. In all this, however, I cannot find anything new. The tasks set do not readily ask for the development of skills in the reading of texts beyond those they might already be able to bring to the text. Certainly the tasks do ask pupils to reflect on the meaning of the text, providing some contextual information – 'What "truths" do you think the writer is trying to get across?' (Walshe 2003: 17) – and to get pupils to think of how it might relate to contemporary issues – 'think about how "free" humans are now' (Walshe 2003: 17). But nowhere does it ask the hard evaluative question such as 'Does this explanation of the relationship between God and Adam and Eve and their disobedience have any significance for how we behave today?' Or better still perhaps, 'How do the ideas of "sin" and "the Fall" in this story question the way in which we live today?' Or better still, 'How does this story question our modern worldview?' (a question for more able students perhaps).

It seems the challenge that Copley makes in his theoretical studies is not fully carried through into the pupil (or teacher's) books. And yet I think Copley is right, pupils should be presented with this challenge and the demand that, if they disagree with the message (and its different Jewish and Christian interpretations), then they should justify their responses.

There is nothing in Copley's approach that goes against the grain of what we might expect good RE to look like, but, it seems to me, he does not present the challenge he advocates that we should make within the classroom material. This is not to deride Copley's attempts. It is most difficult to carry through the sophistication of theory into practice. As we have seen with the classroom material of Jackson, it is difficult to wholly fulfil the promise of the approach. Part of the reason for this, I would suggest, is that we have not fully worked out our pedagogical principles and, within that, there is a tendency not to look beyond the subject of religion and

RE in order to do so. Also, with Copley, there is no attempt to ground the process in explicit conceptual distinctions between a theological and secular worldview. Again, it is narratives that are used to try and convey distinctions but I am not convinced that gives teachers enough pedagogical guidance.

## Constructivist approaches to religious education

### Michael Grimmitt

It is possible to argue that Grimmitt comes closest to a postmodern position, allowing more fluidity in 'textual' engagement, though I suspect that the importance he places on recognising the understanding of the 'text' from the position of the believer might, in part, mitigate against such a judgement.

In his substantial volume *Religious Education and Human Development* (Grimmitt 1987), Grimmitt argued his rationale for religious education being in the service of education rather than in the service of religion. He wrote:

> '[R]eligious' educators are essentially 'secular' educators concerned with the educational value of studying religion and religions. They are 'secular' educators in so far as the educational principles which govern their activities are, in the first instance, those governing all educators, irrespective of their subject disciplines . . . Thus, in order to provide *education in religion* religious educators are constrained to offer an estimate of religion which is compatible with their commitment to education as their *first-order activity*.

> (Grimmitt 1987: 258–259)

Much follows from this statement. First, its import applies specifically and only to religion as a curriculum subject. If you substitute the name of any other subject for religion in the statement, the statement would be exceedingly strange if not absurd. A historian or scientist would have no need to be reminded he was a secular educator – what could exist as contrary to that designation? Indeed the response might well be that he is not a 'secular' educator just an educator. Second, implicit in Grimmitt's statement is the idea that religious educators need to be reminded that they are 'secular' educators, suggesting that many have not taken this on board. Indeed, 'secular religious educator' almost sounds like a contradiction in terms linguistically. Third, an educator enthusiastic about teaching history (as his subject) may be a poor teacher; the same could be true about a religious educator but the import of Grimmitt's statement is that the religious educator could also be guilty of something further – indoctrination into religion, even if he is not proselytising a particular faith. You can't indoctrinate into history. Fourth, Grimmitt's statement raises the spectre of ideological conflict between the religious and the secular. So, for the believing teacher, teaching the parable of the good Samaritan, it can become the Good Samaritan, in the sense that this is a teaching about goodness given by Jesus that turns into a lesson on morality not an enquiry into the nature of the teachings of Jesus. For the Christian believer as RE teacher the implications may go even further in relation to learning outcomes if he confuses his personal and professional identities at this point. In lessons I have observed this is not uncommon and it is worth remembering that the provision for RE in

England and Wales forces this distinction in a way that is not required in most other countries. Fifth, Grimmitt is the only one of the major contemporary theorists who have constructed approaches to RE who has based his pedagogy on educational principles, in the first instance, rather than on those derived from an approach to the study of religion (ethnographic in the case of Jackson and theological in the case of Wright and Copley). As a result the relationship between theory and practice in Grimmitt's work is much more tightly constructed around educational design and learning outcomes that reflect the educational value of the subject (extrinsic justification serving education) rather than responding to the question of how we should study religion (an intrinsic justification as to how religion is best represented).

Grimmitt's approach focuses on human experience first and accommodates religious experience within it. As a result, he states that '[w]hile theology, therefore, cannot provide a *sufficient* understanding of religious education . . . it does provide a *necessary* contribution . . . within [the study of] human beliefs and values' (Grimmitt 1987: 260). As an example he points out that a lack of a theological perspective in enquiring into human experience would entail a lack of consideration given to the idea of transcendence.

In his later work (Grimmitt 2000) he presents his constructivist pedagogy for religious education. Its salient features are as follows:

- ■ Grimmitt highlights the distinction between the instructional model of teaching, which he observes is all too prevalent in RE, and constructivist theories of learning.

- ■ He favours von Glasersfeld's radical constructivism over others (Piagetian constructivism and Vygotsky's social constructivism), which argues that knowledge is 'exclusively an order and organisation of a world constituted by our experience and not a reflection of an objective ontological reality' (Grimmitt 2000: 210). He adds that this makes crucial the role played by language, which von Glasersfeld understands as conveying the meaning of words on the basis of the construction of knowledge derived from 'the subjective experience of the particular person' (Grimmitt 2000: 211). In effect, therefore, knowledge cannot be taught in an instructional way because it is 'constructed by each student individually' and the teacher's role is to '"orient" students' efforts at construction', within which language plays a vital mediating role (i.e. language itself is constructed). The conclusion to this becomes 'that it is absolutely necessary for teachers to have some notion of their students' conceptual networks' (Grimmitt 2000: 211 citing von Glasersfeld 1995: 27). Notice echoes here of features of the variation theory on which Wright drew, but also of a different epistemological position from that of Wright's critical realism. Grimmitt points out the connection between von Glasersfeld's radical constructivism and the French post-structuralist theorist Lyotard (Lyotard 1984). Note also how this puts Grimmitt at odds with those in RE who follow an instructionalist model because it is conveying the truth of a particular religious dogma.

- ■ He illustrates a constructivist approach by using Shiva Nataraj as the item of religious content. He highlights the need to link information to concepts because 'religious knowledge consists of a complex but coherent system of interlocking concepts and categories' (Grimmitt 2000: 212).

■ He applies constructivist theory to how this object can be used by engaging in enquiry rather than instruction; linking students' own experiences to the content being studied; constructing their own meanings and conclusions; responding to those of others and doing collaborative problem solving; reflecting critically on this process and recognising the role that language plays in this in relation to experience and the interpretations conveyed.

■ He presents a three-stage process or pedagogical strategy for applying the above principles: students enquire into and reflect upon their own experience; the item of content is explicitly introduced as a stimulus for hypothesis and meaning construction; additional or supplementary information is introduced to enable students' constructions to be more complex and further embrace alternative perspectives as a critical interpretive process. The supplementary information is not objective knowledge and the learning continues to be based on a dynamic relationship between object and information and the 'critical and reflective thought which pupils undertake as situated or contextualised individuals' (Grimmitt 2000: 217). The sequence of learning moves from 'encouraging egocentric interpretations of experience within *situated thought*, through *alternative contextualised interpretations*, to *evaluative judgements* about the interests which each interpretation serves and expresses' (Grimmitt 2000: 217).

■ When Grimmitt gives the illustration of how this worked in practice with 14–15-year-old students he uses questions that move from encouraging reflection on their own views on death, dying, fulfilment and being reborn through correlating the object to their previous discussion of these issues, through to ones which focused on the Hindu concepts of *maya*, *karma*, *samsara and moksha*, which the supplementary information introduced. In effect, as he points out, his questioning and interventions as a teacher are a form of *scaffolding* their progress in deepening their learning. This acts as an alternative type of intervention to the instructional one of teaching them the 'correct' understanding.

It is clear that Grimmitt has a clear grasp of how religious education can be situated within what is an overall secular educational environment and make a distinctive contribution by maintaining its interest in transcendence. He organises his understanding of learning by placing a pedagogic emphasis on the development of the learner, using a specific constructivist theory which works according to generic principles and skills. In these respects his approach is distinctively different from other approaches considered above. It is surprising that he does not place more emphasis explicitly on a conceptual basis for development, though concepts are presented within his schema, which is more cognitively rather than affectively oriented. In Chapter 4 I shall use Grimmitt's pedagogical understanding to introduce a conceptual basis for the methodology I wish to present based upon enquiry that is not dissimilar to Grimmitt's constructivist method in approach, except in the conceptual nature of its progression.

# SUMMARY OF PART 1

Approaches to religious education can be analysed based on the purpose they seek to pursue. This gives us an understanding of the intrinsic and extrinsic value ascribed to the subject within the curriculum. Whilst differing approaches may not explicitly identify a purpose statement, these can be extrapolated from their ways of characterising the subject. I have identified five different influential projects that give us a range of approaches to the subject. Two of these are explicitly theological, in different ways: Wright and Copley; one is socio-anthropologically based: Jackson; one is experiential: Hay, Hammond and Phillips; one is a liberal constructivist educational model: Grimmitt. These approaches can be situated within the grid presented in Figure 3.1, since they all involve a 'warp and weft' involving the discipline pursued and the method pursued. Jackson's reconstruction of phenomenology, as a method, is situated within social anthropology, as a discipline. Hammond, Hay and Phillips are existential in their method; the discipline is not clearly defined and could be described as an implicit theology linked to psychological features. Wright's discipline is theology but his method is critical realist. Copley has a more straightforward theological agenda. Grimmitt, interestingly, does not have an approach to religion as such, that lies within the discipline prior to its educational rationale, but is concerned with transcendence. Whilst broadly phenomenological in spirit, his emphasis is drawn from constructivist methods in educational psychology.

Having made the above comments in relation to the different approaches used, there is a surprisingly similarity when you consider, beneath the epistemological surface, what they propose educationally. For example:

- the emphasis on critical evaluation and learners' development;
- the importance of learners forming their own worldviews and values;
- the need for learners to critically consider diverse understandings of how to live and principles for living that reflect on/are informed by spiritual or religious perspectives;
- the need to recognise and acknowledge the complexity of ways in which individual and communal identities are constructed;
- the recognition of a spiritual dimension to being human that might involve an idea of transcendence, however that might be formed.

Might there be a way in which to deliver RE in which contesting understandings, different knowledge bases and disciplinary approaches and consistent learning progression might be incorporated to form the purpose of the subject? We shall return to this possibility later in this volume when considering the conceptual enquiry methodology presented in Part 2.

At this point we all have to professionally situate ourselves in relation to what we regard as the purpose(s) of our subject and its significance for learners. We also have to determine how theory translates into educational practice, something that at best has been fitfully accomplished so far. You may wish to determine, at this point, where your allegiances lie in relation to the approaches discussed above.

Despite academic progression over the last thirty years and the way theorists have developed new approaches, RE is in a fairly dire state on the ground, in the classroom. The reasons for this are not because there aren't good teachers, though there aren't enough, but because the subject lacks a sense of two things:

1    its contribution to the primacy of overall educational goals based on the development of young people;

2    its lack of a self-assured understanding of itself as a discipline.

As a result it does not have a clear pedagogic vision or a methodology that gives practical purpose to learning and the outcomes of learning on the ground. I do not mean this in the technicist sense of 'targets' but in relation to what a 'religiously literate' student will be able to achieve – how that quality would make a difference to them as a person.

This lack runs all the way through RE's institutional structures and their fissures, because research and theory have not penetrated practice in any consistent and pervasive way and because most teachers have no inclination or confidence to read theory, which is targeted toward university research exercise achievement. The gap between theory and practice is not just extensive but at present incommensurable. The reasons for this do not lie with individuals or professionals per se but with a system that separates the differing roles of academic and professional classroom practitioner inexorably. Between the two are positioned the centralised agencies, Ofsted, QCDA and the Department for Children, Schools and Families (DCSF), and the local inspector/advisers attached to local authorities and responsible for Locally Agreed Syllabuses. Whilst difficulties in communication could be overcome and bridges made, there is no systemic incentive to do so. Also, at the level of teacher training, through local providers, there is a systemic weakness as a result. In other words, one obvious means of linking up the varying areas of activity in a meaningful way (centralised agencies, agreed syllabi and theory) lacks effectiveness. One of the reasons for this is that the system itself is not linked, i.e. different sectors of the profession send differing messages concerning priorities and they each have varying forms and purchases of authority. For example, local providers delivering PGCEs will be inspected by Ofsted, so clearly Ofsted agendas carry most weight. However, an aspect of that inspection will be to what extent QCDA non-statutory advice and Agreed Syllabuses are included in the training, so they gain authority as a result. But also the shift to Every Child Matters and its outcomes have an overwhelming authority and must be addressed. There are obvious and significant connections between these centralised agendas, and these tend to be addressed and reflected in changes in Agreed Syllabuses over time, but that does not mean that debate over the rationale and direction of RE will be best served as a result. This of course would presume Locally Agreed Syllabuses remain, which will not necessarily be the case. But I return to my point that the problem is systemic. It has developed over a considerable period of years through a mentality of compliance – what you must do, not how you can do it – on which theorists and researchers have made little or no impact.

As a result, there is a systemic malfunction in the system. The overall effect of this malfunction is that new pedagogical ideas rarely reach the classroom, whether they come from RE specialists or from general pedagogic innovations in education. One very important reason for this is that neither inspector/advisers nor teachers are actually attuned to the importance of such innovation as a priority. Specific innovation by creative individuals excepted, which have had no influential effect in a general way, RE has tended to stand still for thirty years; it is in a state of stasis defended by arguments as to its unique place in the curriculum argued on the basis of its extrinsic importance, whether moral, cultural or spiritual, in what it offers to students. It can offer none of these vaunted qualities if it is not pedagogically sufficient in the classroom – which it is not. Also, it needs to think carefully about its intrinsic usefulness to the curriculum overall – why it should be there and what is lost if it is not.

# Living Difference:
# an approach through
# conceptual enquiry

# 4

# A methodology for conceptual enquiry in religious education

## Introduction

Part 2 of the book will introduce a specific conceptual enquiry approach to religious education using a generic methodology that seeks to move the subject forward from the position analysed in Part 1 and specifically addressed in the concluding section of Chapter 3. First, this chapter introduces the initial research from which the methodology was derived and focuses in particular on the idea of what can be called personal or spiritual development that underpins it. Second, it then introduces some epistemological and theoretical issues that follow from the research and inform the pedagogy. Third, it relates the findings of that research and the epistemological and theoretical issues to a specific, but nevertheless generic, pedagogic methodology that serves religious education, as originally presented in the Agreed Syllabus for Hampshire, Portsmouth and Southampton: Living Difference. It contextualises the pedagogical model within recent national initiatives affecting RE and the secondary curriculum and recent pedagogical approaches to the subject, especially that of Michael Grimmitt (introduced in Chapter 3), because it can best be compared to his analysis of educational pedagogy. It then addresses how this model affects progression in learning and the question of how RE can be based on a disciplinary understanding of the subject. The section then goes on to present ways in which this conceptual enquiry pedagogy can be translated into examples of classroom practice. Overall, this section provides an approach to effective learning through conceptual enquiry in religious education.

Behind the structure of this chapter is an attempt to deal with two important aspects of religious education that emerged in Chapter 3:

1 *Narrative*: attention is given to young people's narratives in the first part of this chapter and subsequently to discussion of narrative within a conceptually led methodology.

2 *Hermeneutics*: this is addressed in the third part of this chapter in presenting the conceptual enquiry methodology. Here we are asking how the connection between the learner and the subject material can best be established – a theme central to discussions in Chapter 3.

## The research of the Children and Worldviews Project

Effective learning involves young people speaking their mind but in a serious and informed way. For this to happen we must draw on their experience and provide material or narratives beyond their experience for them to consider and respond to. In the section that follows I present some research conducted by the Children and Worldviews Project that shows what children are capable of by drawing on their own experience and seeking to make sense of it. We shall then consider how this affects the way in which we consider how what we present to children as further material engages with their narratives, can enlarge their perspectives, enrich their reflections and progress their learning in religious education and, hopefully, beyond.

# Children's voices

This research took place with 6–10-year-old children, beginning with my own daughter, between 1992 and 1997. It provides a thread of conversations around the concept of loss and shows how children relate their narratives to that concept.

Although this research was conducted with primary age students I shall show how this has profound implications for the learning and progression of secondary age students as well. Aspects of this research were originally published in Erricker *et al.* 1997 and other academic journals.

## Polly's story

When she was 7 years old my daughter Polly engaged me in an enlightening conversation. Unannounced, as we drove past a local cemetery, she asked me whether her dead grandfather had 'one of those'. She was referring to a headstone. I replied that he did not. She asked why. I replied, with some trepidation, that he had said, in his will, that he did not want one. She asked why and what was a will? I explained about a will containing your final wishes. She then asked what happened to him. With greater trepidation still I explained he wanted to be cremated. She asked, what does cremation mean? I explained it meant you wanted your body to be burned. This moved on to a larger conversation in which she, seeking to make sense of what exactly happened to him, moved into a more philosophical speculation, which I later recorded:

P: Do you remember that question you asked?
Q: What question did I ask?
P: Which part of you is you?
Q: What did you say?
P: OK, I'll tell you . . . Your Being.
Q: What does that mean?
P: It means that is the part of you that is you.
Q: You explained to me, when the body dies what happens to the being, didn't you?
P: Well, you don't really die. The smoke goes up and there are lots of ashes going up like paper . . . As the smoke goes along it crumbles and eventually there is just a little bit that's left.
Q: And that's how small your being is?
P: Well we're not quite sure how big it is.

It is necessary to note that Polly never knew her grandfather; he died two weeks after she was born. We had a photograph of him holding her in his arms just after she was born and just before he died. Also, in the family, we had conversations about him, from time to time, and her elder sister and brother were able to talk from experience of knowing him. Polly could not.

At a later date she asked me to take her to the crematorium. I agreed we would go on a Saturday morning. The day before she wrote a letter to him, emptied the grate in our wood-burning stove. Then she put in her letter and set fire to it. The ashes in the tray beneath she emptied into a carrier bag and we took this with us. At the crematorium, on a rainy morning, she noticed plaques to those who had been cremated. I explained that her grandfather did not wish to have one of those. Nevertheless, we had to see them all before she was convinced. Following this, she found a spot, down by a pond, where she decided to empty the ashes of her letter. Then she said, 'OK, let's go home.' And we did.

The point of this story is that she had to find out for herself. She asked the questions and she decided on the answers. The reason for all this was a question in her own mind which I had no previous awareness of. She settled it in her own way. I could not provide the answer. That is how children learn, we later discovered.

Polly having alerted us to this, we then conducted research with other children to see if this ability of children to make sense of significant life experiences was generalisable. What we took from the experience with Polly was:

- her use of enabling metaphor and conceptual construction;
- the importance of specific relational events in her life-experience;
- her need to construct meaning and resolve issues.

Following this beginning we interviewed children in schools to find out whether this depth of conversation and characteristics of response were replicated. Below is a strand of this research that relates closely to the concept involved in conversations with my daughter: that of loss.

In one school with a group of four 7-year-old children we used the poem 'Looking for Dad', from Brian Patten's collection *Gargling with Jelly* (Patten 1985), as a stimulus because the headteacher said she thought it would resonate with some of the experiences they had encountered. In Patten's poem a young boy is constantly told to tidy his room. He also hears his parents arguing and thinks this is the reason. In time he comes to realise this is not the case but that they are having a quite separate argument, then his dad leaves home. In an effort to bring his dad back he tidies his room. Nineteen days after his dad has left, 29 June, he sits waiting in the hope of his return, and wishing to show him what he has done.

The children responded in various ways in discussion with each other as to what the poem was about. We used the question: where do you think his dad has gone?

In this discussion one child suggested his dad had gone to heaven and another child responded to that by telling her own story about her nan.

## Victoria's story

I think that in heaven you can ride a white pony and have marshmallows. Before my nan died she told me lots of things because she knew she was going to die and she told me about all the things she was going to do and she said she was going to send me a postcard. Before she went she gave me a piece of paper and stuck a photograph on it. I've still got it.

She said she would be happy and she wanted me to be happy when she died. On that day she got a picture of her and all the family, stuck it on a postcard and wrote on the back 'I'll see you in your heart'. Now she's always with me. Now I talk to her all the time. I talk to her when I'm lonely. When I've argued with my friends I go and sit on the wall and think about her and talk to her. When I get fed up I sit there and talk to her about my friends. She tells me that she is riding on things. She says she's having a really nice time. She says she's going to ring me up. She says things in my head, she rings up my brain and talks to me.

The construction of Victoria's response reveals similar features to Polly's:

- the conceptual connection being made;
- the use of figurative language (metaphor);
- a narrative progression that maintains the relationship;
- a basis in experience and making sense of experience.

Our next strategy was to see what the response was when you took one child's story to other children to use as a stimulus. Thus, on one occasion Victoria's story was read to sixty 10-year-old children, during a twenty-minute period within which they were asked to respond. They did so by speaking into a tape recorder and subsequently by writing what their response was on paper, with a decision being made as to whether they wished to speak further about their response (either alone or in pairs). Forty-seven of the children indicated they wished to do this. Amongst their responses were those directed to Victoria asking for more information or relating their own experiences in response. Two of these were from boys whose parents had split up. They had written, on a sheet of paper handed out to each child:

I remember when my mum and dad split up, I was very upset because my mum throw a shoe at my dad and take a chunk of skin out of dads face. I still cry when me and mum meet. Mum gets very upset so she always takes me out a lot to stop her crying and get her mind off this. Please read this.

My mum and dad split up 4 years ago. I feel angry partly with myself but mostly with my dad because he caused the argument here is a picture of what he done to my sister. [Picture of a man standing behind a girl. The man is holding a knife labelled 'stabber' and the girl is labelled 'sister' and saying 'help'.]

At their request we interviewed these two boys together. They were friends aware of each others' circumstances. The interview lasted one and a half hours, moving to four different locations during the school in this time. Below I summarise some important points in this conversation.

## Lee and Glen's stories

Our conversation revolved around the difficulties of dealing without one of your parents and the problems that can cause. They mentioned the feelings that come especially at Christmas, when the family is split up and you can't celebrate properly by having both parents together. Then they described their circumstances in the following way:

L: It's like a key that almost fits the lock but doesn't turn.

Q: What would happen if you could turn the key?

G: You'd see your family back together again.

L: It would open the door.

Q: . . . and that key, can you find a way of turning it or do you think it just will never turn?

L: It will never turn.

G: It will never turn for me either.

Q: It will never turn for you?

G: No, I don't think, even if I do get another person it probably won't be like my mum.

L: No, nothing's like your mum at all.

Q: Would it help to have somebody in school who wasn't a teacher who you could express yourself to?

G: What, like you, or somebody like you?

Q: Yeh.

G: Yeh.

L: Yeh.

Q: Yeh?

G: Even for people who are still like together, but they have an argument in the night and that can upset somebody enough to bring them into tears in school in the morning still, and that needs speaking about, like Zoe, what happened, she split up and the teachers couldn't stop it where she didn't know, they didn't know what to do. Like they couldn't stop it and they couldn't say, 'We'll discuss it,' but like they wouldn't know what to do.

L: Like 'cause they're not involved.

G: And they're not qualified to do it, are they?

L: No, you have to be somebody that knows what it feels like, like in, you don't have to have been through it, but you have to *know* what its like.

Q: Can you sense that in people then?

L: Yeh.

G: You can sense if people like have been through that experience 'cause they're normally upset quite a lot and they're in a lot of stress and they take it out—

L: If people enjoy, enjoy listening, to things like this, then that's a good sign and if they enjoy talking about it with you, then that's good as well.

You will notice how Lee and Glen exhibit similar capacities to Polly and Victoria and how the stimulus of Victoria's story resonated with them at a conceptual level, not just as a particular story with similar characters involved. Also, the imagery of a 7-year-old-child did not deter these 10-year-old children from recognising the seriousness of what she was saying and its importance. In the short piece of interview transcription you will also notice how much they conversed with each other rather than just with me as the interviewer.

# In summary

In this section I have sought to give research examples of children's narratives in order to determine what might be considered educationally necessary but not necessarily sufficient in order to address children's spirituality and their 'spiritual development' or personal development meaningfully. They are:

- conceptual connection;
- use of figurative language (metaphor);
- narrative progression;
- the importance of experience and making sense of experience;
- using narratives to which they can respond;
- a questioning process;
- a process of enquiry;
- acknowledgement and affirmation of subjectivity and interpretation;
- the process involving children in talking with one another not just being taught by an adult.

How does the above relate to creating effective learning in religious education?

Religious education needs to be about how we make sense of the world and our place in it, and responding to how others do so as well. It is about the construction of meaning arising from experience – thus it is about narrative and how our narratives relate to those of others. Underpinning this is the conceptual thread that ties narratives together. In the above that thread was the concept of loss, which made it possible for children to respond to one another regardless of age or differing circumstances. When this happens children show the ability to communicate above their usual 'ability levels' because there is a need to express themselves and be heard. They also listen carefully as they want to hear what is being said. Knowing this it helps us to reconsider our roles as teachers. Teacher is an inadequate term for our role. It suggests we teach something when, in fact, our participation is in facilitating learning, which involves a variety of roles and skills. We need to be able to:

- stimulate pupils with narrative texts (oral, visual and written) that promote responses to issues they raise or raise issues for them to respond to;
- respond to their questions and observations with replies that stimulate their thinking further;
- ask our own thought-provoking questions;
- require pupils to develop skills through activities and tasks that are demanding and require different skills;
- use different learning modes that encourage cooperation, interaction, creativity and debate;
- encourage deep thinking to progress learning.

In doing all this we need to bear in mind that we are seeking to help students develop personally and spiritually. Religious education has both intrinsic and extrinsic educational aims, for example understanding of religious perspectives and behaviour and the development of students' capacities and skills. We need to keep in mind how these can be provided for at one and the same time. Attending to the above issues is the primary task of pedagogy, to which we now turn.

## What do we mean by pedagogy in religious education?

> In short, in the space of less than a decade, liberal educational ideals and a well established and a respected educational consensus for RE teaching has been progressively dismantled by both Conservative and Labour government educational policies.
>
> (Grimmitt 2000: 13)

Here Grimmitt is summarising his critical response to the standards and outcomes driven agenda of these governments based on the delivery of a commodified national curriculum and a centralised approach to education. At this time I shared Grimmitt's anger. My own contribution to his study of pedagogies in RE (Erricker and Erricker 2000) and a volume published later in that same year (Erricker and Erricker 2000a), as well as an earlier report on research by the Children and Worldviews Project (Erricker *et al.* 1997), exemplify why, through the constructivist, person-centred approach they take to learning.

Now, ten years later, much has changed in the approach the QCDA is taking to the idea of curriculum. The most significant shift is the emphasis now placed upon the overall development of the learner as an individual rather than the acquisition of knowledge and understanding within discrete and separate subjects. Also, there is an emphasis, within and across subjects, that learning and teaching should be conceptually based. Both of these things were referred to in Chapter 2. These twin changes recognise the significance of pedagogy, which had previously fallen out of fashion. In turn, this means that the commodified curriculum model railed against by Grimmitt has now been replaced by a more person-centred approach, and his insistence on the centrality of pedagogical thinking in education is now the driver for success. It is an irony perhaps that this thinking has now been taken up from the centre by the QCDA, but this is a result of the Every Child Matters agenda and its five outcomes, as mentioned on p. 28. The need to shift emphasis towards the overall development of the learner is further reinforced by a number of threads running through Ofsted's most recent report on RE, *Making Sense of Religion* (Ofsted 2007), again referred to previously in some detail (see pp. 30–31).

This return to the significance of pedagogy requires us in religious education to clarify our own practice; be clear about what we mean by pedagogy, the relationship between theory and practice, and the similarities or distinctions between RE and other subjects in these respects. Whilst Grimmitt refers to eleven pedagogic models in his work on pedagogies in RE (Grimmitt 2000) he also criticises all of them as being incomplete in various differing respects (Grimmitt 2000: 24–48) and recognises that the pedagogical strategies employed in each are likely to undergo review, revision and refinement. (Grimmitt 2000: 226). At the same time he urges that any pedagogy employed, to be effective, must be constructivist in design (Grimmitt 2000: 222–226). His main point in advancing this claim is against an instructional approach (Grimmitt 2000: 222) and for engagement of pupils in interpretation (Grimmitt 2000: 223). In this sense he is employing constructivist in a broad and general rather than in a theoretical and technical sense, which could apply possibly to any of the approaches he includes in his book, of which I analysed five in Chapter 3. He elaborates on the theory of constructivism as a discrete theoretical approach later in the book by stating:

> Constructivism is a theory (or more accurately a meta-theory) about knowledge and learning . . . At root it identifies knowledge as a human construct which is a consequence of the way in which individuals and communities order their experience. As such, what is conceived of as 'knowledge' does not and cannot reflect some 'objective' ontological reality because that is unknowable. Human knowledge, as a consequence, reflects the way in which individuals and communities order and organise their experience of the world, using concepts which fit the situations they encounter. A characteristic of human knowledge . . . is that it is subject to multiple interpretations or 'constructs' and is controversial or problematic by nature.

(Grimmitt 2000: 208)

The main difference between the general and discrete theoretical use of constructivist, as employed by Grimmitt, centres on whether there is an a priori 'unknowableness' of reality or whether a broadly constructivist approach can be taken that might result in students wishing to affirm the authenticity of a particular 'construct' as being an accurate representation of reality. This distinction is important in relation to the nature of religious truth-claims. The broad use of 'constructivist' implies that an effective definition of a process of learning could be compatible with a range of different approaches – as long as these are based on a principle of open enquiry rather than instruction. The principle behind theoretical constructivism would deny the possibility of fixed universalist and objective truths and thus be in conflict with truth claims made by certain religious groups as being universal and known. At this point I am taking forward Grimmitt's broad use of the term, which would acknowledge that some students might hold to an understanding that the truth-claims of their religion are absolute and not relative, fixed and not open to change, but that the procedures for learning would not be based on this assumption and that their claims are open to challenge. Of course if, on this basis, parents wished to withdraw their children from RE, that is possible, and some may wish to. Historically, this has been the case with some Jehovah's Witness, Brethren and Muslim parents, in particular. At the same time, the methodology of Living Difference, as a model of conceptual enquiry which we turn to on pp. 81–93, does lend itself to constructivist theory in the technical sense as well as in the broader sense. However, this depends upon the way in which it is used and is therefore not a necessary principle of its operation.

In outlining his understanding of pedagogy Grimmitt states: 'a pedagogy is: a theory of teaching and learning encompassing aims, curriculum content and methodology . . . or a science of teaching and learning embodying both curriculum and methodology . . . to relate the process of teaching to that of learning on the part of the child' (Grimmitt 2000: 16–17). He translates this into religious education by considering how religion and education can be brought into a relationship which will reflect how and why pupils will benefit from the study of religion, in terms of what aim, curriculum content and methodology(ies) would enable appropriate learning outcomes to fulfil the aim. He puts it another way by asking what kinds of interaction are required. Importantly he speaks of assimilating and accommodating the content as understood within its faith context and then re-contextualising it within the pupils' own self-understanding (Grimmitt 2000: 18).

Grimmitt then asks three questions which act as a test of the sufficiency of a pedagogy:

1 What kind or kinds of interaction between the pupils and religious content does the model seek to promote?

2 What pedagogical procedures or strategies does the model deploy in order to achieve the kind or kinds of interaction identified above?

3 What pedagogical principles inform the model's pedagogical procedures and strategies, including its approach to the choice of curriculum content?

(Grimmitt 2000: 26)

Unsurprisingly, by definition, Grimmitt's three questions of sufficiency represent a constructivist approach (as opposed to a purely instructional one). However, Grimmitt also uses his 'learning about' and learning from' distinction (as a pedagogical procedure) as an arbiter of the sufficiency of other models (see Grimmitt 2000: 32–34). This alerts us to the fact that the presentation of both pedagogical principles and procedures is not values neutral. Nevertheless the point of Grimmitt's critical analysis of different models is also to consider ways in which their epistemological bases and hermeneutical designs offer pedagogical sufficiency. In doing so he observes, for example, regarding Andrew Wright's model, based on critical realism and a concern for non-relative truth, that:

Despite Wright's fundamental disagreement with the philosophical and epistemological bases of earlier pedagogical models, it is interesting that what he envisages as an appropriate and desirable outcome of RE is closely in accord with, for example, the intentions of both human development [Grimmitt] and ethnographic [Jackson] models.

(Grimmitt 2000: 44)

This distinction, observed by Grimmitt above, alerts us to the need to be able to separate out the philosophical and epistemological positions of a pedagogy from its pedagogic principles and procedures. Grimmitt's analysis of the possible constructions of Wright's pedagogical position on this is a helpful example (Grimmitt 2000: 43–44). Grimmitt's distinction is crucial. It is evident that some of the debates about pedagogy have floundered because the difference between the two has not been fully understood. In practice, for example, the pedagogical model underpinning Living Difference, the Agreed Syllabus in Hampshire, Portsmouth and Southampton, is not tied to a specific philosophical or epistemological position. Rather, it is constructivist in a broad rather than technical sense and as such is compatible with any of the positions Grimmitt reviews, in principle. However, if pedagogical principles and procedures are not rigorous and simply a matter of not being instructional, we can find ourselves with no clarity in the progression of learning and teaching at all.

Regarding my own radical constructivist contribution to Grimmitt's volume on pedagogies (Erricker and Erricker 2000a), developed out of the research of the Children and Worldviews Project, he commented: 'The fact that this theory of human learning challenges contemporary orthodoxy, both religious and educational, is no reason for drawing back from these two

significant areas of human experience and endeavour. But this is what the project does'
(Grimmitt 2000: 46).

What follows is the development of a constructivist pedagogy for religious education in
Hampshire (which may be seen as a response to Grimmitt's criticism and an ongoing dialogue
with QCDA curriculum developments) since I took up the post of County Inspector for
Religious Education in January 2003. This followed my previous employment as a researcher
and Reader in Religious Education at what is now the University of Chichester when I had
written the chapter in Grimmitt's book and conducted my research from an institution of
higher education. I wish to draw attention to a number of insights and failings in the RE
community that have become apparent to me in even greater measure as a result of my new
role, that will both supplement Grimmitt's observations and hopefully signal new possibilities
of which we should be aware as religious educators.

A consequence of having to translate theoretical considerations into policy and practice in
my present role is that it has highlighted a further question which might need to be added to
Grimmitt's three above. That question is:

4  Does the pedagogy translate effectively into a learning process which is accessible to teachers
   and offer a clear definition of progression which can ensure effective planning, teaching and
   learning and assessment?

In order to achieve the above I suggest that a pedagogy must base itself on certain specific
criteria, which underpin constructivism, as outlined below.

## Enquiry

Enquiry involves students actually carrying out an enquiry supported by their teacher. Enquiry
is a process involving an open-ended key evaluative question that the students seek to answer.
This might be best understood in the way John Dewey described it:

> [Dewey] focussed a great deal of attention upon inquiry as a way of making sense of, and giving
> meaning to . . . our world and existence, rather than validating certain objects of knowledge . . . he
> envisaged a global society in which young learners actively experience inquiring through their
> education. Lessons which adopt a Deweyan perspective are not focused upon the learning or
> memorization of facts by which students can be certain. Rather they are characterised by the
> children questioning and trying to become better investigators as 'persons' rather than as 'learners'.
> (Webster 2009)

## Conceptuality

Conceptuality involves focusing the enquiry on one key concept throughout the enquiry
process. This ensures the thread of the enquiry is maintained. The key evaluative question will
be based on the key concept the students are enquiring into. Thus, the outcome of an effective
enquiry will be a more complete and complex understanding of interpretations of that concept,
the value of that concept and students' own evaluation of that concept and its usefulness.

## Integrity

Integrity involves ensuring that the key aspects of the pedagogy are intimately and explicitly related to each other. This is discussed in more detail below but in summary the levels of attainment must clearly reflect the intended learning outcomes of the process of conceptual enquiry and students need to be clear as to what those outcomes involve as they carry out the enquiry. In turn the purpose of the subject, the attainment target and the procedure given for their operation in the classroom must be consistent with one another. Here this consistency is dependent on the methodology employed.

## The Living Difference project: an exercise in pedagogical design

In my role as an RE inspector and adviser it was clear to me that the development of a pedagogical purpose was imperative but that this could not be based on a specific and exclusive philosophical or epistemological base. Thus the pedagogic principles and procedures had to be inclusive of but refine different teachers' understandings of the subject, as long as they were not merely instructional, and pupils' differing worldviews and perspectives, based on their experience. It also had to identify the modes of interaction with the material of the subject and thus the acquisition of capacities and skills required for that interaction to be effective. As a result the review of the Agreed Syllabus in Hampshire, Portsmouth and Southampton in 2003–2004 and the introduction of the new Agreed Syllabus, Living Difference, had to take account of these factors. What follows are the layers of design of the syllabus in order to achieve this.

## Purpose statement

Pedagogy must start by identifying the educational importance and value of a subject in the larger context of educational design. In other words, for religious education, it must establish both its intrinsic credentials and its extrinsic usefulness. The purpose of RE, as identified in Living Difference, is:

- To support students in developing their own coherent patterns of values and principles.
- To support their spiritual, moral, social and cultural development.
- To encourage them to interpret and respond to a variety of concepts, beliefs and practices within religions and their own and other's cultural and life experiences.
- To develop the capacities to interpret, evaluate and respond to differing values and beliefs . . . through extending their thinking and analytical skills and their creative, imaginative and emotional development.
- To foster mutual understanding between students of differing religious and cultural backgrounds.

(Hampshire, Portsmouth and Southampton Councils 2004: 7)

The significance of these statements of educational purpose and pedagogical principle lies in the orientation toward the development of students' capacities, skills and their overall development as empowered individuals. The focus on religion is contextual rather than essential. Put another way, educational development is not *essentially* dependent upon the subject content, rather the subject is a vehicle used for the larger educational development of the learner. If that were not the case the educational rationale for studying the subject would be wholly dependent on the content of the subject (a form of basic catechesis) rather than an open-ended enquiry into the place and value of religion in the modern world.

## Attainment target

The attainment target given in Living Difference is 'Interpreting religion in relation to human experience' (Hampshire, Portsmouth and Southampton Councils 2004: 16). This can be compared with the 'learning about' and 'learning from' attainment targets of the QCDA (at present evident in their non-statutory National Curriculum Framework). An attainment target is, to use Grimmitt's pedagogical understanding, actually an aim or a pedagogical procedure for fulfilling the pedagogical principles, which here are contained in the above Purpose statement. The aim is, therefore, for students to interpret religion in relation to their own and others' experiences. Immediately a hermeneutical circle is constructed. This is subtly different to learning about and learning from religion, in which the primacy is given, in two respects, to religion as the subject of study. First, it is presumed that learning about religion is the precursor to the development of the learner (content comes first); second there is the presumption that this will in some way provide the edification required, in a positive sense, to develop the learner (an implicit assumption that religion is beneficial). No dialectical or evaluative element is explicit in these aims. It is as if the learner is a reactive respondent to the subject studied. The hermeneutical intent of developing the skill of interpretation is, in contrast, both dynamic and ongoing; it is intended to result in a progressive engagement with complexity as a form of dialogue between the learner and the subject of study and for progression to be defined in terms of that learning process. This can be understood as the intention of the pedagogic procedure.

## A methodology for conceptual enquiry

A methodology is a procedural instrument. As such it is to be identified as a pedagogic strategy dependent upon and consistent with pedagogic principle and procedure already established.

Diagrammatically, the process of enquiry methodology that Living Difference proposes is set out in Figure 4.1. However, diagrams, whilst helpful because of their clarity, always require commentary to elucidate the underlying process and intention; which is what I shall provide here.

In Figure 4.1, the process of enquiry methodology, five elements are present, with two possible starting points. There is a need to follow this process systematically and, at the same time, to be aware of the technical association implied in the relationship between the terms

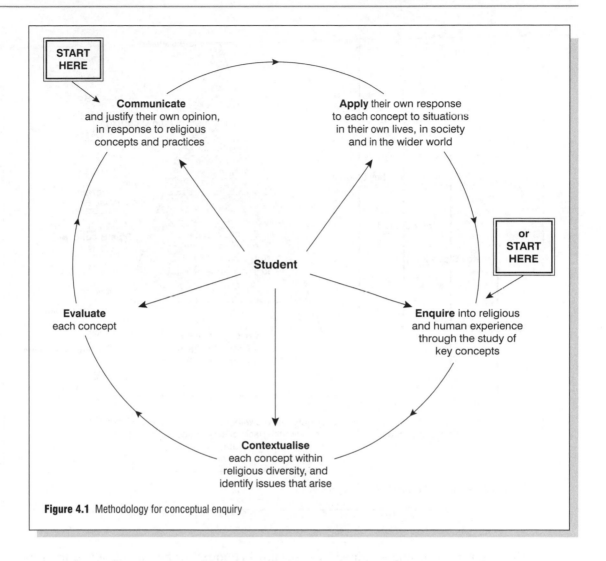

**Figure 4.1** Methodology for conceptual enquiry

used for the elements themselves. It is helpful if we relate these terms to Grimmitt's three-stage pedagogical strategy (Grimmitt 2000: 47–48).

The Communicate and Apply elements relate to Grimmitt's first stage, Preparatory Pedagogical Constructivism, in which 'pupils are engaged in an enquiry into and reflection upon their own *experience* in order to *prepare* them conceptually and linguistically for an encounter with the item of religious content' (Grimmitt 2000: 47).

Communicate and Apply break this process down into two parts. The first is a process of engagement that seeks to facilitate students articulating their own views and understandings. The second builds upon that by presenting students with a situation (a context) within which those views and understandings need to be applied and justified. Necessarily this requires debate focused on interaction between students rather than a didactic approach to learning. However, we need to take account of the Living Difference diagram, Figure 4.2, the hierarchy of concepts, in order to refine what this process entails.

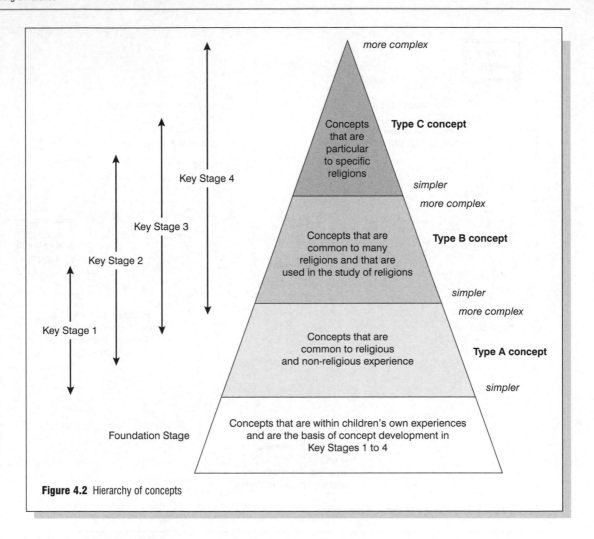

**Figure 4.2** Hierarchy of concepts

The focus for learning is refined by conceptual enquiry not by the introduction of specific content. The way in which this influences the trajectory of learning becomes more apparent once we consider Grimmitt's second stage: Direct Pedagogical Constructivism.

Grimmitt explains this stage as follows: 'In the second stage of the strategy pupils are confronted with the item of religious content *directly*, but without explanation or instruction, so that it becomes the stimulus for them to begin to construct their own meaning and understanding of it' (Grimmitt 2000: 47). Conceptual enquiry alters this process because it is not content that is introduced but a concept that is pursued. At this point it is salient to present examples. I shall restrict myself here to concepts type B and C as presented in Figure 4.2. A type B concept is defined as one that is used in the study of religion and common to many religions. An example of this would be the concept of the sacred. Within Communicate and Apply the enquiry may have centred on that which is sacred to us, in the sense that its loss would have a significant effect on our lives. Here sacred should be used in a broad rather than just a religious sense in order for it to be inclusive of all students' experience.

Thus, it may start by focusing on things of symbolic value but point to relationships of enduring worth.

Grimmitt's second stage relates to the element of Enquire. Here we introduce understandings of sacredness that relate to religious views rather than students' own experience. For example, we may introduce Torah as sacred to Jews. The question is what makes Torah sacred to Jews such that living without Torah would have a significant impact on Jewish identity? Pursuing this question focuses the enquiry on how interpretation of the sacred for religious Jews might differ from our own understanding of the sacred. It is not simply content that changes the focus of learning but the shift in interpretation and use of the concept. The underlying stories and justifications (the narratives) will be different.

Grimmitt's third stage, Supplementary Pedagogical Constructivism, is explained as follows:

> In the third stage of the strategy pupils are provided with additional or supplementary information about the item of religious content which enables their constructions to become more complex and embrace alternative perspectives . . . but [the pupils] continue to engage in an interpretative process in which new knowledge is considered critically and may or may not be accommodated within their own [constructions].
>
> (Grimmitt 2000: 47–48)

We can relate Grimmitt's third stage to the Contextualise and Evaluate elements of the Living Difference methodology. However, the notion of religious content is refined by the focus on the concept. For example, if we stay with the example of Torah as an expression of sacredness, the question may become 'How do different religious Jews regard the Torah in relation to sacredness?' Here, within Contextualise, we can investigate the relationship that Orthodox, Hassidic and Reform Jews have with Torah. This will involve understanding differences between more fundamentalist and literalist interpretations in relation to modernising interpretations, e.g. making behaviour in the world conform to the literal prescriptions of Torah or making decisions in relation to the commands of Torah as applicable to the contemporary world. This will reveal issues and implications with regard to what makes Torah sacred and in what ways its sacredness might seem to be diminished or adaptable (for example by the idea of selectivity with regard to its mitzvot).

The Evaluate element will then provide students with the opportunity to determine to what extent and why Torah is sacred for Jews (an appreciation of differing perspectives), which we can call Evaluate Within, and lead to posing the Evaluate Without question, 'To what extent is sacredness important today?' This leaves the focus of the context (Torah and Judaism) behind. Evaluate Without can obviously follow through into the elements of Communicate and Apply for a second time, having been informed by the enquiry conducted.

Grimmitt makes the point that '[i]t is important . . . that this process is seen as inviting pupils to be *constructivist* in response to . . . new information' (Grimmitt 2000: 47). This is highly important because otherwise the process of enquiry breaks down at the point at which religious content is introduced. He is also clear that the process is not objective and is critical (Grimmitt 2000: 47–48). The Living Difference methodology goes further, through basing enquiry upon concepts, so that the introduction of subject content does not make the enquiry veer off course since its thread is the concept itself and its relation to the learner. Religious content is illustrative but has no prescribed role in the enquiry. The enquiry is firmly rooted in its developmental function for students. This remains the case whether the concept in focus is of type A (common to religious and non-religious experience), B (common to many religions and used in the study of religion) or C (particular to specific religions).

If the enquiry were to focus upon a type C concept the conceptual emphasis would shift. Adapting the example above, within, for example, a unit of work on Judaism, one cycle of learning would be likely to focus on the key concept of Torah. The difference in the process of enquiry would change from that given above, where the key concept was sacred and Torah was illustrative of that. The intention now will be to penetrate the idea of Torah in a more complex way as an important aspect of Jewish identity (for example, in Enquire, through different Jewish understandings of Torah, Oral Torah and rabbinic distillations of Torah). In Contextualise this might lead to different ways in which Jewish groups have applied Torah to situations in which they have found themselves and to ways in which they have adopted or adapted or resisted practices in relation to other groups they have encountered or places in which they have settled and the consequences of that – the Hassidim might provide one example here, as might the exile in Babylon, the diaspora and the establishment of the state of Israel. The Evaluate Within might then weigh the question: 'How has Torah been of value in perpetuating Jewish identity?' The Evaluate Without might pose the question: 'To what extent has Torah helped or hindered Jewish involvement in society (a question of significance within the current debate on community cohesion)?' This would then continue on into Communicate and Apply elements which would constitute a *response* to the idea of Torah in the context of pupils' experience and the wider world. For this the constituent aspects of Torah would need to be unpacked so that its generic characteristics are understood and responded to (e.g. a response to the idea of a normative and prescriptive ethic and way of life that also involves a prescriptive lifestyle and a divinely authored authority).

These two examples do not give an adequate illustration of the scope of the methodology and imaginative ways in which teachers have employed it (see, for example, Hampshire, Portsmouth and Southampton Councils 2006, 2006a; Morgan *et al.* 2007; Morgan 2007; Costambeys 2007; Lowndes and Erricker 2007, 2007a). However, they should indicate that the pedagogical principles on which it is based are free of epistemological restrictions such that it may provide the basis of an inclusive operational curriculum for RE open to different approaches, such as those included in Grimmitt's volume. The important issue is that thinking about ways of enquiring into religious and other worldviews (based on different disciplines and inclusive of different methods, as outlined in Chapter 3) should become part of what students do and thus what any operational curriculum should allow for. The merit of having a number of these methods debated at a theoretical level is that they can also be incorporated into students' learning within the subject.

# The significance of the elements in the methodology

## Communicate, Apply, Enquire

The enquiry may begin at Communicate or Enquire. This might depend on the learning needs of the students in relation to the concept introduced, the prior learning undertaken and the ability level of the students. Teachers in Hampshire have shown preference for starting at either of these points. For example, if the concept is one that is already within the grasp of the students or if the teacher is inclined to introduce the students to something new to be investigated, Enquire might be a good starting point. If the teacher feels his or her students need to build up to the concept through considering it within the context of their own lives, Communicate is preferable. This is often the case with more complex concepts of each type or where a complex type C concept needs a foundation in students' experience.

If we consider the concept of jihad in Islam we might start at Communicate by introducing a prior but related concept within students' experience in Communicate and Apply such as striving. The initial question might be: 'What do we strive for and why?' Jihad then makes sense in Enquire as a striving by Muslims to be closer to Allah. The two types of jihad then make sense of this in terms of personal and social/political practice. However, starting at Enquire with media images of jihad and asking why these events happen and why jihad is used as a term for them would initiate an investigation of the concept and how different Muslims interpret it.

## Contextualise and Evaluate

Continuing with the example of jihad, Contextualise would explore a case study of jihad. The obvious one is the events of 9/11 and the attack on the World Trade Center, but others could be used. Here the question might be: 'What issues does the practice of jihad raise?' This element should include not only media reportage but the justifications and condemnations of this event, from different Muslim perspectives as well as others. It might also include further examples of the justifications of jihad and misinterpretations of the same such as those that can be drawn from Quran and Hadith and by the Prophet Mohammed's words and actions. In other words, the synthesis and analysis of these sources constitute the basis of investigation in order for students to identify and communicate the issues.

Evaluate then focuses on the value of the concept for Muslims as a result. Obviously, this presents the dynamic of the importance of the concept for Muslims but also, in Evaluate Without, the significance of the controversy that can accompany such a concept in a plural modern world in which worldviews and the practices that derive from them can be in tension. How are these to be addressed or overcome?

Communicate and Apply elements may be revisited reverting to the concept of striving. We strive for different things. Can striving be viewed as both a positive and negative idea? If so, on what basis and according to what is being strived for? This invites students to present their own perspectives, taking account of the previous part of the enquiry into jihad.

Most importantly, we must return to the idea of integrity introduced on p. 81. The cycle is an holistic process whereby the enquiry progresses into greater complexity and depends upon using higher level skills of analysis and communication as it moves on, dependent on and reintroducing prior learning in progression from one element to the next. It is not just a structure to be followed.

# Levels of attainment

For learners to be clear as to the expectations in their learning the levels of attainment must reflect the learning process. Thus, returning to the outline of the cycle of enquiry on p. 86 on the key concept of Torah (type C concept) they would be as outlined below.

## Level 4

- Enquire: students can describe the key concept of Torah;
- Contextualise: students can explain how the key concept of Torah is contextualised within the beliefs and practices of Judaism;
- Evaluate: students can evaluate the key concept of Torah by explaining its value to Jews and by identifying and describing some issues raised;
- Communicate: students can describe a personal response to the concept of Torah;
- Apply: students can explain an example of how their response to the concept of Torah can be applied in their own lives and those of others.

## Level 5

- Enquire: students can explain the concept of Torah;
- Contextualise: students can accurately contextualise the concept of Torah within the beliefs and practices of Judaism;
- Evaluate: students can evaluate the concept of Torah by giving more detailed explanations of its value to Jews and by explaining significant issues it raises;
- Communicate: students can explain their own response to Torah;
- Apply: students can explain significant examples of how their response to the concept of Torah would affect their own lives and those of others.

The progressive construction of the five elements of the levels is integrated with the five progressive elements of the conceptual enquiry. Thus students can be clear as to what they are seeking to achieve. They can be supported in identifying the distinction between level 4 and level 5 – moving on from description and basic explanation toward explanation of a more significant and accurate kind. The levels therefore become the intended learning outcomes to direct student learning and of which students can gain ownership. In this way the levels cease to be just a test of the students' ability and become the basis upon which the enquiry is conducted – a means for both student and teacher to measure progression and determine how to progress further.

# The development of skills

Whilst the methodology operates at the level of pedagogic strategy, the development of skills and thus progression through the levels of attainment will only occur if the tasks set and the techniques for learning incorporated within each element of enquiry create an appropriate learning curve that demonstrates student development (see Figure 4.3). In Figure 4.3 notice how the difference between student A and student B is not just knowledge and understanding but the ability to explain rather than just describe. The vertical axis is the critical one, showing higher level skills leading toward greater conceptual awareness. The horizontal axis based on knowledge and understanding is limited in the potential of students to perform at a higher level even if they gain more knowledge. If we teach and students learn only on the basis of the horizontal axis the development of students is not appropriately addressed.

This necessitates that higher order skills should progressively be acquired as students go through each cycle and that tasks should be set that are fit for this purpose. The type and level of skill can be identified from Bloom's taxonomy (see pp. 98–99). Diagnostically, one can determine the fitness of purpose of a task by identifying the skills involved in undertaking it. The overall result can be depicted as in Figure 4.4, spiral progression.

To take an example, when devising the Contextualise element of the cycle using the Jewish concept of Covenant, one could introduce the situation in the concentration camps of the Second World War in which Jews put God on trial. The question would be whether God is responsible for the breaking of the Covenant and allowing Jews to suffer in this way or whether

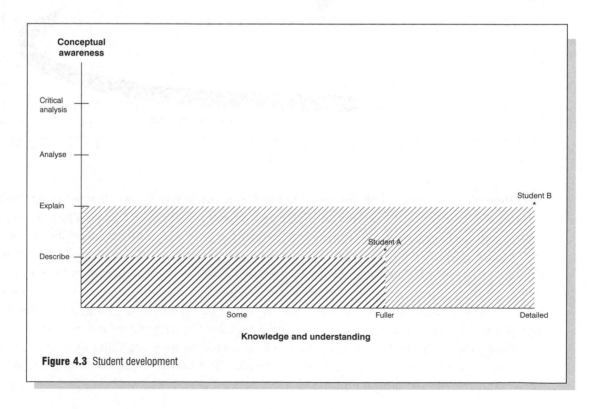

**Figure 4.3** Student development

**Figure 4.4** Spiral progression

Key Stage 4

C

B

A

Foundation Stage

Jews themselves are responsible for breaking the Covenant, in which case their suffering could be seen as self-inflicted, or whether, indeed, the Covenant has not been broken. The task might involve introducing text related to the exile in Babylon as an example of a previous dilemma of a similar kind including prophetic utterance on this issue. It might also involve introducing the original Covenant text(s) in the Torah that defines its terms, as well as introducing more detail of their situation at that time and subsequent reflections from survivors in the concentration camps. This is effectively a Jewish debate that has been ongoing in their history and the students are asked to enter into that by *synthesising* material of different kinds and explaining the issues that arise as a result before *evaluating*, or recognising different Jewish judgements and making their judgement, as a result. The Evaluative question might be: 'Who was responsible for the breaking of the Covenant resulting in Jewish suffering in the concentration camps?' The possible answers might be the Jews, God, neither or it is impossible to tell. Some Jews lost their faith and some held to it. The skills level is high. This would necessitate students being prepared for such a task as they went through the previous elements of the cycle, for example in Communicate, Apply and Enquire. If the learning curve through the cycle up to that point were flat, because of the lack of skills required, they would not cope with this task. Also, if their accumulated knowledge and degree of informed reflection were low that would also significantly affect their ability to perform the task. Contrastingly, a teacher who provided a Contextualise task that asked students to simply *recall* information as to what was involved in the Covenant by *identifying* what was required of the Jews and what was promised by God would not be promoting the higher order skills required at this point in the cycle and there would be nothing of significance, no issues of interpretation, on which to base the following *Evaluative* element. In other words, unless the progression of skills is attended to in the progression of the learning in the cycle the whole cycle becomes flat and students do not progress. This is the difference between complying with the structure of the cycle and understanding that it is a process to enhance progression. This issue will be returned to in Chapter 5.

## Types of concepts

We have devised three categories for these, as mentioned above and as illustrated in Figure 4.2. For religious education conceptual enquiry requires the identification of terms that have importance for believers in specific traditions (type C concepts), terms that are important for the study of religion (type B concepts) and, in a broader sense, terms that are important in the classification of human experience (type A concepts). All of the three types of concepts contain some that are simpler and others that are more complex, but this is particularly true of type A concepts.

Type A concepts focus on concepts that are generic within human experience, therefore, whilst they are wide ranging, there has to be a systematic way of relating them to children's development and experience and linking them explicitly to religious beliefs and practices. Younger children can respond to terms within their own vocabulary and experience. The concepts used have to be readily accessible to them. Belonging, celebrating and special(ness) are the most obvious place to start with those in Foundation Stage and Year 1. They link their own vocabulary and concerns to those that are most transparent within religious behaviour. As children progress further, concepts of a more complex kind can be introduced that build on these: storytelling, community and authority, for example, link their own experience and that of religious groups in an accessible way. Beyond these the most complex of these types of concepts need to be reserved for their upper primary and secondary experience: interpretation, freedom and justice, for example.

Type B concepts focus on concepts that are used in the study of religion and which are common to many religions. These are identifiable by their use of figurative language: symbolism, ritual, sacred, myth and worship are obvious examples. These are the basis of religious literacy.

Type C concepts are those that are specific to a particular religion. As such they are the basis of interpreting worldviews or understanding the way in which a particular tradition makes sense of the world and the way in which different branches of a tradition interpret those concepts to give a distinctive cast to its worldview. These concepts have to be ones that underpin the beliefs and practices of the religion in question, not ones that describe the practices themselves. What we are seeking to get at is the why behind the what of practice and behaviour. Thus, resurrection is a key concept in Christianity but prayer is not. Torah is a key concept in Judaism but Passover is not. Tawhid is a key concept in Islam but salat is not. Dukkha is a key concept in Buddhism but puja is not. Dharma is a key concept in Hinduism but prasad is not. Sewa is a key concept in Sikhism but langar is not.

More will be said on the concepts that can fall into each category in Chapter 5 and tables of these will be provided.

## Developmental considerations

Over the course of six years, since the publication of Living Difference and the inception of the project, new refinements and innovations have been undertaken in recognising the way in which the methodology can be employed as an instrument for progressing learning and development and ways in which it can fail to do so. These have taken place through ongoing development groups, new approaches to conceptual learning being undertaken by teachers and the incorporation of conceptual enquiry into GCSE teaching.

Responses to questionnaires in 2006 indicated the impact the methodology was having, showing an increase in the effectiveness in learning (82.8 per cent primary; 94.8 per cent secondary) by students. Subsequently, a qualitative survey was undertaken, by an independent researcher, with teachers who registered a positive impact of the methodology on teachers' and learners' expectations and progression, the quality of learning, the ethos of the classroom environment and level of engagement by learners. Selected findings from her report are presented later.

Perhaps most significantly a distinction is now being made between conceptual enquiry and the idea of knowledge and understanding of the content of the subject. This means that teachers are thinking very differently about the patterns of their interventions and student interactions within cycles of enquiry to facilitate effective learning and the development of capacities and skills. For some teachers this is a steep learning curve since it involves taking on more sophisticated pedagogic thinking and practice focused upon the learning rather than delivery of subject content.

A last comment on levels of attainment is applicable here. As related on p. 88, the levels of attainment in Living Difference reflect and are integral to its conceptual character (see Hampshire, Portsmouth and Southampton Councils 2006a: 67–69). And these, in turn, become the intended learning outcomes of every cycle of learning, suitably refined to focus on the specific concept and context being enquired into. As a result, attainment is measured against conceptual development not knowledge and understanding, though knowledge and understanding is inevitably the vehicle that supports conceptual development. The distinction is depicted in Figures 4.3 and 4.4, which show how conceptual development is understood in terms of a spiral curriculum, conceptually conceived, and how skills are measured on the vertical scale of conceptuality rather than the horizontal scale of knowledge acquisition.

## Conclusion

This chapter has outlined a discrete conceptual enquiry methodology that is generic but has been specifically applied to religious education. It has shown how, by relating it to the pedagogical principles, procedures and strategies presented by Grimmitt, the methodology can fit with a systematic approach to the subject that is refined by its conceptual focus. It has illustrated some examples of how this approach could be applied in practice. It has provided some quantitative data on the success of its impact on teaching and learning. What is now required is a more detailed consideration of how to plan effective enquiries using the methodology, an analysis of its practical effect in the classroom, and whether it can effectively accommodate differing disciplinary approaches to RE and interdisciplinarity in the curriculum. This will be provided in the following chapters.

# 5

# The Living Difference project

## Curriculum, progression, planning

## Introduction

In Chapter 4 I provided an introduction to the pedagogical process of conceptual enquiry and the structure of its methodology. This was connected, as a pedagogical strategy, to the pedagogical principles laid out in the purpose statement and attainment target provided. Together these gave us the basis for the construction of learning and teaching. In this chapter we shall attend to the detail of how to plan an effective enquiry using the methodology. Also, for the enquiry to be effective we have to attend to a further layer of planning. Whilst the methodology provides purposeful direction to the learning, the actual activity of learning requires effective tasks or activities, which we might call techniques, and appropriate content material in order to achieve the intended learning outcomes. In other words we must pay careful attention to the learning process and its progression and particular techniques for learning such as those associated with Assessment for Learning, Personal Learning and Thinking Skills (PLTS), Community of Enquiry and others. These will also be illustrated at points in the cycles presented in Chapters 6 and 7.

Progression is determined using the eight-level scale in Appendix 5.2 (see pp. 118–121), which is integral to the conceptual enquiry methodology. Further comments on progression will be made later, as will comments on how RE can be regarded as a discipline rather than just a subject on the curriculum. This needs to be urgently addressed and will form a part of the section that follows. We begin by addressing the idea of curriculum.

## Curriculum

If curriculum is only regarded as a matter of what content should be covered it is usually reduced to which religions should be addressed and how many. This is often how planning does start for many teachers and this is the result of the dominance of a reductive form of a descriptive phenomenological approach concerned with religious representation. This then tends to result in a defensive attitude adopted by teachers because they can't fit all the content into the curriculum time available. This defensiveness then results in not only issues concerning the reduction of Key Stage 3 to two years rather than three (an issue I do not want to address here) but also the completely non-educational attitude of having to cover everything quickly with no time for student reflection, debate or engaging with students' own experience, to create relevance or the capacity to reflect on their learning. At its most crass what emerges is the woeful learning about religions (and plenty of them) that has been a commonplace for a good number of years. Such a form of religious education is not worthy of curriculum space. We need to go back to educational principles that can justify the subject's curriculum time.

First, what can the subject offer that will develop young people such that without it being on the curriculum their development would be impoverished? This takes us back to the discussions within Part 1 of this book. Religious education is derived from religious studies. Religious studies is a multidisciplinary endeavour: sociological, phenomenological, philosophical, psychological, ethical and theological. Unfortunately, the dominance of a phenomenological approach largely emerging from a reductionism of the writings of Ninian Smart in the late 1960s and 1970s has resulted in overlooking the richness of disciplinary approaches to the subject. Nevertheless, when Smart propounded different dimensions to the study of religions, first six then seven, there was a sense in which he was suggesting that religions themselves, by virtue of having these different dimensions, within his typology, had to be studied in more than one way. Religions had, for example, doctrinal, ethical, mythic and experiential dimensions. But no systematic attention was paid to this in religious education. What gained precedence was the idea that students should empathise with religions and that to do this they would need to bracket out their own enculturised perceptions and value systems, their preconceptions (the idea of eidetic vision in phenomenological terms, as promoted originally in the writings of the phenomenologist philosopher Edmund Husserl).

In RE this translated into an overall aim of the subject, students empathising with religious believers, without any significant attention (if any) being given to how students could develop the difficult skill of 'bracketing out' their own worldview (though at a theoretical level Robert Jackson's attempts to rectify this through addressing cultural grammar are to be applauded). The RE that resulted was dominated by content and justified by the dubious claim that the subject promoted empathy. This does not amount to a justification for a discipline that needs to be on the curriculum because of the way in which it provides a unique but complementary facet of development for young people.

In Chapter 3 we noted some approaches to RE that have taken seriously the need to refine and develop RE by taking account of and developing different disciplinary approaches but also that these have not translated extensively or effectively enough into the classroom. This is because either the theory has not found its classroom expression or the way it translated into textbook resources did not adequately reflect its theoretical principles, or these approaches have simply been ignored because of the competing demands of compliance to such bodies as Ofsted and GCSE syllabi that do not require theoretical innovation to be taken on board.

The other factor that complements a disciplinary approach, which I drew attention to at the end of Chapter 3 and the beginning of Chapter 4 is relevance to children's experience and narratives. This is a pedagogical matter that should complement disciplinarity. It is not an alternative acting as a panacea for lack of student engagement with religion. Thus, for example, whilst experiential approaches, as presented in Chapter 3, provide such engagement, they are not, in a disciplinary sense or in a pedagogic sense (as discussed in both Chapters 2 and 4), sufficient.

There are two aspects to this pedagogical conundrum: disciplinarity and relevance. If I give an example using history I hope a contrast becomes clear. Whilst I have been in charge of history in Hampshire it has become abundantly clear that good history teachers do regard their subject as a discipline because:

- they are training students to be historians by developing the skills of investigating the past (an intrinsic criterion by which the subject becomes justified);
- they have conceptual criteria for success: chronology, sources, significance, etc.;
- they understand that history is always about enquiry and how you carry out that enquiry;
- they recognise the importance of scrutiny of texts, weighing of evidence and interpretation;
- the emphasis is on student progression and developing an understanding of period and themes (which I would prefer to call concepts) such as power, empire, migration;
- they use levels of attainment that relate to the skills of historical enquiry.

In RE the tendency is quite different and often diverse. The aim has tended to be extrinsic to the academic nature of the subject, whether that be:

- defending the importance of religion or its values (selectively chosen);
- or avoiding religion per se to engage students in ethical and values issues more relevant to them;
- or using adapted spiritual practices taken from selected branches of religious traditions to enhance students' own spiritual development as in experiential methods;
- or avoiding higher level skills such as evaluation;
- or not drawing on the disciplines by which the study of religion is informed;
- or not recognising the importance of enquiry;
- or not scrutinising texts but rather presenting them as givens;
- or not recognising the importance of progression, assessment and using levels of attainment that relate to the subject as a discipline and to students' academic development.

The purpose in introducing a methodology for conceptual enquiry in Hampshire in 2004 was to give the subject direction as a discipline that had an enquiry approach, emphasised progression, skills and the importance of students understanding, engaging with and using concepts. A further step down this road is to then use the disciplines by which the subject is informed to carry out various types of enquiry (theological, socio-anthropological, philosophical, for example) harnessed to the generic conceptual enquiry methodology already in place.

The second aspect of this, which I referred to above, is to then determine how using the discipline (RE or history, for example) can contribute to extrinsic aims. By this I mean the overall development of students, for example spiritual, moral, social and cultural (SMSC) development or the QCDA's 'successful learners, confident individuals, responsible citizens' (QCA 2006). My point is that this can only start to happen effectively once the subject understands itself as a discipline and what that entails. You don't decide between pursuing intrinsic academic goals or the extrinsic overall development of young people; you have to regard these as complementary. In this respect it is not only RE that is deficient but most subjects across the curriculum.

In relation to the above analysis, when we consider how the curriculum should be put in place we need to consider the following:

- what disciplines (in the context of the overall disciplinary area of religious studies) will be addressed;
- how this will relate to the development of students' skills of enquiry;
- how this will be relevant to their own lifeworlds and experiences;
- how this will promote their overall personal development;
- what religions and religious material will be included.

## Progression in religious enquiry

Progression in RE is a traditional weakness, alongside assessment. One of the reasons for this is that practitioners in the subject have not been clear about what progression means. This can be traced to the confusion and insufficiency I have mentioned above that pertain to the academic and educational designs of the subject.

If a subject is not focused on how it can contribute to the development of the skills of a learner, it is hard to see how it can argue for its place in the curriculum. It is not enough to say it will happen; the point is how you can demonstrate that it does. At its most basic the evidence is provided with reference to the levels of attainment a subject uses to determine the capabilities that students have acquired. That is the measure by which we can advise students on what they have achieved and how they can progress further.

## Levels of attainment

The attainment levels are not an irrelevance for RE, they are a means of its justification. For this reason they have to be fit for purpose. In effect they define what the educational mission of the subject is. Across all subjects there are certain generic requirements identified by 'trigger words' and phrases such as 'describe in simple terms', 'describe', 'explain', 'give a coherent explanation' and so on (see the levels of attainment exemplified in Appendix 5.2, pp. 118–121). Once you set an attainment level learning has to be geared to achieving that. Thus progression is exemplified on the basis that, in a particular piece of work, the student has achieved that. This is why the 'levelling' of student work is so important. It is not simply a judgement; it is an explanation of what has been achieved which acts as the diagnostic platform for what has to be achieved next.

If levels were solely based on the acquisition of information we would not be enabling students to progress in their skills and thus the subject would contribute little to student progression – it would be like a 'mastermind' contest. That is not the point of education. What we have to show is that RE contributes to the overall skills development of learners in the fullest sense such that its omission from the curriculum would disempower them – make them less able and prevent them from fulfilling their potential.

## Conceptual enquiry

Levels of attainment predicated upon conceptual enquiry are not just another, alternative way of ensuring progression; they are a way of changing RE from a subject that is not skills based to one that is. They are a way of ensuring progression and evidencing that it is taking place in a systematic fashion that is intelligible to and can benefit students. The result should be that students can tell us how the subject has benefited them. This approach is developmental rather than judgemental, in that it provides a measure of progress in skills acquisition. In a broader sense this provides a means by which students can realise how by studying this subject they are enhancing their ability to understand themselves and their world. However, they have to make connections between what RE gives them and what other subjects give them in realising their potential. This means levels of attainment focus on learning not teaching: it is not about our performance but theirs. Our capacity as teachers needs to be judged by what students achieve.

## A taxonomy of skills

It is important to identify the skills that relate to both the employment of a conceptual enquiry methodology and the levels of attainment in which progression is reflected. One easy diagnostic test as to whether a cycle of conceptual enquiry will be effective is to apply Bloom's taxonomy to the way in which skills are planned into a conceptual cycle. Bloom's taxonomy ranks skills in an hierarchical fashion (from lowest to highest), as follows: knowledge, comprehension, application, analysis, synthesis, evaluation. In a newer version the corresponding skills, stated as verbs rather than nouns, read: remembering, understanding, applying, analysing, evaluating, creating (see Atherton 2009, http://www.odu.edu/educ/roverbau/Bloom/blooms_taxonomy.htm).

Either way, the message is clear: the conceptual cycle only works to create progression if the higher order skills are present to create a 'learning curve' that ensures skills progression. As a result you can diagnostically test the elements of a cycle against the level of skills required within it. Put bluntly, if your cycle consistently relies on tasks based on remembering and understanding rather than the higher skills, then it is not fit for purpose. Since the cycle will culminate in either Evaluate or Communicate and Apply it should be challenging learners to be evaluative and creative. That is the basis of progression.

It follows that analysis and synthesis are necessary skills in order for evaluating and creativity to be carried out effectively. Therefore if the Contextualise part of the cycle does not promote these skills there will be a subsequent deficiency. If teaching and learning solely relies on remembering and understanding, the learning curve will be flat, the work produced 'unlevellable' and progression minimal at best. This provides us with a diagnostic tool to check whether our 'teaching' provides the possibility of student progression in learning based on our understanding of the process-oriented pedagogy the conceptual enquiry methodology provides.

## Progression and the use of texts

We can illustrate how progression is related to the development of skills through focusing on the use of texts. In Chapter 2 I referred to Julian Stern's book *Teaching Religious Education* (Stern 2006), which has a chapter on 'Investigating text and context'. On page 8 he cites a study carried out by the Association of Religious Education Inspectors and Advisers (AREIAC), which can be found on their website (www.areiac.org.uk). It compares the use of texts in history and RE, with the results outlined below:

**History**

Tasks tend to require pupils to:

■ read multiple source materials;

■ make decisions and choices about the material they are reading;

■ work with original texts;

■ handle challenging text material;

■ process reading so that their writing output is significantly different from the material they have read.

**RE**

Tasks tend to require pupils to:

■ rarely use multiple texts;

■ simply recycle their reading;

■ use second-hand rather than original texts;

■ engage with over-processed simplified language;

■ reading for understanding doing little with the original: too much emphasis on low level comprehension and recall.

(Stern 2006: 8)

If we ask why there should be such a disparity between the skilful reading of texts in history and the lack of the same in RE, the following springs to mind:

■ History teachers understand themselves to be historians and the purpose of their teaching to be that of developing their pupil's abilities to perform the same role. Thus, the study of history is a *discipline* based on the skills required for critical enquiry. Texts are sources that are indispensible to carrying out this endeavour. Texts are investigated with the idea in mind that they provide evidence and that, in this respect, some texts are more reliable than others. The outcome of textual enquiry must contribute to the overall process of reliably interpreting the past and explaining its significance.

■ It is an interesting undertaking to try and provide a similar paragraph to the above for RE teachers. Do RE teachers understand what they do as a *discipline*? Do they regard their teaching role to be that of developing pupils' ability to critically enquire? In what sense are texts regarded as 'sources' in RE? What is the overall process to which the reading of texts contributes in RE?

Generally speaking, the findings of the AREIAC study suggest that RE has, as discussed above, lost its sense of being a discipline at all (if indeed it had such a sense). As a result the acquisition of skills is not paramount and is even neglected. As a further result there is a lack of progression because the idea of progression therefore becomes meaningless apart from in relation to the further accumulation of information. Thus the low level skills of comprehension and recall become the drivers of many tasks undertaken by pupils.

In order to correct this we have to ask ourselves how we ask pupils to engage with texts with progression and the idea of a discipline in mind.

## Planning

When planning cycles of conceptual enquiry the five bullet points posited at the end of the above section on curriculum must be borne in mind. Here I address the specifics of how to construct a conceptual cycle of enquiry. First consider the students for whom you are planning the cycle and their capabilities and needs. As an example we can start with Year 7.

## Planning for Year 7 students

What is the prior learning of the pupils that come to you from their experience in primary school? Have they been engaged in conceptual enquiry? If not, then what has been expected of them? Do you know? If they have, then what concepts have they studied and what contexts have been introduced in relation to what religious traditions? Being able to answer these questions confidently is highly important to how you can progress their learning and build on the skills they have already developed. It is not surprising that transition, along with progression and assessment, is a weakness in RE. Many secondary teachers start with the assumption that students have learned nothing of importance in their primary experience, but that is often based on a measure of content or information acquisition on which they may initially be tested and found wanting. It is also the case that students coming from different feeder primary schools have had very different RE experiences. However, determining their RE knowledge is not a measure of students' overall development and the latter (the quality of RE experience students have had in their primary school) provides a better measure than the former (the amount of information they have acquired).

In primary schools where conceptual enquiry has been embedded they would be dealing with simple type A concepts in Year 1, such as belonging in relation to the context of Church, and celebration in relation to the context of Diwali. The concepts are within their experience and allow them to move out to how they operate in the contexts of others. They might then progress to type B concepts by Year 3 or 4, such as worship in relation to the context of Hindu or Sikh puja, and more complex type A concepts, such as freedom in relation to the festival of Passover. Then they even move on to some type C concepts in Year 6, such as umma in the context of Hajj. Even if their RE experience has not provided them with this foundation it does not mean they are not capable of it, simply that they have not been given the opportunity.

Therefore, at the beginning of their secondary education, students should be given the opportunity to work at the generic level of ability they have achieved in primary school, at least as recorded in their English. Relate this to the specific conceptual enquiry levels in Appendix 5.2 (pp. 118–121) and this will give you a starting point. As a general rule, the need for students in Year 7 is to begin to engage with type B concepts and more complex type A concepts to ensure they gain the capacity to understand and use figurative expression: simile, symbolism, metaphor, etc., on which their comprehension of religious language will depend. Chapter 6 explicitly deals with religious literacy and gives examples of cycles that engage with this.

To recap so far: we have covered what students might have done in primary school and the importance of knowing about their previous learning experience. We have affirmed the importance of knowing the level of attainment achieved to date and matching that to the levels of attainment in Appendix 5.2. Now we begin the process of planning a cycle.

## Planning a cycle of conceptual enquiry

1 Consult the list of illustrative concepts A, B and C in Appendix 5.1 (pp. 112–118) and decide on an appropriate concept for a new Year 7 class.

2 Next we need to provide the context for that concept. This will be related to the religious tradition you have decided to engage with and we need to ensure the compatibility of concept and context. In order to do this, consider the material you will introduce in the context and its relevance to the concept.

3 Now decide on the key evaluative question students will have to answer in Evaluate having completed the Contextualise element of the cycle. It is important that the Contextualise element raises issues upon which the evaluative question will be based.

4 Having done this, fill in the rest of the cycle by deciding whether the Communicate and Apply elements are to come at the beginning or the end. Then determine what needs to be included in the Enquire element as an introduction to the concept, so that it has been engaged with prior to its instrumentality in the Contextualise element. Note that if Communicate and Apply precede Enquire and if the concept is type C, or even some type B, then the Communicate and Apply will need to have a lead-in concept, and appropriate learning activity, to bridge to the key concept introduced in Enquire.

5 Once you have the full cycle established in outline, determine/firm up the teaching and learning techniques that will be fitted to each of its elements.

6 Now check around each element of the cycle to determine the skills required at each point. Measure against Bloom's taxonomy to diagnose whether the skills level required is fit for purpose.

7 Ensure you now insert, or previously have inserted, a lead question in every element of the cycle that signals the purpose and end point of enquiry within that element and that these lead questions proceed logically and progressively toward the key evaluative question.

8 Last (though once you have become adept at constructing cycles it will be a first consideration), ask yourself what is the disciplinary approach to the study of religion that your cycle primarily draws upon.

# Examples of two cycles of enquiry for Year 7 students

These two cycles were linked together under the unit of work heading: 'What is the problem with the world?' (Costambeys and Timms-Blanche 2006: 271–287).

The unit draws on Hindu and Christian beliefs related to the underlying concepts of change and cause and effect. It introduces the development of skills in interpretation associated with written and visual texts in which symbolic and mythic ideas are conveyed in order to explain reasons for important characteristics in human existence. As a baseline unit of work in Year 7 it will determine and develop students' appreciation of differing explanations of change and cause and effect within human existence offered by different religions and develop their own appreciation of these concepts.

## Cycle of learning 1

Lessons 1–2
Key concept: samsara
Key question: How effective is the concept of samsara as an explanation of change?

*Communicate* a response to the concept of change

Students are asked to reflect on changes in their own life and the most significant changes:

- What created these changes and how did they affect you?
- What does this tell you about the effects of change?
- How is death a moment of change and what effect do you think it brings about? Is it the final change?
- Is there any connection between being born and dying or dying and being born?

Answers are written on cards and read out anonymously.

*Apply* the response to their own lives and those of others

Students are asked to consider when changes occurred whether and to what extent they were the agents of change or experienced its effects and to note whether this made a difference. Students note their responses on Post-Its, which are then, with their permission, displayed on a board.

To consolidate and promote mutual sharing of ideas students are divided into groups to discuss their views:

- What creates significant changes in our lives?
- What types of effects do these changes create?
- To what extent are we the agents of change?

These collective views and differences in view are then fed back to the class. This prepares students for understanding the concept of samsara in Enquire.

### *Enquire* into the key concept of samsara

The concept of samsara introduces students to the idea of cyclical change and change as a constant rather than intermittent activity. It also broadens the scope of change going across lives rather than just within one life.

Here verses from the Upanishads are analysed to draw out exactly what are the specifics of change in the concept of samsara. In the original set of resources eleven verses are used and students are asked to determine how the idea of change presented in the concept of samsara presents new understandings of change and the reasons for it.

Here I present three of the verses used as examples of the nature of the task undertaken:

> The soul is born and unfolds in a body, with dreams and desires . . . And then it is reborn in a new body, according to its former works.

> The quality of the soul decides its future body. Its thoughts and actions can lead it to freedom, or lead it to bondage in life after life.

> When a man knows God, the God of love, then he leaves behind his bodies of transmigration.

Students are asked to identify: what changes occur, how and why changes occur and what the results of change are from the verses given. Then they are asked:

- How does this understanding of change differ from the ones you gave previously and why?

It is important that this task takes place in pairs or groups and that then the observations are shared amongst the class to arrive at an agreed 'commentary' on these verses. Students are encouraged to ask questions to seek further information or clarify statements, both amongst themselves and through the guidance of the teacher.

### *Contextualise* the Hindu concept of samsara within the Hindu symbol of Shiva Nataraj

Here an image of Shiva Nataraj (the dancing Shiva) is introduced, either as a statue or from the internet. Students are asked to speculate on how it symbolically relates to the concept of samsara:

- How does it manifest change?
- What are the features of the image that suggest change?
- What sort of change is occurring?

They are then given an information sheet to link to the image:

> Shiva Nataraj represents the great *dance* of life. His *many arms* show his great power. He is the God of creation and destruction.
>
> He stands inside a never-ending *circle of fire*. All life moves through a circle of creation and destruction. Things come to life, they change and they die. That is how life is. It is a circle of fire because fire shows the idea of creating and destroying. A fire creates as it destroys. That is how life is.
>
> The *drum* represents the beat of life. If you want to hear the life within you, listen to your heart beating. As the drum beats, Shiva Nataraj dances. Life is a dance, always changing, never standing still, always moving.
>
> *Shiva Nataraj holds a piece of fire* but his face does not show pain. This shows that if we understand that everything is being created and destroyed, then we can cope with life; we can be peaceful and calm.
>
> *Shiva Nataraj's hair* is the great river Ganga (Ganges). This is our sacred river, the river that brings life to Northern India. A river is like a circle or a dance. It is always changing; it never stays the same. You can never step into the same river twice. It starts; flows to the sea; the water evaporates; it rains; it begins again. A great circle!
>
> The *tiny figure* under his feet is ignorance. If you do not understand the circle of life you are ignorant and you will find life hard. So Shiva Nataraj tramples on ignorance and destroys it.

***Evaluate*** *the concept of samsara by showing an appreciation of the value of the Shiva Nataraj image and making a judgement on its interpretation of samsara as an explanation of change*

Here students must both explain the image and how it offers a representation of samsara (Evaluate Within) and comment from their own perspective (Evaluate Without).

One student wrote:

> For me, Shiva Nataraj is a symbol to show that my life is always changing. If I try to stop it changing, I will fail. You cannot stop change. This is difficult sometimes because you don't want things to change. Maybe we were worried about going to a new school. We don't want to grow older. We don't want to leave our family. We don't want to die. But we will, and we have to accept it. We will die, but Shiva Nataraj reminds me that I will be born again. I believe in reincarnation – that I will return and be born again. Everything changes, nothing remains the same. That is what life is like.

It is an interesting exercise to determine how you would level these comments and what feedback you would give to the student. For example, a strength of the piece is her ability to explain rather than just describe and relate it to her own life. Additional feedback might be that though she has related the concept of change to the image of Shiva Nataraj she has not explicitly related this to the concept of samsara. Also, she has positively evaluated but there is a lack of critical commentary. Interestingly, too, it is worth noting this student is not Hindu.

# Cycle of learning 2

Lessons 3–4

Key concept: free will

Key question: Could God have made a better job of designing people if he hadn't invented free will?

***Communicate*** *a response to the concept of free will by answering the question: What does free will mean to you?*

Students are given the stimulus below to help them construct their response:

In writing your answer you should consider these points:

1   What is the difference between ordinary, everyday choices and moral choices?
2   Do you really have a choice if you don't have real options to choose from?
3   Does having a real choice mean having the option to do the wrong thing?
4   Do people need to make bad/wrong choices simply because they have that choice?
5   Are people restricted in their choices? Restricted, for example, by:

- society and its laws (e.g. you have to come to school, people must pay taxes);
- their genetic make-up (a 7 foot man weighing 95 kg can't be a ballet dancer);
- their commitments (someone with a family to support must work);
- their age (a 90-year-old woman can't be a teenage fashion model);
- their social conditions (choices are very limited for some people in the third world).

6   Do people have the wrong understanding of free will? Does it, in fact, mean more than just the ability to choose? Does it mean the freedom of will to choose what to do with your life through your actions?

This was given as a homework task to bring to their next lesson.

***Apply*** *their response to their own lives and those of others*

Here students share in groups the responses they have given. They have to interpret different ways in which free will has been understood and the implications. They then draw out the most important issues raised.

***Enquire*** *into the Christian understanding of free will*

Here a picture of Adam and Eve is introduced and students speculate on the image in relation to the concept. The skills focus is the interpretation of a visual text depicting an interpretation of an event. What, in this case, is the understanding of free will being presented and its consequences? Students 'hot seat' Adam and Eve to explore different ways of interpreting this story in relation to what is involved in the concept of free will.

***Contextualise*** *the concept of free will within the story of the Fall and Christian teachings based on it*

Here two texts are introduced: first, the biblical story. Here students study the story in groups and identify what they think are the reasons for Adam and Eve having free will and how that was expressed. Then they comment on the consequences in the story, the banishment from the Garden of Eden. They then feed back their reflections on the story as a teaching on free will, its consequences and disobedience. What issues does this raise for the concept of free will and the authority of God?

Second, the visual depiction by William Blake is introduced of God creating Adam. This is analysed and the students' attention is drawn to the snake already being woven around his leg. Discuss the implications of this. The question is then posed whether God actually planned the Fall within his creation and what the implications are for a reinterpretation of the story and God's intention, which students now discuss to see if they can now come up with a new interpretation of the story in relation to God's plan.

## *Evaluate*

The key question is reintroduced: Could God have made a better job of designing people?
   The following argument is put:

- God created humans and made them special by giving them *free will*;
- free will allows people to make their own choices and mistakes;
- people often make mistakes which lead to suffering and problems;
- God loves people and does not want people to suffer;
- so, why didn't God design people so that they wouldn't make mistakes?

Students are now required to respond to this argument, and specifically the last question, drawing on their understanding of free will (Evaluate Within) and are given an information sheet to draw on in order to construct their answer.

Then they are asked to reconsider the concept of free will and whether they think this story provides a plausible explanation for free will and what is involved in having free will (Evaluate Without).

A further step in the enquiry would be to compare the samsaric explanation of change and the biblical explanation of free will. What issues and further reflections and questions are raised by this comparison?

I have suggested that each of these cycles may take the equivalent of two lessons but this can vary according to the depth of complexity engaged with and the ability of students that you are working with.

## Reflections on curriculum, progression and planning

1   Check on the planning of the two cycles presented above in relation to the planning guidance given previously. To what extent are these cycles fit for purpose and could they be improved?

2   Identify, according to the descriptors against each element of the cycles employed, at what level these cycles are expecting students to work and achieve. Consult the levels of attainment in Appendix 5.2 (pp. 118-121) to determine this.

3   What disciplinary aspects of the study of religions are these cycles focused on and what skills are being addressed?

It is important to note that students' capacities are more important than their age, though maturity can also be an issue in relation to material presented. If student entry at Year 7 suggests that a considerable number of students are only achieving level 3, then the cycles presented above will be too difficult and should be introduced in Year 8. If they are level 4 they should be appropriate. Also bear in mind that students may be operating across levels 4–6 and, therefore, work presented to them should be commensurate with their ability to achieve across all these levels. Where differentiation is required it should be in relation to support given to achieve the tasks at their own level and providing material in an appropriate form. It should not be by removing the requirement to develop skills.

When planning the curriculum across a key stage attention needs to be paid to:

■   Appropriate complexity of the type A, B and C concepts introduced. Key Stage 3 should contain all three and certainly types B and C. There should also be a progressive movement to more complex concepts.

■   Complexity can also be introduced through both the nature of the task employed in the Contextualise element of the cycle, the complexity of the evaluative question and the skills level demanded.

■   Whether cycles should be stand alone or part of a larger unit of work. Type C concepts should be used with others from the same religion when seeking to build up an interpretation of a religious tradition.

■   Cycles should be planned across a key stage to ensure that students engage with different disciplines used in the Study of Religion and the commensurate skills involved.

## The Living Difference Evaluation Project Report

Subtitle: *How Far Does the Hampshire, Portsmouth and Southampton Councils Agreed Syllabus 'Living Difference' Facilitate Effective Teaching and Successful Learning in RE? An Exploratory Study.*

Katherine Wedell's commissioned independent report produced in February 2009 gave us a means to reflect on the extent to which Living Difference had made a significant impact on the practice of a selective number of RE teachers and the learning of their students and to construct a meaningful development plan based on evidence as a result. Below I quote from the summary of this report, which she structured according to planning, progression, attainment and training. This should help readers to reflect on how best the conceptual enquiry methodology can be used to good effect and what pitfalls may be avoided. Twenty Hampshire teachers were interviewed, across the primary and secondary phases, all of whom had stated that Living Difference had had a positive effect. The quoted part of the report indicates the impact of Living Difference, offers suggestions for further improvement in its implementation and suggests some national implications:

> This research indicates that Living Difference can facilitate significantly more effective teaching and successful learning in RE in a number of ways. However, this is not happening fully in all cases and the implementation of Living Difference needs some further development.
>
> Living Difference is an enabling framework. It supports teachers' planning. The concept and the process of learning make clear what the aim of learning is and how to get there. Learning is therefore purposeful for students and this raises attainment.
>
> Living Difference enables teachers and students to see attainment and progression. Teachers assess one aspect of learning at a time and this is consistent across units of work. The specific skill progression in the level descriptors makes clear what students have achieved and what they need to do next to progress.
>
> Living Difference sets out how to enable students to learn at a higher order level. Students are investigating and applying concepts at every stage in the process of learning. This enables a far higher level of attainment than students were reaching before Living Difference.
>
> Living Difference engages students in their learning. The concept links the religious material and students' ideas and experience and thus makes learning relevant and meaningful. Students' own voices are integral in the learning process. Students have more opportunities to achieve in a variety of ways.
>
> The findings suggest that the following are areas for further development.
>
> 1   The provision of more exemplars of evaluative questions teachers can use in units of work: examples of the kinds of question format which will help students to evaluate the concept.
>
> 2   The provision of a formula, a technique, to help 'unpack' concepts: more guidance in analysing concepts, in order to see their significance beyond the religious context.
>
> 3   Support to integrate the level descriptors into planning; specifically, to see that the level descriptors dovetail with teaching as intended learning outcomes.
>
> 4   Support to plan Contextualise in terms of higher order thinking skills. In the Contextualise element, students actively investigate the significance of the concept in the context, in order to evaluate its significance. Contextualise is not just the bit where you put the 'learning about religions.
>
> Arising from the findings of this research are questions for RE nationally.
>
> ■   Is Living Difference a pedagogical model which could underpin the National Framework for RE and RE in the secondary and now primary curriculum reviews? Living Difference is entirely compatible with the intentions for RE set out in these documents and supplies the 'how' of how to realise those intentions. Teachers in this sample valued the fact that Living Difference does give the 'how': a process of learning and not just the intention. As one interviewee commented, '*It's a way of doing, not just an intention and you don't have to reinvent the wheel*'.

■ Does Living Difference provide the model for learning in RE most appropriate in a curriculum led by concepts and skills? Is it more appropriate to RE than other models of learning because, specifically, it provides an approach to religious concepts and a process of analysing them?

■ Is one Attainment Target better than two in practice? Should RE practitioners see the concepts of 'learning about' and 'learning from' as helpful in having moved us beyond confessional RE, but unwieldy when applied to assessment in practice? 'Learning about' and 'learning from' inform an understanding of the subject at a general philosophical level. Living Difference is not incompatible with that general conception of RE. Assessment in the Living Difference model, however, is grounded in the learning process. The learning process sets out one way in which you can 'interpret religion in relation to human experience'. There is one intended learning outcome at each stage in the learning process. Through these intended learning outcomes students attain the attainment target. Teachers are clearer than they were before about whether they are addressing the attainment target in their assessment, because they are only assessing one thing at a time and because the attainment target and the learning process together form one indivisible whole.

■ Does Initial Teacher Training and Continuing Professional Development need to give greater emphasis to learning theory? Should they give teachers opportunities explicitly to try out pedagogical approaches in practice? This could enable teachers to have a much greater critical command of the 'how' of learning, across the subjects. Students are learning to learn, in a skills- and concepts-led curriculum. Teachers can only facilitate students' learning to learn if they are clear about the processes of learning.

■ Should all Agreed Syllabi provide a pedagogical framework like Living Difference does? Planning and implementing effective RE is challenging for teachers. Living Difference sets out good practice systematically at a pedagogical level and thereby supports teachers in their good practice. One teacher commented:

*LD tightens the whole thing of what would make an outstanding lesson; it helps to bring it all together.*

And if Agreed Syllabi provide underpinning guidance at a pedagogical level, should Local Authorities and/or other institutions support training of the kind which is going on in Hampshire, in the development groups and the steering groups and the work of the advisors? Teachers in this sample overwhelmingly benefited from their training. Their students have hugely benefited as a result. Can we afford to do less if we want quality RE which enables our young people to realise their abilities?

(Wedell 2009: 33–34)

## National guidance and Living Difference

It is important that national guidance and pedagogy in RE should be aligned. Otherwise it is not possible to speak with authority of the right of RE to be considered as a significant aspect of the curriculum and as integral to young people's development. This is the case whether the pedagogy emerges from research in higher education or through Locally Agreed Syllabuses. Fundamentally, that distinction, in itself, would be erased if the agencies involved were working with common intent together. Whilst, at present, Locally Agreed Syllabuses have statutory deter-mination the components of their statute that have any relevance relate to the demographics of religious adherence. It is right that where, in one authority, a particular religious group has significant representation that should receive attention in the Locally Agreed Syllabus. However, it is wrong that those syllabi should be different in other respects, with regard to overall purposes that reflect standards, achievement and pedagogical value. This would be regarded as absurd in any other subject. With this in mind I show below how some of the key concepts in the Living Difference pedagogy focused on conceptual enquiry can be aligned with the QCDA's 'compound concepts' within its secondary curriculum.

## Compound concepts and key concepts

This list presents some examples of key concepts in Living Difference according to the compound classification provided by QCDA in its conceptual guidance in order to provide focus for the learning experience and progression of students:

1  Beliefs, teachings and sources

- Type A: change, wisdom, authority, interpretation;
- Type B: God, salvation, scripture;
- Type C: redemption, resurrection, incarnation, Torah, Covenant, Moksha, nirvana.

2  Practices and ways of life

- Type A: altruism, charity, benevolence, environmentalism, commitment, hedonism;
- Type B: initiation, discipleship, stewardship, pilgrimage;
- Type C: mitzvot, amrit, communion, eucharist, darshan.

3  Expressing meaning

- Type A: hope, justification, interdependence;
- Type B: symbolism, ritual, myth;
- Type C: sacrament, holy matrimony, ibadah.

4  Identity, diversity and belonging

- Type A: community, identity, difference;
- Type B: rites of passage, ordination, worship;
- Type C: baptism, church, umma, sangha, khalsa, Israel, varna.

5  Meaning, purpose and truth

- Type A: truth, purpose, destiny, fate, free will, contingency;
- Type B: revelation, faith, transcendence, omnipotence, theism, monism, panentheism;
- Type C: dharma, maya, samsara, tawheed, trinity.

6  Values and commitments

- Type A: toleration, justice, forgiveness, freedom, love, compassion, obedience;
- Type B: sacred(ness), prophecy, martyrdom;
- Type C: atonement, reconciliation, repentance, agape, karuna, sila, ahimsa, shirk, jihad, khalifah.

Whilst this list exemplifies a compatibility between the QCDA compound concepts or thematic areas of study it does not mean that there is a linear alignment between those and key concepts in the conceptual enquiry methodology. If you return to the two cycles of enquiry presented above and identify the differing QCDA compound concepts involved, then it will give a better understanding of how different cycles of enquiry can address those areas denoted by the QCDA but not simply according to one being addressed in any specific conceptual cycle.

For example, the cycles presented above together address aspects of 1, 3 and 5 of the six compound concepts. This suggests there should be some alignment between these compound concepts and different disciplinary approaches to the study of religion in RE, commensurate with the idea of it being a discipline.

Similarly, in addressing the QCDA eight level scale for levels of attainment in RE it is not problematic to derive a compatibility with the levels presented in Appendix 5.2 (on pp. 118-121). But the way in which this can be done is to take a particular level in Appendix 5.2, for example level 4, then turn to the level 4 QCDA scale (as contained in the non-statuary national framework) and identify what, within that, can be added to the conceptual enquiry level by focusing on any specific conceptual enquiry, such as those given above, and incorporating the relevant material under the supplementary heading: 'this will be achieved through . . .' (and adding the requisite text). For example, the cycle on samsara is intended to be used by students at level 4 and above. Including the QCDA non-statutory eight level scale in the Non-Statutory National Framework, level 4 would read as follows, incorporating both the conceptual enquiry methodology levels and then the supplementary Non-Statutory National Framework descriptors:

Students will be able to:

- describe a personal response to the concept of change;

- explain examples of how their response to the concept can be applied in their own lives and the lives of others;

- describe the key Hindu concept of samsara as an expression of change;

- explain how samsara is contextualised within the Hindu image of Shiva Nataraj;

- evaluate the concept of samsara by explaining its value to believers and by identifying and describing some issues it raises.

Note how the order of the statements changes if the cycle begins with Communicate and ends with Evaluate.

They will be able to do this through:

- using a developing religious vocabulary to describe and show understanding of sources, beliefs, ideas, feelings and experiences; making links between them (Attainment Target 1: Learning about religion)

- raising and suggesting answers to questions of identity, meaning and purpose; applying their ideas to their own and other people's lives; describing what inspires and influences themselves and others (Attainment Target 2: Learning from religion).

Note what is mentioned and what is omitted from these two attainment targets and how that relates to different approaches taken, in a disciplinary sense, in any particular cycle of learning. Don't try to cover everything in one go but recognise the complementarity and differences in what is addressed in different cycles across a cycle of learning, a unit of work, a year and a key stage.

## Conclusion

This chapter has considered how curriculum planning can address progression, skills and disciplinarity in the RE curriculum through conceptual enquiry. It has also provided an exercise in how to plan a conceptual cycle and an example of a unit of work based on two conceptual cycles. Reflections on the impact on teachers' approach to, planning and delivery of RE and the effect on their students' learning was presented in the context of an independent survey on the implementation of Living Difference conducted by Katherine Wedell. Also, the compatibility of QCDA non-statutory guidance and its alignment with the conceptual enquiry methodology and levels of attainment were addressed. The following two chapters focus on religious literacy and interpreting worldviews as the prime objectives of religious education. In doing so they provide further examples of effective planning according to conceptual enquiry. Before moving on to Chapter 6 you might well want to devise a cycle of enquiry of your own as an exercise in planning.

## Appendix 5.1

## Type A concept

Examples of concepts common to religious and non-religious experience. These are illustrative not exhaustive. As with the other types of concepts they are not in alphabetical order. The important thing is to decide on how progression and continuity between concepts can best be established.

- suffering
- loyalty
- belief
- identity
- change
- good and evil
- devotion
- community
- sacrifice
- submission
- remembrance
- freedom
- wisdom
- power
- creation
- forgiveness
- justice
- peace
- love
- interpretation
- hope
- authority
- prejudice
- persecution
- justification
- hedonism
- environmentalism

# Type B concept

Examples of concepts that are common to many religions and that are used in the study of religion:

- God
- worship
- symbolism
- ritual
- prophethood
- sacred
- holy
- myth
- initiation
- rites of passage

- prophecy
- pilgrimage
- martyrdom
- discipleship
- stewardship
- faith
- salvation
- covenant
- revelation

# Type C concept

Examples of key concepts that are particular to specific religions.

## Christianity

- *Trinity*: the doctrine of the threefold nature of God as Father, Son and Holy Spirit. Three persons (or forms) in one God;

- *Incarnation*: the doctrine that God took human form in Jesus Christ and the belief that God in Christ is active in the Church and the world through the Holy Spirit;

- *Church*: the whole community of Christians in the world throughout time as the body of Christ or the body of believers; also a particular congregation or denomination of Christianity; also, the congregation of a particular church or worshipping community;

- *Salvation*: the belief that all believers will be saved and live in God's presence;

- *Atonement*: reconciliation between God and humanity through Christ, restoring a relationship broken by sin;

- *Sin*: act or acts of rebellion against the known will of God; an understanding of the human condition as being severed from its relationship with God because of disobedience;

- *Resurrection*: the rising from the dead of Jesus Christ, leading to the rising from the dead of all believers at the Last Day, and the belief in the new, or risen, life of Christians;

- *Redemption*: the effect of the death on the cross of Jesus Christ in setting people free from sin;

- *Repentance*: the acceptance of our unworthiness before God and recognition of the need to be saved from sin by his love;

- *Reconciliation*: the uniting of believers with God through the sacrifice of Jesus Christ; the process of reconciling Christians with one another;

- *Grace*: the freely given and unmerited favour of God's love for humanity; the means to salvation through faith in Jesus Christ;

- *Logos*: the Word; the pre-existent Word of God incarnate as Jesus Christ;

- *Agape*: the love of God for humanity, which Christians should seek to emulate;

- *Sacrament*: an outward sign of a blessing given by God (Protestant) or the actual presence of God (Catholic); in the Roman Catholic Church these represent a means to salvation.

A unit of work on Christianity, or one including the Christian tradition, would be expected to draw on some of these key concepts. Further beliefs and practices included should be related back to the key concepts.

## Buddhism

- *Dukkha*: suffering or dis-ease; the unsatisfactoriness of worldly existence;

- *Tanha*: thirst or craving; attachment to desiring;

- *Anicca*: change, the continual changing nature of worldly existence;

- *Anatta*: the lack of a substantial and unchanging self, soul or identity;

- *Nirvana (nibbana)*: enlightenment; the extinguishing of ignorance and attachment that binds one to worldly existence;

- *Karma (kamma)*: the state of rebirth through one's attachment to the world and the self;

- *Buddha*: enlightened or awakened one; one who sees things as they really are;

- *Sangha*: the Buddhist community; sometimes used specifically about the monastic community (arya sangha);

- *Dharma (Dhamma)*: teachings of the Buddha; also, the Truth about the way things are;

- *Bhavana*: mental culture or mental development/discipline; also, meditation/formal training; the seventh and eighth steps on the eightfold path, or middle way, taught by the historical Buddha;

- *Karuna*: compassion, one of the two (inter-related) aspects of enlightenment;

- *Prajna*: wisdom; the second of the aspects of enlightenment; the first three steps on the eightfold path, or middle way, taught by the historical Buddha;

- *Sila*: ethical conduct; the fourth, fifth and sixth steps on the eightfold path, or middle way, taught by the historical Buddha;

- *Upaya*: skilfulness/skill in means; an attribute of the Buddha; also, the ability to adapt the teachings to an audience, and one's actions and advice to individuals and situations.

A unit of work on Buddhism, or one including the Buddhist tradition, would be expected to draw on some of these key concepts. Further beliefs and practices included should be related back to the key concepts.

# Hinduism

- *Brahman*: ultimate Reality, the formless understanding of God;

- *Avatar*: an incarnation (or descent) of God; for example, followers of Vishnu believe he was incarnated in 10 different forms, of which the most famous are Rama, Krishna and the Buddha;

- *Atman*: the presence of ultimate formless reality in a person or living being;

- *Brahmin*: the highest caste entrusted with the knowledge of the Vedas;

- *Brahma*: the Hindu God responsible for creation and creative power; one of the trimurti (the three deities who control the gunas: the three functions of creation, preservation and destruction);

- *Vishnu*: the Hindu God responsible for the preservation of creation; one of the trimurti;

- *Shiva*: the Hindu God responsible for the destructive aspect of creation; one of the trimurti;

- *Murti*: the manifestation of God in a particular form and with a particular function;

- *Darshan*: literally *seeing*. Refers to being seen by God, and thus blessed; Hindus refer to *going for darshan* when going to the mandir (temple) for worship;

- *Samsara*: the created world, ultimately temporal and limited – even illusory; it consists of nama-rupa (name and form); it is the cycle of life, death and rebirth;

- *Maya*: the form and nature of the created world, ultimately illusory or masking the true reality;

- *Guna*: rope or quality; specifically refers to the three qualities that make up and influence matter: sattva (goodness), rajas (passion) and tamas (ignorance);

- *Moksha*: liberation or release from samsara;

- *Yoga*: the paths (marg) to moksha; literally means 'to yoke' or bind;

- *Bhakti yoga*: the yoga of loving devotion;

- *Jnana yoga*: the path of knowledge;

- *Karma yoga*: the path of ethical works or actions;

- *Karma*: the law by which one's actions result in a higher or lower rebirth according to whether one's actions have good or bad effects;

- *Vedas*: the ancient scriptures that contain the revealed knowledge of reality;

- *Dharma*: religious duty, according to one's status or place in society (see jati); it also refers to the intrinsic quality of the self or truth (see karma);

- *Varna*: colour; this refers to the four vedic caste sub-divisions in Hindu society; these are Brahmins (priests), Kshatriyas (ruling or warrior class), Vaishyas (merchant class) and Shudras (labouring class);

- *Jati*: this refers to the occupational kinship group to which one belongs in Indian society; it is a form of social regulation and hierarchy derived from that of varna;

- *Ahimsa*: non-violence.

A unit of work on Hinduism, or one including the Hindu tradition, would be expected to draw on some of these key concepts. Further beliefs and practices included should be related back to the key concepts.

## Islam

*Islam*: submission to the will of Allah, leading to peace;

*Muslim*: one who submits;

*Tawheed*: the oneness of God and His creation;

*Risalah*: prophethood, the messengers of Allah;

*Akhirah*: life after death, the hereafter;

*Yawmuddin*: the day of judgement;

*Jihad*: individual striving toward Allah (greater jihad), preventing the corruption of Allah's creation (lesser jihad);

*Shirk*: forgetfulness of Allah, putting someone or something as being equal to or above Allah;

*Umma*: the community of Muslims worldwide;

*Iman*: faith;

*Ibadah*: worship;

*Akhlaq*: ethics governing conduct, character and attitudes.

A unit of work on Islam, or one including the Muslim tradition, would be expected to draw on some of these key concepts. Further beliefs and practices included should be related back to the key concepts.

## Judaism

*Mitzvah/mitzvot* (pl.): commandment in Torah;

*Torah*: law, teaching, God's word; the five books of Moses;

*Shekhinah*: the presence of God;

*Zion*: expression of perfection in the Messianic Age;

*Mashiach*: Messiah, the anointed one to deliver the world into the Messianic Age;

*Israel*: one who struggles with God; this refers to the worldwide Jewish community; the land of Israel and the modern state of Israel;

*Rabbi*: ordained teacher of Torah (the Law); often the religious leader of a Jewish community;

*Kedusha*: holiness – *You should be holy, for I, the Lord your God, am holy*;

*Tzelem Elokim*: in the image of God;

■ *Covenant*: the agreement made between God and the Jewish people involving promise and obligation;

■ *Redemption*: God's promise, in the Covenant, to release the world from its fallen, sinful state.

A unit of work on Judaism, or one including the Jewish tradition, would be expected to draw on some of these key concepts. Further beliefs and practices included should be related back to the key concepts.

## Sikhism

■ *Niguna*: concept of God as One and formless, without attributes;

■ *Ik Onkar*: the symbol representing God as One;

■ *Bani/shabad*: the word of revelation;

■ *Nam simran*: personal meditation;

■ *Haumai*: the human condition of self-reliance;

■ *Manmukh*: self-centredness;

■ *Gurmukh*: God-centredness;

■ *Sewa*: service as an essential response to gurmukh;

■ *Guru*: God manifest, as in Guru Granth Sahib;

■ *Nadar*: the grace of the Guru;

■ *Panth*: the Sikh community;

■ *Khalsa*: fellowship of those who have taken amrit (both men and women);

■ *Amrit*: the Sikh rite of initiation into the Khalsa; also the sanctified sugar and water liquid (nectar) used in the initiation ceremony;

■ *Jot*: the divine light indwelling everyone;

■ *Mukti*: liberation from the world and union with God;

■ *Maya*: the illusion that the world has an essential reality instead of being temporary; the implication being that the soul has no true dwelling in the world.

A unit of work on Sikhism, or one including the Sikh tradition, would be expected to draw on some of these key concepts. Further beliefs and practices included should be related back to the key concepts.

## Humanism

Humanism is not a religion. It does, however, share many of the values held by the world religions, such as a number of those listed below, but without a belief in God:

■ *Value of life*: seeking to make the best of the one life humans have by creating meaning and purpose;

*Rationalism*: explanation of human and natural phenomena based on reason, verifiable evidence and scientific method;

*Moral values*: derived from human knowledge and experience alone; central to civilised living for both individuals and societies;

*Responsibility*: self-reliance and independence of thought; responsibility of humans for their own destiny; treating others in a way one would like to be treated; care for the environment, now and for the future;

*Evolution*: acceptance that human beings have evolved naturally over millions of years, as have all other forms of life;

*The human spirit*: nourished and fulfilled in the appreciation of natural beauty, in human creativity and through human relationships;

*The human heritage*: respect for the inheritance of human achievement – intellectual, philosophical, artistic, technological and scientific;

*Human co-operation*: the importance of international agreements such as those on Human Rights, the Rights of the Child and Protection of the Environment; the support for voluntary organisations which seek to help people (e.g. Amnesty International, Samaritans, Citizens Advice Bureau);

*Toleration*: need for mutual understanding and respect between all human groups; this involves opposition to extremes of belief which seek to impose their own creeds on others and thereby deny basic human freedoms;

*Secularism*: impartiality towards, and equal treatment of, individuals and groups with different religious and non-religious beliefs.

## Appendix 5.2

## Levels of attainment

### Level 1

| | |
|---|---|
| *Enquire* | Pupils can identify and talk about key concepts studied that are common to non-religious and religious experience (type A concept). |
| *Contextualise* | They can recognise that the concept is expressed in the practices of the religion studied. |
| *Evaluate* | They can evaluate the concepts by talking about their importance to believers in simple terms, and by identifying an issue raised. |
| *Communicate* | They can talk about their own response to these concepts. |
| *Apply* | They can identify how their response relates to their own lives. |

## Level 2

*Enquire*        Pupils can describe in simple terms key concepts studied that are common to non-religious and religious experience (type A concept); they can identify and talk about concepts that are common to many religions and used in the study of religion (type B concept).

*Contextualise*  They simply describe ways in which these concepts are expressed in the context of the practices of the religion studied.

*Evaluate*       They can evaluate the concepts by describing in simple terms their value to believers and by talking about an issue raised.

*Communicate*    They can describe in simple terms their response to these concepts.

*Apply*          They can identify simple examples of how their response relates to their own lives and those of others.

## Level 3

*Enquire*        Pupils can describe key concepts that are common to many religions and used in the study of religion (type B concept).

*Contextualise*  They can describe how these concepts are contextualised within some of the beliefs and practices of the religion studied.

*Evaluate*       They can evaluate the concepts by describing their value to believers and by identifying and describing an issue raised.

*Communicate*    They can describe their own response to the concepts.

*Apply*          They can describe examples of how their response is or can be applied in their own lives and the lives of others.

## Level 4

*Enquire*        Pupils can explain key concepts that are common to many religions and used in the study of religion (type B concept); they can describe some key concepts specific to the religions studied (type C concept).

*Contextualise*  They can explain how these concepts are contextualised within the beliefs and practices of the religions studied.

*Evaluate*       They can evaluate the concepts by explaining their value to believers and by identifying and describing some issues they raise.

*Communicate*    They can explain a personal response to type B concepts and describe a personal response to type C concepts.

*Apply*          They can explain examples of how their responses to the concepts can be applied in their own lives and the lives of others.

## Level 5

| | |
|---|---|
| *Enquire* | Students can explain key concepts specific to the religions studied (type C concept); they can explain some connections between different concepts. |
| *Contextualise* | They can accurately contextualise them within key beliefs and practices of the religion in which they are expressed. |
| *Evaluate* | They can evaluate the concepts by explaining their value to believers and by identifying and explaining some important issues they raise. |
| *Communicate* | They can explain their own response to religious concepts. |
| *Apply* | They can explain significant examples of how their response does or would affect their own lives and the lives of others. |

## Level 6

| | |
|---|---|
| *Enquire* | Students can give more detailed explanations of a range of key concepts specific to the religions studied. |
| *Contextualise* | They can accurately contextualise them within key beliefs and practices of different branches of the religion in which they are expressed, and explain connections between different concepts. |
| *Evaluate* | They can evaluate the concepts by giving more detailed explanations of their value to believers and by explaining significant issues they raise. |
| *Communicate* | They can explain their own response to religious concepts with a justification for their response. |
| *Apply* | They can give well-chosen examples of how their response would affect their own lives, those of others, and wider society. |

## Level 7

| | |
|---|---|
| *Enquire* | Students can give coherent, detailed explanations of a wider range of key concepts specific to the religions studied. They can explain how concepts within a religion are related to one another. |
| *Contextualise* | They can accurately contextualise them within the beliefs and practices of different branches of the religion in which they are expressed; they can analyse some conceptual differences and similarities across religions. |
| *Evaluate* | They can evaluate the concepts by giving coherent explanations of the importance of the concepts to the lives and values of believers and by identifying and explaining issues that affect the wider society. |
| *Communicate* | They can give a coherent explanation for their own response to religious concepts with a justification. |
| *Apply* | They can apply their response by giving some evidence of how their response would affect their own lives, those of others, and wider society; students are beginning to draw on a range of sources to appropriately present and evidence their arguments. |

# Level 8

| | |
|---|---|
| *Enquire* | Students can interpret a wide range of key concepts specific to the religions studied. They can give more complex explanations as to how concepts within a religion are related to one another. |
| *Contextualise* | They can accurately contextualise them within the beliefs and practices of different branches of the religion in which they are expressed, and analyse conceptual differences and similarities within and across religions. |
| *Evaluate* | They can evaluate the concepts by justifying how and why the concepts are important to the lives and values of believers and by analysing how issues arising will affect the wider society. |
| *Communicate* | They can give a detailed explanation for their own response to religious concepts, with a justification for their response based upon a coherent argument. |
| *Apply* | They can apply their response by giving carefully selected supporting evidence of how their response would affect their own lives, those of others, wider society and global affairs; students are drawing on a wider range of appropriately selected sources to present and evidence their arguments. |

# 6

# Case studies in religious literacy

## Introduction: what do we mean by religious literacy?

What do we mean when we speak of religious literacy? It is clear that we are referring to the need for students to know the meaning of religious vocabulary but it is much more than this. The idea of meaning is embodied in the notion of understanding how a word operates and has significance within a whole language within which it is contextualised. For example, I may know some French words but I may stumble when I seek to put them into a sentence and I may be embarrassed if I do not know their cultural associations or the 'grammar' (as used by Jackson following Geertz) of the culture. By knowing the literal meaning of words I do not therefore become culturally literate. Beyond this I may also lack an overall understanding of the worldview within which they operate, a matter of translation. I need to be aware that languages do not simply translate words existent in one culture to another but that there is a different conception of the world involved that is communicated by words within a language in which they sit and have their role. As an example, Claude Lévi-Strauss' *Tristes Tropiques* cannot be translated into English as 'the sad tropics', which ceases to convey the melancholy association of the meaning of the French word 'triste'. Bear in mind of course that 'the melancholy tropics' doesn't work either, and that the designation given by a French anthropologist of their condition would not necessarily be recognised by the inhabitants as a description of their condition that resonated with them. He was writing for a sophisticated Western readership in French.

Equally, when we refer to religious literacy we mean grasping the intimate connection between a word, its cultural habitat and therefore the conception of the world that has formed its meaning. In this way we work toward what is called, in Chapter 7, interpreting worldviews, and in Chapter 8, worldview analysis. Before that can happen we need to start by introducing students to the levels on which language operates, a more generic understanding conveying the idea that when we seek to imbue meaning we have to use language that is not just literal but figurative. We find this everywhere in religious utterance, as we do in literature, whether religious or not, and in everyday speech. Students also need to recognise that objects take on figurative meaning such that they have a value beyond their material worth.

# Initial examples of practice

At a simple level, taking an example from my own experience with some Year 10 students in a Hampshire school, I asked them to consider the meaning of phrases in common usage that they might also employ. We discussed the meaning behind the phrase 'My heart is broken'. The question I posed was 'Do you call a doctor if someone says this to you?' The example is trite; of course, no one said, 'Yes.' Why not? Because they know the figurative meaning of the phrase by virtue of it being embedded in their enculturation. Who might say this? I asked. 'Someone whose boyfriend has left them,' came the reply. So, this is an example of literacy at its most basic, which uses figurative language in order to convey meaning. They knew what I was on about but would not normally have reflected upon the fact that they knew. When you move into explicitly trying to convey meaning beyond the cultural associations of literacy with which you are familiar a whole new learning task is posed. The problem becomes transparent when learning is explicit and has to move beyond our normal cultural boundaries and ways of using language to convey experience.

Here is a different example. In a special needs school with 13-year-old students who are bordering on severe learning difficulties the teacher is teaching the concept of symbolism. This is beyond these students. She is valiant. She starts with signs and displays a triangle on the whiteboard. 'What does this tell us?' she asks. Nobody knows. The triangle is clear to me because of what surrounds it. It is the sign used to indicate that a campsite is near. It operates by showing the traditional outline of a tent. Why don't they know this? Because they have never been in a car looking for a campsite with their parents and they are not aware of the campsite sign in the guidebook. There is no association. They are not, in this respect, literate. How could they know? But this is a sign, not a symbol. We move on to the students identifying clubs that they belong to or activities that they do and then describing and drawing a depiction of them being there or doing that activity. Now we have drawings that identify activity, for example swimming in a swimming pool. We are no closer to symbolism but we do have association with images they have produced. I wrack my brains; how do we move this on toward the concept and can we? I notice a pot of flowers on a windowsill. I ask the teacher if I can join in and take the pot of flowers to the front of the class. I ask the question, 'I have some flowers here, what should I do with them?' Richard, at the front of the class, answers, 'Give them to teacher.' His answer is not surprising, and of course I was waiting for it. He knows the cultural convention of men giving flowers to women or people making a gift of flowers to one another. I say to the teacher, 'Here, Claire, these are for you,' and she says, 'Thank you, Clive.' I now ask the class, 'If I go away and Claire looks at the flowers, what will she think?' Richard again, 'She will think of you.' Thus, Richard knows the symbolism of the act and that flowers are symbolic. But he does not explicitly understand symbolism. He cannot generalise this knowledge; it is learned behaviour of a cultural grammar. However, what this alerts us to is that symbols, unlike signs, involve a story (the act of giving), an object being imbued with symbolism (when Claire looks at the flowers she thinks of me despite the fact that I look nothing like the flowers), subjectivity (what the flowers symbolise for Claire is unique to her) and a cultural code (in which flowers carry specific symbolic association).

In another school a teacher, who was Spanish, used chrysanthemums to convey to a Year 7 class how in Spain they were given at times of death, but that this was not the case in England. Thus, the symbolism becomes even more specific and not knowing the cultural code could get you into trouble if you use the wrong sort of flowers for the wrong occasion in the wrong culture. In fact, we need to recognise it is only because we know our own symbolic cultural codes that we are able to send the right messages at the right time, which is why, for example, we lay wreaths at funerals rather than giving them to someone with whom we are out on a date: wreaths of flowers convey a different sense of affection than that we might try to convey in a romantic way. We could go on and on. Roland Barthes' well-known example of red roses to demonstrate semiology is a case in point (Barthes 1972), as is the distinction between red poppies and white poppies on Remembrance Day in Britain.

Visiting another school I was helping the teacher plan a lesson. His initial idea was to give the students a textbook with different religious symbols in it (the Cross, the Star of David, etc.). They were to copy these and colour them! This was a lesson on symbols (but not on figurative expression). We started again. We downloaded three images from the internet. One was of young Muslim women wearing headscarves (hijab) but otherwise in Western dress. A second was of the young Muslim woman who had been suspended from attending a school in Luton, where hijab was commonly worn by other female Muslim pupils, because she wore a more demonstrative statement of Muslim identity, in the form of the jilbab, a fuller, more enveloping form of dress that is distinctively Muslim. A third was of a scantily dressed young white teenager in provocative pose and short skirt. The concept was symbolic dress. The evaluative question was: 'Which of these people would you allow to attend your school, in these forms of dress?' One of the reasons for choosing this question was to do with the nature of the students. This was a school in a white, working class catchment area where schooling was not valued by many or by their parents, and multiculturalism was something that existed elsewhere. The question had to be directly relevant to their location and experience.

In the course of the lesson students were introduced to the differing images and discussed the account of the young Muslim woman who was suspended from school and took the school and local authority to court and won. It was intriguing to watch two boys who were friends debating whether the school principle of wearing uniform should take precedence over the religious principle of dress: 'If our school has a uniform policy it has to be obeyed by all students' versus 'If it is her religious obligation she must be allowed to follow it'. Many of these students resented wearing uniform and did their best to subvert it: ties at half-mast and shirts worn outside trousers or skirts, of course. The question was: 'Did they get the idea that dress could be symbolic?' When I was working with three girls at the back of the class they told me that the skimpily clad girl was just wearing what she wanted but the other two were wearing Muslim dress. I pushed them on this. 'But aren't the images actually different?' They replied, with more thought, that one image was saying 'I am Muslim', the other was saying 'We are Muslim and British'. Bingo, they had started to recognise how symbolic dress works, why it amounts to a significant statement of identity and thus can become controversial. The vote on who could come to school and who couldn't, dressed as they were, resulted in the Muslims being allowed, including the young woman from Luton, but the scantily dressed young woman being excluded because, as one boy put it, 'She is dressed like a tart and that is not allowed!' This, I think, owed more to the fact that they had to wear uniform than anything else.

## Case studies

## A case study based on the concept of symbolism: Hats Off!

This example was produced by a Hampshire RE Advanced Skills Teacher, Penny Morgan, from Beaufort Technology College (Morgan 2007a).

### Communicate

A number of different hats are introduced, either in pictures or actual hats to be worn by students. These can range from police helmets to 'Ascot hats', to Father Christmas hats, and the like. Students have to decide who might wear these hats and what they might wear them for. Examples of reasons for wearing hats and their associated significance are given: practical, authority, protection, fashion, warmth, status and so on. Students make the associations and this draws out how hats can have different associations and, sometimes, symbolic value.

### Apply

Students are asked: 'What if a hat is changed?' For example, if a police officer in uniform substitutes his or her helmet for a different hat, what has changed? Why does the new hat (an 'Ascot' hat, for example) affect our view of the police officer, and perhaps make us laugh? Here the point of the symbolism of a piece of headgear is reflected upon.

Here students discuss ways in which items of headgear and other items of dress become symbolic and why and how incongruousness is linked to symbolic distinctions: wrong messages are sent.

### Enquire

Enquire requires an input of information to allow the enquiry to proceed further into a particular area. Here the kippah is used to show its symbolic significance in Orthodox Judaism.

A picture of a Jewish boy wearing a kippah is shown at this point, with the following commentary:

> This kippah is a type of headgear worn by men and boys of the Jewish faith. In Judaism, putting on a head covering is a mark of respect.
>
> The Talmud says that the purpose of wearing a kippah is to remind Jews of Gd, who is the Higher Authority 'above us' (Kiddushin 31a). External actions create internal awareness; wearing a symbolic, tangible 'something above us' reinforces that idea that Gd is always watching. The kippah is a means to draw out one's inner sense of respect for Gd.

It's easy to remember Gd while at the synagogue or around the Shabbat table. But Jewish consciousness is meant to be part of all aspects of their lives – how they treat others, and how they look at the world.

Students are then asked to explain how and why, through the example of the kippah, symbolism can take on religious significance and how that might be different to other forms of non-religious symbolic expression.

## Contextualise

A particular scenario is then presented based on an incident at the Pinkas Synagogue in Prague:

During the Second World War, the Nazis killed over six million Jews in a deliberate attempt to destroy all the Jews in Europe. This is known as the Holocaust. In the Pinkas Synagogue, the walls have been inscribed with the names of all the Holocaust victims from the region. The synagogue has thus come to represent something that is important not only to Jewish people but to huge numbers of others as well.

A group of students were visiting the synagogue where all the names of victims of the Holocaust from the region are listed. Male visitors were required to wear a kippah and they were available to buy for a small cost. Each of the male students bought one and put it on. As soon as they had passed through the entrance into the inner rooms, one of the boys took his kippah off and put it in his pocket.

Students are now asked to discuss and respond to the following questions, giving their justifications for their points of view:

1    Did he do anything wrong?
2    What did his action symbolise?
3    Should the wearing of a kippah symbolise anything to someone who is not Jewish?

## Evaluate

The evaluate element asks students to make decisions based on the learning so far but in a transferable way:

To complete the cycle of learning on the key concept of symbolism you need to evaluate the concept. This means that you need to 'weigh up' the significance of the concept for Jews and for others.

*Evaluate Within*

These pictures [included in the original text] are of the Jewish cemetery in Prague.

1    Explain how this place might be symbolic.
2    Would this place still be symbolic if there were no Jews in Prague?

*Evaluate Without*

The following questions move away from the specific context used and ask for more generic judgements:

1    Why is symbolism an important concept in religion?
2    Explain why symbolism might be important to people who are not religious.
3    If a symbol has no meaning to you personally, is it still to be respected as symbolic?

# A case study based on the concept of the sacred

Here I elaborate further on a concept introduced in Chapter 4. Taking sacred or sacredness as an example, the significance of how something can be sacred for some people and not others shows how figurative understanding can result in significant religious and political ramifications. It is not just a private matter. A land that is sacred to some and not others – Israel, for example – is so by virtue of its identification with a people called Israel. Thus there is a direct correspondence between the identity of the people and the land, as a geographical space. The reason for this is the story that gives the people their identity: the Exodus from Egypt, the promise of the land to the Chosen People, the taking of it, its defence with the interventions of Gd. The diaspora and the establishment of the state of Israel follow, with all the problems that have since arisen. The sacredness of Israel for religious Jews is a given because it is so bound up with their identity as a people and the revealed nature that underpins the justification of their claim. Story, subjectivity, symbolism and the socio-cultural/religious code all come into play to establish sacredness, in the same way as symbolism – but with the idea of the sacred the stakes are even higher, the poignancy is intense and the issues complex.

However, for students to enquire into the concept of the sacred with Israel as the context it would not be appropriate to leave uncontested the Jewish claim to inhabit the land (whether from a Palestinian or Jewish anti-Zionist point of view) and its consequences. This is a facet of the enquiry that raises issues and introduces further complexity, as is required for the Contextualise elements of the cycle to be effective. The point is not just to understand why some religious Jews regard the land of Israel as sacred but to investigate the complexity and implications of the concept itself. Thus, a cycle of learning based on this might be planned as follows.

## Enquire

*Question: What do people regard as sacred and why?*

Present a range of statements in which the term sacred/sacredness is used and discuss the similarities and differences in the meaning of the term and the differing things/people/relationships to which it is applied.

This can include images that accompany quotations and can range to the idea that the earth/environment is sacred. That a relationship with someone close to me is sacred, the sacredness of a loving relationship, which may involve carrying a picture of them. That God and his creation are sacred. It should involve challenging students as to what sacred or sacredness amounts to in each case – why this term, rather than any other, is applied. It should end by discussing what we have learned about the use of this concept and how interpretations of it compare or differ and why.

## Contextualise

*Question: Why do religious Jews regard the land of Israel as sacred and what issues does that raise?*

Introduce texts that reveal why the land of Israel should be considered sacred by religious Jews. These could include excerpts from biblical texts such as reference to the people of Israel as a Chosen people and the giving to them of their own land by Gd as part of the Covenant. Students need to study these and determine what makes the land of Israel sacred for religious Jews, i.e. how sacredness is determined by them and the consequences of that in terms of rights that they have. Next, texts and images can be introduced concerning exile, as in Babylon, and the diaspora that led to them not having that land and going through periods of suffering and persecution, as in the Holocaust. This sets the scene for the Balfour Declaration and Jews returning to their homeland or, in the case of anti-Zionist Jews, refusing to return, based on the idea that it does not fulfil the Covenant. Students need to discuss the issues that arise as a result: religious, political and moral.

## Evaluate

*Evaluate Within*

*Question: Should Jews be allowed to keep the land of Israel because they regard it as sacred?*

Answers to this question arise out of students' considerations of the issues arising in the Contextualise element of the cycle and should be focused on whether the fact that some religious Jews regard Israel as sacred means that they should own it. This element of the enquiry should include mention of what difference it makes as to whether the land is called Israel or Palestine, and what the rival claims of Palestinians are.

*Evaluate Without*

*Question: Is sacredness a blessing or a curse?*

This returns us to the concept outside the Contextualise element and broadens the focus. What is the effect of sacredness being abused? Can we arrive at a conclusion as to whether 'sacredness' should always be respected? Or does the idea of regarding something important to us as sacred actually prevent us from moving on and adapting to a changing world? Are there limits to the respect we can show to what others regard as sacred, and if so, why? Are there historical or contemporary examples that can help us focus on this: Native American peoples or Australian Aboriginal peoples?

## Communicate

*Question: What do we regard as sacred, if anything, and why/why not?*

Here we are dependent on students' personal contributions and their initiative but we can stimulate this by providing further examples of the way in which the idea of 'sacredness' is used in the modern world, e.g. in relation to wild animals and their survival, rainforests and their importance, and the survival of peoples and their land when threatened by outside agencies. Here we are drawing on the progression in the learning so far. In recognising why Jews regard the land of Israel as sacred it is important to grapple with how the idea of sacred can be used and sacredness can be justified in other ways. It is not just about something being special.

## Apply

*Question: What examples can we give to show the importance of or issues raised by sacredness in our own lives and those of others and the consequences of these?*

This allows the issues raised in Communicate to spill over into justifications for the use of the concept in relation to specific situations and needs to involve students reflecting on their own learning, for example by discussing issues such as:

- To what extent is the idea of the sacred important to us today?
- To what extent does it hinder or advance our progress?
- To what extent does it oppose our tendency to exploitation, greed and material concerns?

Throughout this enquiry the aim is to challenge students to reflect on their own values and identity, consider those of others and determine the usefulness of the concept in relation to the complex question of what we value and why, and what issues are raised as a result.

This example is only one element in engaging students with the idea of religious literacy but it shows how pervasive and significant this engagement is. It also shows us that it goes beyond being religious, in the more prescriptive, narrow and traditional meaning of the term. It introduces us to the wider function of religious literacy as an engagement with contested values. It introduces the idea that religious literacy needs to be understood as a means of engaging with differing perspectives on the human condition and the issues that it raises. It also signals that understanding the world and human language literally is inadequate to deal with its existential concerns and political motivations, even if these motivations are derived by some religious groups from a literal understanding of textual formulations.

# A case study based on the concept of myth

There is a close relation between type B concepts in that they are all concerned with conveying meaning that cannot be expressed as matters of fact. With myth this is especially true because it is the concept most likely to be dismissed for this reason. As a result it is important to engage students with the significance of myths for the continuity of purpose and identity that myths convey. Factually, anything called a myth is untrue but we are seeking to take students beyond this understanding to a more complex appreciation of the concept, as conveyed in the study of religions. This case study is an adaptation of a cycle of enquiry developed from a unit of work in *Living Difference: The Secondary Handbook* by the RE Department at the Mountbatten School, Romsey, Hampshire (Hampshire, Portsmouth and Southampton Councils 2006a: 291–314).

## Enquire

*Question: What is a myth?*

Present students with a series of statements and ask them to categorise these into facts (those which can be evidenced as correct), untruths (those that can be evidenced as incorrect) and others (which will be statements of meaning, values and purpose).

Simplistically, for example: the world is flat; the earth revolves around the sun; humans should look after the earth.

Students themselves can come up with other examples falling into each category and explain why they do.

Present students with an excerpt from a story (this can be a written text or a film) in which a message of the third category is being presented. These are ubiquitous: Harry Potter, Philip Pullman's trilogy *His Dark Materials*, C.S. Lewis' *The Lion, the Witch and the Wardrobe* and many others. Ask students to explain the message conveyed and comment on its value. Is it a fact? Is it an untruth? What category does it fall into? What are the characteristics of such messages?

Here it will be necessary to explain the function of the concept of myth in referring to such messages because they cannot be called facts or untruths but are considered important. For different people different messages or myths are important. This enquiry is to find out what myths (messages) are considered important by whom and why.

## Contextualise

*How do the Christian myth of stewardship and the Aboriginal myth of the Dreamtime differ and what are their essential messages?*

Contextualise the concept of myth in the Christian understanding of stewardship and the Australian Aboriginal understanding of the Dreamtime.

For the Christian concept of stewardship use an abbreviated version of the Genesis account of creation, which introduces the idea of stewardship of the creation by humankind (Genesis 1.1–2.3). Also use contemporary statements on Christian stewardship such as the following:

> God's kingdom is here, but is a long way from its full and perfect completion . . . We remain the stewards of creation. In fact, if the whole cosmos is somehow included in God's saving plan . . . then creation-care is kingdom work – it brings glory to God.
>
> (A Rocha website: http://en.arocha.org/bible/index7.html)

For the Aboriginal idea of the Dreamtime use the Aboriginal creation story (see Palmer and Bisset 1999) and ask students to determine its importance for Aborigines by consulting historical and recent reports on ways in which losing their land has impacted on the fragmentation of Aboriginal culture and society (for example the Mabo and Wick case and the ruling at the Commonwealth conference in 1937, in which the aim of Aboriginal assimilation was affirmed (see the Australian Aborigines website at: http://members.tripod.com/siekman/british.html; http://members.tripod.com/siekman/presentday.html).

Students need to decide what are the significant characteristics of these two different myths and important ways in which they differ. They can do this by creating two message bottles, one for Christian stewardship and the other for the Aboriginal Dreamtime. They need to distil the essential messages from each of these and write the respective message for each bottle.

## Evaluate

### Evaluate Within

*Question: Why are the myths of stewardship and the Dreamtime important for Christians and for Australian Aborigines?*

Students will have determined the differences between the myths in Contextualise; now they have to decide on why these are of value to the believers in question. For example, if stewardship were removed from Christian belief what impact would that have? Here the relationship between stewardship and the Christian belief in creation can be explored, and the role they believe they have been given by God. Further, this can be related to the way Christians exercise this role in the world, for example in relation to the environment. For Aborigines, the impact of losing their territory can be further explored, and the effect of that on their identity and purpose.

### Evaluate Without

*Question: Why are myths important to us or can we live without them?*

Here students have to reflect on what their learning so far has taught them and debate the value of myths to our sense of purpose and identity as humans. Are there other myths we have lived by? What were they and what other myths do we have now and what is their value?

## Communicate

Students are introduced to modern messages and campaigns that are pursued today. Here the websites of pressure groups and other organisations can be consulted, for example Greenpeace and Friends of the Earth. What are their messages and what are the arguments for their importance? Are these examples of modern myths? Where does their authority come from?

## Apply

Students decide on their own message to put in a bottle. What is their important myth that they think should be conveyed to the world today. Ask them to try and agree this, and where they disagree they need to try and form themselves into groups. If they can't find a group they can fit with they write their own message. Discuss with students the outcome of this and what that might say about the characteristics of myths and their importance.

# Review

It can be seen how closely the three type B concepts above of symbolism, sacred and myth are interrelated. Thus, the aim is to develop students' abilities to recognise this inter-relationship as a means of recognising how the language of religious expression works and how it can be understood. In turn they need to become aware of how this type of figurative expression also operates in their own lives and how understanding these forms of figurative expression constitute the foundation of religious literacy and create the means for interpreting worldviews, the subject of Chapter 7. In the case studies below, using a type A then type C concept, I shall show how both of these are also instrumental to religious literacy.

# A case study based on the concept of suffering

Suffering is a type A concept but here we can see how, used with a specific theological context, the story of Job, it contributes to religious literacy and demands some understanding of figurative expression for the learning to be effective. This cycle was devised by Jo Maule, Head of RE at Cowplain School in Hampshire (Maule 2006). It was part of a Welsh Board (WJEC) GCSE course which students began in Year 9. The cycle was planned to extend over two one-hour lessons. The school uses the accelerated learning programme and thus Assessment for Learning (AfL) is an overt feature of the planning. Prior to this cycle students had completed a previous enquiry into the concept of free will.

## Communicate

As a starter activity students are asked:

> Think about your parents or carers. At times, their action or inaction means you feel pain – physical, psychological and emotional.

- Why do your parents or carers allow you to feel that pain?
- Can you make a list of at least five examples and try to explain why you think they have behaved in this way.

They are also asked: What do I think about this? What are my reasons for thinking this? They are reminded of prior learning from the last lesson, in which they enquired into free will as a response to suffering, in order to ensure they connect up the previous learning to that done in this cycle on suffering.

Student responses to the first task are then reviewed and discussed, starting with the following prompt:

What examples have you listed?

- Your parents may have taken away your Playstation.
- You may have been stopped from visiting your friends.

The idea that parents/carers may sometimes have to be cruel to be kind is then introduced for reflection and comment.

## Apply

Here the following question is introduced: What if there were no suffering in the world?

Students consider what issues this might raise and whether a case can be made for suffering having positive effects or not, for example in relation to pain telling us we may need medical attention, or whether without suffering at times we would not be able to appreciate good things and experiences. Are the two necessarily inter-related?

Students work in pairs on the ideas they have written down and complete a PMI (plus, minus, interesting) against these.

## Enquire

The learning outcomes for the cycle are introduced. By the end of the enquiry (level 4):

- you must be able to explain the problem of suffering;
- you should be able to explain reasons why God might allow suffering to exist;
- you might be able to evaluate how religious believers reconcile the nature of God with the problem of suffering.

A 'Big Picture' or Mind Map is introduced that outlines the concepts, words and religious teachings that will be explored during the unit. In addition students are presented with a focus on five key questions:

1   Why do people suffer?
2   In what ways do people suffer?
3   How do people cope with suffering?

4    What is evil?

5    Why is there evil?

The following text then acts as a stimulus for students to grapple with the central question for this cycle of enquiry:

> Christians and Muslims believe that God is omniscient (all-knowing), omnipotent (all-powerful) and benevolent (all-loving) but, despite this, He allows evil and suffering to exist in his world. We have looked at free will as an explanation but this does not fully explain why a God who is all-knowing, all-powerful and all-loving would allow us to suffer.

The point of this input is to recognise a particular point of view held by believers from these religions and the question with which they have to grapple as a result. Students are asked to consider how bringing together the concepts of omniscience, omnipotence and benevolence affect interpretations of and explanations for suffering. Here they can draw on the prior learning in the Communicate and Apply elements of this enquiry and the concept of free will in the previous enquiry to suggest ways in which these may provide some means of explaining suffering from this perspective and some new issues this raises. This provides an entry into the Contextualise element based on the story of Job.

## Contextualise

*Question: (How) can the story of Job help religious people to understand the purposes of suffering?*

1    Create a fortune line in your book. It will look like this [Figure 6.1].

2    Plot the events of Job's life against the horizontal fortune line.

3    In your own words, explain what lessons Job might have learned from this experience.

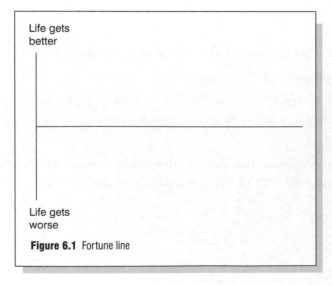

**Figure 6.1** Fortune line

In order to do this students need either to have a truncated account of the events of Job's life or, preferably, to consult specific pieces of significant text directly. The latter approach can be made by identifying specific verses in the Book of Job, placing them in an envelope and distributing one envelope to each of a number of groups of students. You would expect the events to include:

1  The conversation between God and Satan on the testing of Job's faith.

2  The afflictions of Job.

3  The conversation between Job and his wife in which she encourages him to curse God.

4  The judgements of Job's friends on why he has been the object of misfortune.

5  The final restoration of Job's life and prosperity.

These events should be numbered in chronological order. Students now have to plot them on the fortune line in their groups, deciding where exactly they should go. This discussion is an important aspect of the learning. To extend this aspect of the learning further, ask a group of students to now make a living graph. First, they need to form a line, representing the 'fortune line' in Figure 6.1. Then each student steps further in front of or behind the line to indicate how good or bad each event is that he/she represents. Students from the other groups can now quiz them on their decisions and how they made them. This, effectively, demands a dialogue representing a theological commentary on the Book of Job.

It is also interesting to ask students, 'What if the story lacked a particular component?' For example, if the end was changed and Job did not become prosperous again would that change the sense and interpretation of the story in relation to why Job suffered?

## Evaluate

Here God is put on trial. Students are given the following instruction:

1    Your task is to defend God's decision to allow suffering and evil in his world.

2    You and your partner must decide upon at least five reasons why God would allow it to exist. You must give your reasons and explain how they could be used to defend God.

Finally, the following explanations can be used to determine the best interpretation of why suffering occurs and students have to debate the merits of each one:

■    Free will: evil is caused by people making the wrong decisions. We were given free will by God. If we decide to act in a certain way we can't blame God.

■    Punishment: all suffering is punishment for the things we do, say or think that are wrong. All suffering is punishment for our own badness. Everybody does things wrong but not everybody seems to get what they deserve.

■    Test: suffering is a test of our faith in God.

■    Education: suffering is an education for us. It makes us better people, teaches us the difference between right and wrong and may prepare us for an afterlife in which we are more worthy.

- Appreciation: there has to be badness in order to appreciate goodness. This means we recognise the good. So we have to suffer in order to do good.

- God's will: we cannot know God's will so we cannot question what happens to us but accept God has reasons for our suffering and have faith in him.

- The Devil: when something bad or evil happens it is the Devil that causes it and suffering is the result.

Students might well ask, 'Is the story of Job true?' By this they might well mean 'Did it really [historically] happen?' This brings us back to figurative understanding. Whether or not it is literally true (it happened), does the story inform us about certain 'truths' that we need to consider in life?

## A case study based on the Buddhist concept of karuna (compassion)

For this example I am indebted to Lat Blaylock and his work on Aung San Suu Kyi, which uses the resources and some of the activities presented below (Blaylock 2005). In an issue of the *Hampshire RE Secondary News* (Erricker 2006) I reorganised Lat's example to fit with a conceptual enquiry approach. It represents an ethical enquiry but taking account of the Buddhist principle of karuna (compassion) as the key concept and the basis of ethical conduct (sila). As a result it is an exercise in religious literacy and provides the beginnings of worldview analysis because it is based on a type C concept (one that is particular to a specific religion) rather than being dependent on students' own understanding of compassion. This is the most important development in learning that conceptual enquiry provides. Since the enquiry is now driven throughout as an enquiry into the Buddhist concept of karuna it challenges students to compare and contrast the Buddhist interpretation of the concept with their own understanding of compassion. As a result it affects how they understand Aung San Suu Kyi's decision and their response to it; they don't just make up their own minds or come to see her as simply an inspirational figure.

### Enquire

This teaching comes from the Buddhist scholar Shantideva:

> May I be a protector of the helpless
> A guide to those travelling the path
> A boat to those wishing to cross over
> Or a bridge or a raft.
> May I be a lamp for those in darkness
> A home for the homeless
> A servant to the world.

The key to understanding this text is through its use of metaphor. It alerts us that a key basic skill students have to acquire is understanding the use of figurative expression. We cannot assume the meaningfulness of this text to pupils if they do not know how to read it and how to interpret that meaning. What the students need to be able to do is provide a commentary on the text. The key to this lies in the author's use of the images of protector, guide, boat, bridge, raft, lamp, home and servant. The meaning he gives to these terms needs to be understood within the context of Buddhist teachings that make clear the meaning of the terms helpless, path, cross over, darkness and homeless, and especially in relating these to the Bodhisattva ideal. If we do not do this, then any understanding of compassion students gain will not be from the Buddhist interpretation of the term (karuna), but from how it can be understood within the context of the students' worldviews.

Immediately we become aware that this is a very dense passage appreciation of which relies on knowledge of the Buddhist teachings to which it alludes. Thus worldview analysis is involved. We also become aware that because of its use of metaphor the pupils need to be able to handle this generic form of textual artifice. Thus religious literacy is involved.

It follows that if we place this text within the Enquire element of the cycle we might preface it in Communicate and Apply with a more accessible text that is within the pupils' own cultural context in order to start to understand this figurative mode of expression. An obvious choice might be 'Like a bridge over troubled waters' by Paul Simon, and this might involve analysing what the lyrics of that song are saying. The pupils could then be asked what image other than 'bridge' could have been used and whether it might be more effective. Other textual images could be provided to support this task. Then they might be asked what that would mean in relation to actions. Again, accounts of what people have done based on compassionate motives could be scrutinised, such as forms of charity, and the consequences and value of these determined. They can also be asked whether they have acted compassionately and, if so, how and why. This again would draw out the characteristics of compassion and the sorts of sacrificial elements involved. Ultimately, you are asking to what extent we are capable of compassion in our own lives and what the results of that are and how compassion is expressed within textual sources (which can include visual ones), prior to enquiring into why it is such an important virtue to which Buddhists aspire.

In Enquire, to fully understand the import of Shantideva's Buddhist text we need to focus on his images of helpless, path, crossing over, darkness and homelessness. For Buddhists these have particular resonance in their teachings. Thus, for example, the parable of the raft, the image of samsara as a turbulent sea, darkness as a state of ignorance, helplessness being a result of ignorance and heedlessness, the path as the eightfold path that leads to enlightenment or nirvana (the other shore), homelessness as the condition of us all (as opposed to literal homelessness), the refuges as a means to moving beyond this condition characterised by dukkha (unsatisfactoriness or suffering).

Therefore it makes sense for pupils to engage in group activities where each group analyses, for example, the meaning of each metaphor in relation to other texts that shed light on its meaning. Collectively, bringing together the work of each group will create a fuller understanding of why Shantideva used these images, what their import is, leading to an explanation of the Buddhist concept of compassion (karuna) and its depth, multifacetedness and complexity from a Buddhist perspective. This perspective will amount to a basic grasp of the bodhisattva ideal in Buddhism. It will also challenge the understanding of compassion students espoused in the Communicate and Apply elements of the cycle previously and raise the question of the extent to which the differing concepts of compassion can be compared and contrasted.

The question that follows is: 'How do Buddhists develop compassion?' One means is meditation as a discipline to calm and enquire into the mind. Here we can use Lat Blaylock's example of walking meditation. Students can be asked to carry out a walking meditation. Reflecting on this experience students can be asked to consider how the qualities they experienced in slow walking meditation might be linked to Shantideva's text on compassion. Further commentary on the purposes and types of meditation could also be provided if required to deepen the enquiry, for example through metta (loving kindness) meditation, which is directly relevant to Aung San Suu Kyi's situation.

## Contextualise

Here Aung San Suu Kyi's situation is introduced, with some biographical background. She is under house arrest in Burma. Her husband is in England seriously ill with cancer. Her two sons are also in England. The Burmese authorities will allow her to visit them but she will not be allowed to return to Burma, where she was democratically elected as leader. Should she stay or should she go? Nine 'Advice Cards' are provided giving advice from a number of different sources: her husband Michael, the Burmese generals, a song about her written by U2, one of her sons, a statement by the Buddha on compassion, and advice by friends. Students are asked to rank the value of the advice from least helpful to most helpful. However, it is important that these pieces of advice are ranked on the basis of the concept of karuna; otherwise the Buddhist orientation of the cycle, along with the concept itself, is lost. This forces students into a much more difficult interpretive exercise as they start to realise the implications of the concept on practical decision making. If Aung San Suu Kyi wants to do the most compassionate thing when both choices can be understood as compassionate, which choice should she make?

## Evaluate

*Evaluate Within*

Here students, in groups, are asked to construct their own advice, based on the concept of karuna. What advice would they give? This activity forces them to try and adopt a Buddhist perspective and enter more fully into Aung San Suu Kyi's situation as a Buddhist. Here they really do have to discriminate between their own view and understanding of compassion and what they have come to understand as the implications of karuna. Following this, students can be told Aung San Suu Kyi's own decision, to stay in Burma, and some of the consequences of that; for example, she never saw her husband again before he died and she is still under house arrest. Reflection on this is very useful since it draws out that karuna, as a motivation, does not necessarily bring you your desired outcome.

*Evaluate Without*

At this point we can pose a key evaluative question that goes beyond the context itself, but draws directly upon it, and which tests the complexity of students' own learning and asks them to formulate a response to the key concept, having also developed a Buddhist understanding of it: 'Acting compassionately can be both selfless and fruitless, do you agree?'

## Reviewing provision for religious literacy in conceptual enquiry

In the above examples I hope I have shown how relevant understanding and communicating through figurative expression is; also how this is essential to addressing religious literacy through conceptual enquiry, whether using type A, B or C concepts. Figurative expression and religious literacy generally are prevalent forms of communication at an everyday level and demand student engagement with concepts initially beyond their awareness. Also, I hope this has shown how students can engage with religious literacy quite easily once the right approach is applied, the right questions asked and the right concepts employed as the driving force and focus of learning throughout.

Religious literacy, and cultural literacy in some of the above examples, is the underlying developmental learning purpose for these types of lessons or conceptual cycles, which will then move on into interpreting worldviews in a fuller sense. When studying religion there are other concepts of equal importance and some of often greater sophistication. In the above examples, some type B category concepts such as symbolism and sacred have been explicitly introduced. The point of identifying concepts of this type is that they both are in a category used, in a generic sense, within the study of religion and they all rely upon understanding figurative expression for their explication. However, generic type A concepts presented, such as suffering, also demand figurative understanding, due to the nature of the context used. Also, type C concepts such as karuna will require analysis of their figurative meaning, in order to make sense of metaphoric texts that demand we do not translate such concepts out into our own terms, here for example compassion as we might already understand it, and retain the distinctive quality and rigour of the Buddhist concept.

The case studies presented above are of different kinds, not only in relation to the type of key concept used but also in the way they make different disciplinary demands on students. Whilst all focused on developing religious literacy in different ways the symbolism cycle 'Hats Off!' demands a recognition of socio–anthropological understanding; the sacred cycle demands a recognition of political awareness; the suffering and karuna cycles demand an understanding of textual analysis and theological reasoning. All of these also focus on values questions and ethical demands.

## Provision and progression at Key Stage 4

At Key Stage 4 it is common for schools to do ethics options from GCSE boards. Within these are studies of medical ethics, especially, for example abortion and euthanasia. When approached through conceptual enquiry the focus on religious literacy makes the issues involved much clearer. For example, the concept of sanctity of life is a driving force behind religious views on these matters: it is not just a term to be learned or understood; it is the 'orthodox' or 'pre-modern' position from which others depart or derive. Sanctity itself references to sacred. Therefore to make studies of these issues meaningful religious literacy and a conceptual awareness of these terms are essential.

Penny Morgan at Beaufort College, Winchester, has reported on how she introduced conceptual enquiry in her GCSE option on Christian Ethics. In Year 8 students had already studied her unit of work on Aspects of Christianity (Morgan 2006). Now, six months later, she remarks, 'they confidently came up with the key concepts of redemption, resurrection and atonement and could clearly explain them in context' (Morgan 2007: 26). In the Christian Ethics module she wanted their religious literacy to be applied within answers to GCSE questions. Here is an example of a student's response to a question on cloning:

> Most Christians aren't against cloning animals if the animals are treated with respect and well looked after. They think it is important to try to solve the problem of people in the developing world not having enough to eat and this might be one way of doing it. The attitude to cloning humans is different for many Christians. This is because they think everyone is created by God and that cloning goes against the sanctity of life because it doesn't show respect for human beings and their special relationship with God. Christians who are in favour of cloning think that it must be carefully controlled so that they don't try to create super beings.
>
> (Morgan 2007: 27)

Here is another example of a student's response to a question on research using human embryos:

> Christians such as the Roman Catholics believe that life begins at the moment of conception so think that using embryos for research is a sin. On the other hand, some Christians think that because Jesus showed that it is important to help the sick, research on embryos might help this. The Methodist Church supports this type of research if it is for health reasons.
>
> (Morgan 2007: 27)

It is an interesting exercise to scrutinise these students' responses, as we did in one instance in Chapter 5, and decide how we would level them according to the Living Difference level descriptors (Chapter 5, Appendix 5.2; see pp. 118-121) and according to GCSE mark schemes. You might also want to plot them according to the student development model introduced in Figure 4.3 (see p. 89). In the answer on cloning sanctity of life is made explicit, in the answer on using human embryos sin is made explicit. Both are what we would call Evaluate Within responses but neither are Evaluate without (stating with justification your own view). To what extent do these answers exhibit a level of religious literacy and conceptual awareness? What feedback would we give to these students for improvement?

Lorraine King, the Head of RE at Wyvern College, Fair Oak, in Hampshire has also commented on the changes that introducing conceptual enquiry at GCSE has made, having already reconstructed her Key Stage 3 curriculum. She states that, despite being worried initially 'about the possible impact it would have for GCSE results',

> conceptual thinking has great potential for students doing GCSE. Here, for years, I had been focusing on the content of the syllabus rather than the concept, whereas in reality it should be the

concepts we really focus on using the content to enable the students to understand the concept. For example, when studying Martin Luther King is it really necessary that the students give a potted history of his life? No – what they should be focusing on are the concepts of agape or non-violent protest or injustice . . . I have found that the cycle fits well with the Welsh Examination Board, and I can see that the conceptual methodology allows for sleeker more focused lessons, where the students have the opportunity to think at a higher level.

(King 2008: 24)

The problem initially encountered by Lorraine, as for many teachers, is that Key Stage 3 and GCSE do not marry up. The challenge is to progress learning development through GCSE with Key Stage 4 years building on Key Stage 3. But you have to have specific principles on which this is based and practised, which can accommodate the requirements of GCSE even if they are lower than what you seek to achieve for your students. Developing religious literacy through conceptual enquiry is the way in which we have sought to address this issue. Progression should not stop when GCSE starts.

## Levels of religious literacy and progression

Religious literacy operates at a number of levels and these should be reflected in the idea of student progression:

- At its most basic it is about being familiar with terms and vocabulary and being able to connect them with stories and other religious material and practices. Conceptually, this would also involve connecting these to ideas that are common to religious and non-religious groups and generally relevant to human experience, such as those of suffering, and different ways in which these are explained and interpreted (type A concepts).

- At a higher level it is about having a more sophisticated and broader grasp of religious material, practices and behaviours. Conceptually, this would involve the introduction of more focus on figurative expression and concepts like symbolism and sacred(ness) which place greater stress on perspectives, interpretation, meaning and transcendence, and use figures of speech such as simile and metaphor in a more explicit fashion.

- Higher still, it is about gaining a more complex grasp of the interconnections and differences prevalent within religious material, practices and behaviours, and their figurative and sometimes political significance. Conceptually the stress is increasingly on interpreting worldviews, in which connections are made with and between type C concepts, those that are specific to a particular religious worldview. Here sense is made of the holistic and systematic nature of the thinking of specific religious groups and differences in interpretation are encountered in relation to specific worldviews. We shall address this in Chapter 7. At the same time we encounter different interpretations of generic (type A) concepts between worldviews, such as freedom, which will be exemplified in Chapter 8.

## Conclusion

This chapter has sought to demonstrate how religious literacy can be enhanced by using a conceptual enquiry approach to learning and how that can benefit students in enhancing their disciplinary understanding of religious interpretations. Type B concepts have been identified as a way of doing this through introducing the need to engage with forms of figurative expression, but type A and C concepts have been included to show how religious literacy extends to recognising the basis on which different worldviews express their understanding of human experience and the values that underpin that. We have also considered how religious literacy can be progressed at Key Stage 4 to ensure that there is no disjuncture in student progression across key stages when embarking on GCSE.

At this point you may wish to construct your own cycle of enquiry, based on a type B concept, that exemplifies how students' religious literacy can be progressed within Key Stage 3.

# Interpreting worldviews

## Introduction

Attending to the interpretation of worldviews takes us beyond a basic religious literacy, which might be defined as understanding how religious language works in general and how it relates to different conceptual interpretations of experience. The particulars of this were analysed in Chapter 6. To be able to dialogue with worldviews is to understand the conceptual bases on which worldviews are constructed and ways in which those concepts are interpreted differently by differing groups of believers. Indeed it also involves understanding why some concepts are held dear by some believers and radically changed or even dismissed by others; the idea of priesthood in Christianity would be a case in point. Importantly, however, it is the distinctive and particular concepts that pertain to a tradition that reveal the originality of its mentality, what we have referred to as type C concepts. These were presented for some of the main traditions in Chapter 5, Appendix 5.1 (see pp. 112–118). Therefore, to understand and engage with a particular worldview you must engage with it on the level of these concepts, not more generic ones. Also, since these concepts are not simply literal statements but ones, in the case of religious worldviews at least, that often demand figurative understanding and abstract thinking pointing to some transcendent idea of truth, they can be challenging. Beyond this the concepts together represent a pattern of ideas that combine into an original interpretation of human experience. Therefore, it is grasping how the concepts work together that constitutes the overall ambition of the project. Within the levels of attainment, provided in Chapter 5, Appendix 5.2, this begins as an expectation at level 5 and becomes an ever more refined requirement from then on. This expectation has, generally speaking, not been present in RE previously and radically refines the way in which planning and expectations need to be considered.

When teaching a concept within a tradition, finding effective, engaging tasks or activities and appropriate content is often the way in which teachers begin their planning but this is pedagogically insufficient since the learning, as a result, lacks appropriate progression, is not sufficiently disciplined and does not actually engage appropriately with the concept. For example, students can find a task interesting and engaging because it requires them to be active decision makers or conduct an exercise in which they have to arrive at a judgement, but this does not, in itself, constitute effective learning.

A common example is one that concerns Jesus' resurrection. In this activity students are given the roles of detectives. They are assigned to the case and have to decide what the likely outcome was. They are presented with types of 'evidence' and possible conclusions. They then, in groups, have to make a decision as to what outcome was the most likely. I saw this undertaken in one class with a good teacher who made the lesson fun and the students were fully engaged. There were a number of possibilities as to what had happened:

- the disciples stole the body;
- the Romans took the body;
- the Jewish authorities took the body;
- Jesus didn't really die and escaped from the tomb;
- Jesus was resurrected.

And so on.

You can do this activity using excerpts of biblical text or, for less able students, paraphrasing them. But that is not the point. Although students were fully engaged and enjoyed the lesson we have to ask: 'What did they learn?' I went around talking to the groups and listened to the feedback of the lead member of each group. Remarkably, most of them came to the conclusion that Jesus was resurrected, or, to put it more accurately, came back from the dead. I asked one group, after they had delivered this verdict, what they thought their station sergeant, or even a judge at a trial, would say when they presented their evidence and the conclusion that they had solved the case and, yes, the most reliable conclusion was resurrection!

This, of course, is nonsense on more than one level. First, it confuses the idea of evidence derived from empirical investigation and detective procedures. Second, coming back from the dead is not an equivalent of resurrection. In the Gospels Jesus himself derides this in the story of Lazarus, which we consider on pp. 145–149. Also, resurrection is, in the fullest sense, miraculous. It is premised on the direct intervention of God and its implication is the overcoming of sin, as St Paul announces. The existentialist philosopher Kierkegaard deserves the last word. In his commentary on the raising of Lazarus he said, 'And what would it profit Lazarus to live again if he only has to die as a result?' (Kierkegaard 1989: 4). Most importantly, resurrection is a theological 'event' set within the Christian story of redemption and Christ as redeemer. Therefore the activity above does nothing to elucidate what the concept of resurrection means or why Christians believe it: whether they believe in physical resurrection or not.

I give this example as one instance of what can happen when you start planning from the idea of an engaging activity and import content to fit with it. Pedagogically, this is at least irrelevant and, potentially, disastrous if we are seeking to help students enquire into the worldviews of religious believers and treat our subject as a discipline. One reason why this happens is that we do not know what to do with the subject. It is actually rather embarrassing because the conceptual premises on which religious worldviews are based are often so far removed from students' own worldviews and the way in which they reason as to seem implausible. That is not surprising in a modern society dominated by scientific thinking. However, we do not do the subject of religion any service by distorting it to make it palatable. Engagement should come from meaningful enquiry.

Below are three examples of conceptual cycles based on three different type C concepts taken from three different religions: Christianity, Islam and Buddhism. These are followed by three examples of cycles from units of work involving a number of cycles based on type C concepts from Christianity, Judaism and Humanism.

## Conceptual cycles on type C concepts

## Christianity: an approach using theological textual enquiry – resurrection and the raising of Lazarus

### Communicate

Ask students to observe the image in Figure 7.1, reflect on what they see in the image and discuss their reading of it. Here you are seeking to draw out from them the description of the facial expression, how it has been constructed and the emotions conveyed. Discuss the reasons for the descriptions that the students give, the quality and detail of description and what that tells us about the man being viewed.

**Figure 7.1** The face of Christ

*Source:* Reproduced with kind permission from a Postcard by Judges of Hastings. www.judges.co.uk

## Apply

Ask students to enter the picture and take on the emotions observed. What are they observing that produces these emotions? What are they looking at and how is this affecting them? What does the scene beyond the frame reveal – the context they are in? Ask them to draw on their own experience and record then retell their thoughts, feelings and questions

Reflect on the responses given and discuss these (here the point is to reflect on student interpretation and the richness of language description used and the variety of response).

Reflect on the concepts that the students use to make sense of the narrative expressed by the image for them: for example loss, suffering and so on. Ask them to try and decide which is the most significant concept that applies to their narrative based on the stimulus of the image (i.e. what is the most important idea behind it that they think the artist is conveying and which they can relate to).

Finally, ask students whether the scene they created, the emotions involved and the idea they identified was inevitable: what caused it, can it be overcome, and if so how?

This process is one we could refer to as 'reading' pictures; it is not just about looking at religious art.

## Enquire

Here the key concept is introduced: resurrection.

*Key question: What is the meaning of resurrection?*

Give the students the following texts to work out an explanation of the Christian understandings of the concept:

> I handed on to you the facts which had been imparted to me: that Christ died for our sins . . . that he was buried; that he was raised to life on the third day.
>
> (1 Corinthians 15: 3–4, *The New English Bible*)

> If it is for this life only that Christ has given us hope, we of all men are most to be pitied.
>
> (1 Corinthians 15: 19, *The New English Bible*)

> Listen! I will unfold a mystery: we shall not all die, but we shall all be changed in a flash, in the twinkling of an eye, at the last trumpet call. For the trumpet will sound and the dead will rise immortal, and we shall be changed. This perishable being will be clothed with the imperishable, and what is mortal must be clothed with immortality . . . then the saying of Scripture will come true: Death is swallowed up; victory is won! O Death where is your sting? The sting of death is sin . . . but God be praised, he gives us victory through our Lord Jesus Christ.
>
> (1 Corinthians 15: 51–57, *The New English Bible*)

Ask students to identify the main points about resurrection in the texts that make it a unique event and why they choose the statements they do.

Ask them how this relates to their previous learning in terms of finding solutions or causes in the scenes they constructed in the Apply element and the emotions they discerned in the image of the face used.

Draw out the idea of sin and its relationship with resurrection. Sin may well have been a concept focused on earlier in their learning with the story of the Fall as the context. Also focus on students' explanations of the scene they created and the resurrection explanation – for example whether there are earthly solutions or eventually only transcendent (beyond death) ones.

The first intended learning outcome (at level 5) is to explain the meaning of the concept of resurrection. Share with them the issue of the extent to which their responses do this.

## Contextualise

*Key question: Was Lazarus resurrected or just raised from the dead?*

Reintroduce the first image (Figure 7.1), put alongside it the second scene (Figure 7.2) and ask students to explain the connections between them. This is a simple observation exercise in the first instance. They need to identify that Figure 7.1 is a detail in Figure 7.2.

They can also observe the emotions of any different characters in the scene and seek to describe those. Notice particularly the faces of Martha and Mary in the top left corner.

Now they have the context that the artist has painted, within which he crafted the face and its expression. It will be too difficult for students to work out the meaning of the scene. Therefore introduce the story which it is depicting – the raising of Lazarus:

**Figure 7.2** The raising of Lazarus

*Source:* Reproduced with kind permission from a Postcard by Judges of Hastings. www.judges.co.uk

There was a man named Lazarus who had fallen ill. [His] sisters [Martha and Mary] sent a message to him [Jesus], 'Sir, you should know that your friend lies ill.' When Jesus heard this he said, 'This illness will not end in death' . . . And therefore, though he loved Martha and her sister and Lazarus, after hearing of his illness Jesus waited for two days in the place where he was.

Following this wait he said:

'Our friend Lazarus has fallen asleep, but I shall go and wake him.' The disciples said, 'Master, if he has fallen asleep he will recover.' Jesus, however, had been speaking of his death, but they thought he meant natural sleep. Then Jesus spoke out plainly: 'Lazarus is dead. I am glad not to have been there; it will be for your good and the good of your faith. But let us go to him.'

On his arrival Jesus found that Lazarus had already been four days in the tomb. Martha said to Jesus, 'If you had been here, sir, my brother would not have died. Even now I know that whatever you ask of God, God will grant you.' Jesus said, 'Your brother will rise again.' 'I know that he will rise again,' said Martha, 'at the resurrection on the last day.'

Jesus said, 'I am the resurrection and I am life. If a man has faith in me, even though he die he shall come to life; and no one who is alive and has faith shall ever die. Do you believe this?'

'Lord I do,' she answered . . . With these words she went to call her sister Mary . . . So Mary came to the place where Jesus was. As soon as she caught sight of him she fell at his feet and said, 'Oh sir, if you had only been here my brother would not have died.' When Jesus saw her weeping and the Jews her companions weeping he sighed heavily and was deeply moved. 'Where have you laid him?' he asked. They replied, 'Come and see sir.' Jesus wept. The Jews said, 'How dearly he must have loved him!' . . .

Jesus again sighed deeply; then he went over to the tomb. It was a cave with a stone placed against it. Jesus said, 'Take away the stone.' Martha, the dead man's sister, said to him, 'Sir by now there will be a stench; he has been there for four days.'

Jesus said, 'Did I not tell you that if you have faith you will see the glory of God?' So they removed the stone. Then Jesus looked upward and said, 'Father I thank thee; thou hast heard me. I knew already that thou always hearest me, but I spoke for the sake of the people standing round, that they might believe that though didst send me.'

Then he raised his voice in a great cry: 'Lazarus, come forth.' The dead man came out, his hands and feet swathed in linen bands, his face wrapped in a cloth. Jesus said, 'Loose him, let him go.'

(John 11: 1–44 abbreviated, *The New English Bible*)

Now students need to work with synthesising information from the different texts: written and visual.

Also, at a deeper level, these different texts rely on layers of interpretation. For example, what did the writer of the Gospel of John seek to convey as his message about resurrection and Lazarus? How is the artist seeking to represent/interpret this event? What sense can we make of both the concept of resurrection and the question whether Lazarus was resurrected in this narrative?

It is important to ask students to observe the detail of the artist's scene carefully and articulate their observations. Then relate those to a careful reading of the written text in which the most important sections and statements are determined and commented on. Then puzzle out some of the conundrums of this account by asking questions about the text for reflection. Then decide what are the most important issues that remain about resurrection and what are the essential ingredients to resurrection that this enquiry throws up in relation to the question: 'Was Lazarus resurrected?'

You may also want to introduce Kierkegaard's comment that we mentioned earlier:

And what would it profit Lazarus to live again if he only has to die as a result?

(Kierkegaard 1989: 4)

## Evaluate

*Evaluate Within*

*Key question: What is the significance of resurrection for Christians?*

Here you may want to introduce other stimuli from contemporary Christians, on DVD or by having a visitor from the faith. What needs to be brought out is the necessary connection between resurrection and faith. Also, the question needs to be engaged with whether resurrection needs to be a 'literal' event.

*Evaluate Without*

*Key question: Can resurrection be of significance for others today?*

The point of this question is to question whether resurrection, as seen by other than Christians, in today's world can still make sense. Or has the world changed so much, through science and other understandings we have, that it is simply not believable in the same way as it might have been in earlier times. Alternatively, it could be said that there is still a need for faith in a life beyond death despite these other advances.

Within Evaluate it can be important to recognise what has emerged from each element of the cycle as the enquiry has progressed, and the Evaluate Without may well move into a second Communicate and Apply session as students give their own responses to the concept of resurrection today. This can also involve examples of texts in which 'resurrection' is used but not in the same theological sense.

Of course this enquiry can be simplified by using a shorter and simpler text for the raising of Lazarus and for the other biblical quotations, and for some students reading the story out, enacting it, etc. may be more engaging and less taxing than textual scrutiny. The important thing is not to lose the thread of the enquiry and engagement with the concept.

# Islam: a socio-anthropologically oriented phenomenological enquiry – taqwa in Ramadan

This cycle is based on the Muslim concept of taqwa: the ability to refrain from all that is forbidden and to perform all that is wajib (obligatory). The aim is to engage students with what this means for Muslims and the practices that it underpins. Taqwa is close to the concept of greater jihad in that it is a striving to come closer to Allah by doing those things that Allah has prescribed in order to be obedient to Him. It is an aspect of fiqh (law).

In this cycle the intention is to draw out the difficulties faced by Muslims living in non-Muslim countries in carrying out the discipline and practices associated with taqwa and fiqh. For Shia Muslims (on whom this example is based) this will also involve seeking a ruling (fatwah) from a jurist (a mujtahid, normally an ayatollah) when they are unsure what to do. This is called doing taqleed. Here we want the students to be engaged with working out the dilemmas presented to Muslims.

The intended learning outcomes are for students to be able to (level 5):

- explain the concept of taqwa and its connection to other Muslim concepts;

- explain how it is contextualised in fasting during Ramadan;

- evaluate taqwa by explaining its value for Muslims and some issues it raises;

- explain a response to the concept of taqwa;

- explain examples of how their response would or does influence their own lives and the lives of others.

*Key evaluative question: Why is taqwa important for Muslims fasting during Ramadan?*

## Enquire

For this element of the cycle you will need to provide students with information related to salaat (prayer, times of prayer and the direction of prayer) and halal and haram in relation to food. They can then use the information to help work out the dilemmas below.

The situation below is taken from the Introduction to *A Code of Practice for Muslims in the West* (Hadi al-Hakim 1999: 17–24). Pages 17–24 are the basis of the story for the students to respond to and to consider the issues raised by the author in making his way to the West by aeroplane. This allows the students to work on the sorts of issues that living in the West, after previously only living in a Muslim country, raise and why having a source of authority and guidance is important. It can also, subsequently, act as giving permission to the students to raise their own issues and questions, related to their lives, and create a forum for informed and engaged discussion.

*Coming to the West: on the aeroplane*

Imagine you were coming to the West, for the first time, as the person in this story is. We are going to follow his journey and the difficulties he faced. We are going to discuss and consider what he should do in each situation to give him our advice. Then we shall see what he decided, how he made his decision and why.

The story takes place on an aeroplane. He is travelling to London. He has on him the following items: a copy of the Holy Quran, a comb and a small bottle of perfume.

It is now midday and close to the time for noon prayer. Put yourself in his situation. What does he have to do? How is he going to do it? What difficulties may he have? In what ways may he be feeling uncomfortable? What guidance may he need and how will he get it?

Issues you may wish to prompt on in discussion: where does he do wudhu (washing)? Where can he stand for prayer? Does he need to stand for prayer? Where is the direction of qibla? Does he need something to pray on? Does he need to ask for help from anyone; if so who?

> After doing Salat an announcement comes that food will be served soon. What should he do?
>> The airhostess asks him if he wants fish or chicken. What shall he have? Is there any problem with either of these? How will he work out the answers to these questions?

Get the students to make decisions, in groups, as to what they would do faced with these situations, in role as Muslims, and pay special attention, in discussion of their answers feeding back to the whole class, to: the way in which they decided; their motivations, how deep into the issues they were willing to go; any self-conscious concerns they would have had in these situations; any disagreement within the groups and across the groups.

The point about this part of the process is to bring out the idea that they are like an umma, a community of Muslims trying to deal with problems arising within a Western secular situation. Seek to bring out where the students feel they have difficulty with any decision because they lack knowledge or guidance. Make it a positive contribution to be able to identify exactly where problems lie and list these.

A different and more active way of presenting this is to dramatise it. Make the classroom into an aeroplane and act out the situation with characters.

At the end of this element students need to feed back what this activity has taught them about the Muslim idea of taqwa and the difficulties Muslims can face in a non-Muslim environment. They might also want to speculate on how the situation might have been different on a plane run by a Muslim airline.


## Contextualise: a Muslim family at Ramadan

Muslims do sawm (fasting) for taqwa (spiritual training) to become better Muslims and stronger persons. It can be likened to an athlete's training to be a better performer and have more self-control.

Doing the fast and still being kind to others and keeping our emotions under control shows our strength. If we cannot do this we cannot notice ways in which we have to improve ourselves.

*Vocabulary*

The following vocabulary will need to be introduced and through this students will be able to connect the key concept of taqwa to other Muslim concepts related to Ramadan, the month of fasting:

- sawm (pl. siyaam): fasting;
- Sa'eem: one who fasts;
- fidya: redemption made for not fasting;
- qadha: fasting at a later date to make up the fast;

- kaffara: expiation;
- umma: the Muslim community.

Students need to be organised in groups of six.

Instructions to the class are as follows:

You are a Muslim family in Ramadan going through the fast. Each of you will have a card with a brief description of yourself (character card). There is another set of cards describing events that happen during the period of fasting (events cards). Together you make decisions as you receive information from each card in turn about the things that happen during this time. There are also cards to guide you in making your decisions (advice/instruction cards) and a 'Fasting Guidance sheet' explaining the rules.

Character cards should be handed out at the beginning of the activity.

Events cards should sit in a pile, face down, and be turned over one by one. The issues raised by each event card should be dealt with in turn.

The advice/instruction cards can be laid out at the beginning so they can be seen all the way through. Though the numbering of these relates to the numbering of the other cards, each advice card also contains information that could be used more broadly. The cards could be numbered or not depending on how much you want to help the students.

*Characters*

- an elderly grandmother;
- father;
- mother;
- son aged 14;
- younger daughter aged 5;
- elder daughter aged 18.

*Character cards: 'Who are you going to be?'*

1    Grandmother: you have fasted during Ramadan all your adult life but now you are quite old and rather frail. You wish to continue fasting but are not sure you are strong enough to last through Ramadan. You wonder what to do. On the one hand fasting is important to you; on the other you do not want to injure your health.

2    Son: you are 14 years old. You are doing the fast but finding it hard. You have to do a lot of work at school and homework. The teachers and other students don't understand why you are doing it. You don't want to discuss this with your parents because you think they won't understand and they will think you are not very strong.

3    Younger daughter: you are 5 years old. You want to join in the fast like your mother and you feel left out but you have not spoken about this. Also, you do not really understand what is going on and why your family are doing this.

4   Elder daughter: you are 18 years old and at university, away from home most of the time. There is not a Muslim community near you and you are wondering whether to fast or not. Where you are it does not make sense and nobody else does it. Also, you think you are trying to be a good and kind person anyway. You come home quite a lot but you do not feel part of the local Muslim community any more.

5   Father: you are finding life difficult during the fast. You have to work hard and there is a lot of pressure. Sometimes you have to work very late. This is making you cross and you get irritable a lot, especially at home with your family. You are aware this is wrong and that it means you are not doing the fast properly.

6   Mother: amongst other things you are responsible for shopping for the family. Also, as you enter Ramadan you have not been feeling very well. Both of these things affect the events of Ramadan for you.

*Event cards: 'What will happen next?'*

1   Grandmother: you are not sure whether to fast or not but you want to. You explain this to the family as Ramadan approaches. Have the family talk to her about this and give what advice they think best. She has to make the decision.

2   Son: your teacher in school is worried because you are not concentrating very well. She thinks you should stop fasting. She doesn't understand why you do it and it is interfering with your work. She thinks you will do badly in the tests that are coming soon. She wants to talk with your parents. What should you do? What can you say to the teacher? How can you discuss it with your family?

3   Younger daughter: you decide to ask your family if you can try fasting too. Have a family discussion about this and decide what is the best way to respond. Have the family help her the child to understand why they are fasting. Think about how she can understand this for herself. Remember that the fast is about taqwa. Think about a practical way of teaching her.

4   Elder daughter: you are visiting home during Ramadan and you have not been fasting regularly. At home you are fasting because your parents are and you don't want them to think you are not. Your parents ask you about being at university and you decide to tell them that you are finding keeping the fast difficult. How can the parents deal with this situation? What should they do and how should they respond?

5   Father: you get very cross with the family and they are upset. How should you and the family deal with this situation? Think of the best way to help the father in this situation and some practical ways to make things better.

6   Mother: at the beginning of Ramadan you were shopping in the supermarket. There was a woman with a stall giving away free chocolate to taste. You forgot it was the time of the fast and ate some. What should you do? A few days later you became ill with the flu. Should you continue fasting or not? Your illness lasted five days.

*Advice/instruction cards: 'What are the rules?'*

1   Men and women who are incapable of fasting because of advanced old age are totally exempted. They do not have to give any qadha (make up the missed fast).

Those elderly people who find it extremely trying and difficult to fast are also exempted; but they have to pay a redemption (fidya) of 3/4 kg of food to the poor and needy in lieu of each fast.

2 Every baligh Muslim (one who has reached puberty, normally 14 and over) must fast during the whole month of Ramadan.

Anyone who leaves out a fast on purpose has to give qadha (make up the missed fast) together with kaffara (expiation) for each fast. The kaffara (expiation) is either:

■ to free a slave;

■ to fast for two months instead of each fast of Holy Ramadan;

■ to feed sixty poor people.

3 'Oh you who believe! Fasting has been prescribed upon you as it was prescribed upon those before you so that you may have Taqwa' (*Qur'an-Suratul Baqara* 2: 183).

Taqwa is an active force which strengthens a person's spiritual power. It is a sign that a person is master of his own self.

4 There is no obligation in religion.

One must obey one's parents.

5 There is no guarantee that one who observes sawm (the fast) will definitely have taqwa. In fact, he/she cannot have taqwa if he/she continues to backbite, slander, tell lies, harm others and deal with others with no akhlaq (morality).

6 If a person forgets that he/she is a sa'eem (one who is fasting) and eats or drinks, then his/her sawm (fast) is correct.

Allah does not desire hardship. Therefore if someone is sick or travelling, then he/she is not allowed to fast.

A person who, due to certain illness, is unable to sustain and endure thirst is exempted. However, in view of the sanctity of the holy month, he or she should not drink water to quench the thirst fully. Such a person will pay fidya (of 3/4 kg of food to the poor and needy) in lieu of each fast and will give qadha (making up each day of not fasting later) if the illness is later remedied.

## Evaluate

*Evaluate Within*

*Key evaluative question: Why is taqwa important for Muslims fasting during Ramadan?*

An answer to this question can be achieved by reflecting upon and analysing issues arising from the learning process in the activity that students performed in their groups in the Contextualise element of the cycle and what issues that raised. For example, what decisions did they come to? How did they arrive at those decisions? How did they play their characters? Did different groups arrive at different results? What does this tell you about what is important to Muslims when they fast? Are there ways in which fasting in a non-Muslim society is more difficult than fasting in a Muslim society and why? This should challenge the pupils to use higher order skills of comparison and evaluation.

*Evaluate Without*

To what extent should and could non–Muslims assist Muslims with taqwa in striving to obey Allah and perform their religious duties?

The Enquire and Contextualise scenarios will have provided examples to consider here and students may be able to introduce others, dependent on other prior learning, into Muslim concepts. This should be a genuine debate as to what is and is not possible or reasonable. For example, do you provide spaces for prayer in schools, or at airports. Do you provide halal menu items? Do you even provide separate bathing beaches? This, of course, addresses questions of community cohesion.

## Communicate

Here students are responding from their own opinions and experience and applying their learning to their own lives and those of others:

■ Ask students to consider what things they strive for and what is so important in their own lives that they would be or are prepared to give up other things for it. What do they give up and why? Give examples of when and why? What rules do they make for themselves and why?

■ Consider ways in which their striving is similar to or different from that of taqwa for Muslims in terms of motivation and practice.

## Apply

■ What if they were in a situation where it was difficult to follow their own goals and practices? How would they adapt or not?

# Buddhism: an approach using experiential learning techniques and philosophical enquiry – bhavana and the Wheel of Becoming

## Communicate and Apply

Why do we greet people in the way that we do?

Ask students to stand in pairs facing one another and to greet each other in the manner they would normally use. This will involve handshakes, slaps on the back or just saying, 'Hi!'

Ask them how it felt to do this. They tend to say it felt uncomfortable, odd, etc. When asked why they often respond with the idea that it is normally something they do when they first see each other, not later. Drawing out this point further we can see that what we have just done was artificial since it did not perform the function it was intended for.

Now introduce an adapted more formal Buddhist-oriented style of greeting in which the students stand facing one another with palms together in front of their chests, first look directly into each other's eyes and then lower them and bow slightly with their body. This is done in silence. In commenting upon this they tend to say it is more respectful and intense or focused because of the formality and the looking directly at one another at the beginning. They may also comment that it was done in silence and that this had an effect.

The Apply is about reflecting further on this and on other types of greeting, such as a salute by the military. Here we draw out the way in which different greetings convey different messages and relationships and are bound by a known cultural function. So we come to understand that certain types of greetings seem strange for very definite reasons. At a deeper level we start to recognise that greetings are enmeshed in very specific values being conveyed and are part of the web of cultural experience. We also start to realise that cognitive and affective understandings are involved; in other words, it is about both what we know and how we feel. These introductory activities give us a basis of reflection on which to start to consider Buddhist ideas, especially that of bhavana (mental culture of development), and the way in which they are related to Buddhist practices.

## Enquire

What does bhavana mean?

The focus in this cycle is on the Buddhist concept of bhavana: mental culture or mental development. Introducing it at the beginning of the Enquire element we can ask how it might be related to the greetings we did earlier. How are greetings part of the way in which we develop 'mentally'? How is this related to what we tend to call both our minds and hearts? The teaching point to develop here is that for Buddhists the term 'citta' (mind) encompasses what we separately call mind and heart. Therefore bhavana or mental development does the same.

The point now is to show how this is related to Buddhist practice so that the idea makes sense. Introduce the saying 'When bowing dies, Zen (or Buddhism) dies' (Shunryu Suzuki 1982). After doing the next activity we shall reflect on what this means in relation to bhavana.

Here students can be taken out of the classroom. In the classroom a mock Buddhist shrine will be set up or, if you are nervous about the idea of this activity being taken for worship, just a meditation cushion. The idea now is to walk back into the classroom, having removed our shoes, and, in silence, bow three times, in Buddhist fashion, to the shrine or the cushion. Do this in a line, with teacher or lead student first (having prepared that student for what he or she has to do). Each student must carefully observe the student in front and copy his or her actions. The idea is to have all the students finally sitting in front of the cushion or shrine together and to hold that situation for a brief period before ending the exercise. This can be done using a bell.

After the activity students then comment on its effect. They tend to comment on the effects of the silence and the formality of the activity and how it has created a calm atmosphere and made them feel peaceful, relaxed and focused. Also, that it has created a feeling of respect and of being together in a deeper way. They may even comment on its effect on the sense of time – perhaps even as if time becomes suspended or goes more slowly. The teaching points are to draw out the idea that we have changed the character of the environment we are in, and that we have created change in our minds as well. Also, that silence, from a Buddhist point of view, is what is there when noise ceases – it is a natural condition not an awkward one. All this can now be related back to the statement 'When bowing dies, Zen dies' and what that might mean. Then, how is this related to bhavana?

The next activities are two meditations (note that Zen means the same as the Sanskrit word dhyana, which we can equate with meditation). These involve sitting in a meditation posture. The point of the posture can be explained through the teacher trying to sit in that posture (unsuccessfully) on the floor and using a Buddha rupa from the shrine for the students to decide how successful the teacher has been. Is the teacher as upright, calm, relaxed, etc. as the Buddha? What advice can they give to the teacher to help improve the posture? What is the difference in effect between the teacher's and Buddha's posture? Here the teaching points are to draw out the effect on our state of mind of being in a relaxed, upright, self-supporting posture, and to make us aware that our usual distinction between mind and body does not apply in the same way for Buddhists, i.e. that for Buddhists the idea of consciousness affects the body as well as the mind – there is an interdependence and inter-relationship. (The further, more significant point this is leading to is that consciousness is not located in 'individual minds', therefore bhavana eventually points to this idea and the overall idea of interdependence.) Thus, the idea is to be in a comfortable relationship with our body, not one that causes pain. Here the difference in posture that is created by using the meditation cushion can be shown. The body creates a triangular shape; the knees are on the ground; the back is straight; the person relaxes.

The first meditation involves ringing the bell and listening to its sound until it disappears, then listening to the silence. After doing this, invite comments on the experience. The second meditation involves doing as before but now noticing the thoughts that go through the head and trying to let go of them so they pass through but do not remain. Again, invite comments on this experience. Student comments often mention the difficulty of letting go of thoughts; the surprising thoughts (anticipating lunch, for example), memories and feelings that arise; the difficulty of being distracted by other quiet sounds that they hear in the silence or the serenity that comes with letting things come and go. The first meditation is a calming one (samatha). The second asks them to become more aware of thoughts that the mind creates and is the beginning of insight meditation (vipassana). Students again comment on the quality of silence but can also mention the discomfort of not being in control of their minds. Here the teaching point relates to the importance of observation or awareness and the idea of being mindful. The fact that everything changes all the time, nothing abides, not even in the mind, can be introduced and the idea that we are not our thoughts.

Now, at the end of Enquire we can reflect on what we have learned concerning the concept of bhavana (go back to the initial question) and how it is related to what we have been trying to do. In terms of intended learning outcomes the Enquire element, at level 5, will mean students are able to explain the concept of bhavana. That is what they now have to try and do. This is best done as a group activity so they can share observations and input with one another to come up with the richest explanation.

## Contextualise

How does the Buddhist Wheel of Becoming convey teachings on bhavana?

Contextualise involves interpreting the Buddhist Wheel of Becoming (see http://en. wikipedia.org/wiki/Bhavacakra) in relation to bhavana and raising issues to evaluate. It is important that a Contextualise task does not become just a speculating activity since it needs to involve higher order skills. Thus, it would not be enough to ask students to make sense of the text without some focusing intention. The point is they need to be aware that this is meant to extend their understanding of the concept of bhavana further and that this task will therefore be related to the previous learning accomplished. Also, they need to know what this text is called. Therefore they need to discern why it is called a wheel and how that influences the way in which they read the text. If we need to scaffold this we can think through the components of a wheel – axel, hub, rim, spokes – and discern them in the image presented. Also there is the function of a wheel: to turn. How does this affect our reading? Initially, students' observations and interpretations should be the impetus, but some teaching points will then need to be drawn out in relation to these: the five distinct realms and reflection on what it is like to be in these realms (related to their own experience). For example, the heavenly realm of pleasure and happiness can be related to their own ideas of when they have been happy and why, and how that changed and why. Similarly with the hell realm, where there is pain and agony. What have they experienced to approximate to this? What is worse, toothache or heartache, and why? Each realm has a corresponding psychological condition attached to it. The realm of the jealous gods (devas) is associated with envy and this is depicted in the image by a tree with fruit growing in the heavenly realm but with its trunk is in the deva realm and with someone striving to chop it down with an axe. What does this tell us about envy? At the hub are three animals: pig, cockerel and snake. They represent ignorance, greed (desire) and aversion (hatred), which drive the wheel on, so it turns. What is the implication of that? The visual text depicts our worldly existence based on illusion and our creating of that world out of desire (samsara). Thus bhavana is the means of bringing it to a stop, breaking the chain of ignorance, desire and aversion such that the momentum ceases and change stops. The result is nirvana. Another way to understand the image is as a mirror rather than a wheel. By holding it up to a student as a mirror you can ask, 'What are you seeing?' Thus, reflection is taken a turn further in realising the subjective implications of the investigation and the final interpretive conclusions. All this is done to progress learning and enquiry into the concept by using student-led investigation, responses to questions by students, questioning back to them and making the relevant teaching points or informational interventions at appropriate times, and teacher intervention in the form of further information at specific relevant points. Students are now in a position to think about the issues the concept raises in relation to the context given.

## Evaluate

The Evaluation element of the enquiry can be based on the issues the students raise, or others you may wish to use based on the questions below, for example:

- What self is there to develop if we are not our thoughts and the self is an illusion (the Buddhist concept of anatta – no self)?

- What remains if the world we know ceases (the issue of nirvana not having any positive description)?

- How does this result in Buddhists acting in the world? What is the point? (This invites the need to understand the Buddhist quality of compassion – karuna – in relation to bhavana.) One way of addressing this would be to use material such as internet footage and articles related to such events as the Buddhist monks' protests in Myanmar or the self-immolation of a Buddhist monk during the Vietnam War.

- How is it possible for creatures to move from one realm to another through karma (especially in relation to the animal world, which is driven by instinct)?

These are genuine questions and some further stimuli may be required to take students' thinking to this level but that does not mean that the issues raised have to be answered in a positive fashion, defending the Buddhist point of view. For example, the depictions and message of the Wheel of Becoming can be understood psychologically but also cosmologically. If the depiction of realms is not held cosmologically (which would mean that the idea of rebirth is thrown into doubt), how can one progress to nirvana over many lifetimes? And how would it be possible to do so in one lifetime? And what happens to those in other realms than the human one?

The evaluative questions should focus on:

- What is the value of bhavana to Buddhists (Evaluate Within)?

- Is bhavana useful to us, outside a Buddhist context, in our own lives?

It is possible to proceed again to Communicate and Apply by considering our response to bhavana. What is our idea of mental development (Communicate)? How does that affect us and the society we live in (Apply)?

This is a complex enquiry because it is focused on a large Buddhist concept. It could be changed and simplified by altering the concept – to meditation, for example. The cycle would then be reconstructed as a result, with some activities moved to a different place in the cycle and some left out or replaced. That is the point of working in a process way – nothing is fixed, it is about the inter-relationship of parts and constantly moving students' understanding and reflection forward incrementally, focused on the concept.

## Units of work on different religions

These units of work are presented in outline, and in truncated form rather than in detail because of their length. The aim is to show how concepts specific to a particular tradition can be used to create conceptual cycles that combine to create a systematic unit of work on a tradition. This presentation will focus on the logic of the enquiry more than the learning techniques employed in the different elements of the cycles and units overall.

# Christianity

This unit of work was produced by Penny Morgan, Advanced Skills Teacher in RE at Beaufort Technology College, Winchester (Morgan 2006: 205–236). Here I shall focus on two of the seven conceptual cycles included: Atonement and Redemption. The unit is intended for Year 7 students (level 4 upwards). These cycles are mainly focused on theological enquiry.

## Atonement

*Communicate and Apply*

Students express a personal response to the concept of atonement as trying to make up for (atone) for doing wrong, through drawing on up to three of their own experiences. This leads on to a discussion of whether it is always possible to atone for something. For example, can you atone for committing a murder? Can we always atone for what we have done? Who decides whether we have atoned for our actions? How does it feel if we cannot atone for them?

*Enquire*

Focuses on the Christian concept of atonement. The students have to put into order a card sort identifying different parts of the Christian story, in which atonement is one part. They must identify which part of the story relates to atonement and which part caused the need for atonement then answer the question: 'Why is atonement a necessary part of the Christian story?' They can then explain what atonement means for Christians.

*Contextualise*

This probes deeper into the Christian understanding of atonement and the issues it raises by examining the story of the Fall in more detail. Here the correlation between sin and atonement is drawn out. What was the nature of the sin of Adam and Eve in the story of the Fall? Why couldn't they atone for it? How does the event of Jesus' crucifixion provide for atonement and what does that signify? Here the importance of obedience, sacrifice and God's forgiveness needs to be identified. The final question is who atoned and for what and why?

*Evaluate*

*Key question: What issues are raised by the Christian concept of atonement?*

Here consider how the Apostles' Creed expresses the idea of atonement. Then consider why Christians can't atone for something just by doing good works: why can't we atone for an action just by being good? Finally, focus on issues in world affairs: why can't we create the world we want or a world without suffering? Link this back to the logic involved in the Christian idea of atonement as an explanation of why only God can rectify what we can't atone for. Then share ideas on further issues this concept raises.

# Redemption

This is linked to the above cycle on atonement.

*Enquire*

Begin by focusing on the idea of redeeming as in paying in order to get back what you own, as with getting things back that you previously gave up by taking things to a pawnbroker, or in being given back something that was confiscated due to your bad behaviour, which you 'redeemed' through good behaviour. Tease out what you have to do and what is required before something can be 'redeemed' or re-owned. Then apply that to relationships; for example, what do you have to do to regain someone's trust if you have lost it and can that be done by you alone? What exactly is involved?

*Contextualise*

Introduce the Haitian Hunger Cloth as a depiction of redemption. With the concept of redemption in mind ask students to study it and decide what question they wish to raise about it. Then have a question and answer session around it. How is the concept of redemption involved in this depiction of the Christian story? How might redemption be achieved? How is it linked to other concepts we have worked with? How might it be understood by different Christians in different ways?

*Evaluate*

*Key question: Why is redemption important for Christians?*

Ask students to feed back what the Hunger Cloth is saying about redemption and how it is achieved. What significance would this have for Christians? How might it affect their attitudes and actions? What would Christians hope or expect might happen in the future, as a result (what promise is entailed)? You can feed in what responsibilities might be placed upon Christians by the concept of redemption and why the world is still corrupt if Christ has redeemed it. You may also want to include other written texts for students to synthesise with the Hunger Cloth depiction to augment their understanding. This could be done in groups.

*Communicate*

Students discuss how the concept of redemption might or might not be applicable to their own lives and those of others (this can be taken out of the Christian context). They should relate these to the modern world and issues within it. Can the world be redeemed, does it need to be, and if so how?

*Apply*

Students produce their own version of the Hunger Cloth, with reference to their own response to redemption. They can do this in groups or pairs so this involves negotiation. It needs to depict their vision for change and how that can be achieved, depicted in a symbolic fashion.

Finally students need to discuss and show how the concepts of atonement and redemption are related, from a Christian perspective, and to what extent they can be from their own point of view. The pedagogical point is not just to be able to explain Christian interpretations of these ideas and their connections but also how they still resonate or not with human experience in wider contexts.

# Judaism

This unit of work was produced by Toni Sambrook and her colleagues at Wildern College for the Performing Arts, Hedge End, Hampshire (see Sambrook *et al.* 2006: 505–534). Here I shall focus on two of the six conceptual cycles included: Covenant and Mitzvah. The unit is intended for Year 8 students (level 4 upwards). These cycles are mainly focused on socio-anthropological enquiry.

## Covenant

*Communicate*

An assortment of packs is provided that contain various items related to everyday and lifetime agreements. Students, in groups, have to sort the contents by what sort of agreement is shown in each pack and what that agreement entails. These can involve mortgages, marriages, etc.

*Apply*

Students must now determine who the agreements benefit and how; whether it is easy to keep the agreements, what is entailed and what are the consequences of breaking the agreement. They need to record ideas and draw out the key points.

*Enquire*

Students now enquire into the key concept of covenant: what makes a covenant different from just an agreement and what covenants are they likely to enter into in life. The key point needs to be established that covenants are legally binding agreements. Ask students to decide on a covenant they think the world benefits from and one it might not. For example, is marriage a valuable covenant or is it better just to live with a partner?

*Contextualise*

Here the focus is on the Jewish Covenant made between Abraham and God. Using the biblical text or a paraphrased version of it students need to highlight the nature of the agreements involved; what, exactly, makes it a covenant, and what makes it unique as a covenant. Ask students to raise issues about why Abraham would have entered into this Covenant: why would he agree to sacrifice his son Isaac? What does this Covenant require in terms of the nature of obedience? Why do they think Abraham would enter into it? What is distinctive about it?

*Evaluate*

*Key question: What is the significance of the Covenant between God and Abraham?*

Focus on three key aspects of this and introduce supplementary material as required. Do you think Abraham benefited from this Covenant? Why would God want to make this Covenant with Abraham? How might this Covenant affect Jews today? The last question can involve supplementary material on Orthodox Jewish lifestyles based on the Covenant to show its radical effect over time and how it still determines ways in which some religious Jews live their life.

## Mitzvah

This cycle focuses on the way the Covenant involved specific commandments and asks if one of them, the ritual act of circumcision, is still relevant today.

*Communicate*

What outward signs do we show of our belonging to a group? Show a PowerPoint slideshow of distinctive signs of belonging and identity. Ask students to identify and explain these signs: who has them, what do they denote in terms of belonging and values, what rituals, dress, types of greeting or other features might accompany them? Some of these could be provided for correlation.

*Apply*

Ask students to explain how significant examples of signs of belonging are also an expression of obeying specific commitments. They can draw on the work above and others can be added. Specific examples of connection can be shown and commented upon. What would happen if you did not wear what you are expected to wear? When might that happen and why? What happens if you do not behave as you are expected to and why? Can you still belong if you do not show signs of commitment?

*Enquire*

The concept of mitzvah is explicitly introduced as a commandment that is a sign of keeping the Covenant. Here the focus will be specifically on circumcision as a sign of the Jewish Covenant.

This is an outward and visible sign so recap on the work done in Apply on the nature of such signs and their implications in relation to identity and belonging. Then discuss why, for Jews, circumcision should be a mitzvah and how that may differ from the signs discussed earlier, for example its physicality and non-reversibility: you can't remove the sign once it has been done – what are the implications of that?

*Contextualise*

Introduce the Brit Milah ceremony and what it entails. Use selected passages from the first chapter of Jonathan Freedland's (2006) book *Jacob's Gift: A Journey into the Heart of Belonging* to help students understand how a non-religious Jew could still decide to circumcise his son. Discuss the issues and implications that arise from this. Does circumcision still have meaning for Jews in the twenty-first century, and if so why? Why is such a mitzvah still so important even if the religious sense of the Covenant no longer has significance?

*Evaluate*

Is circumcision still important today as a mitzvah of the Covenant? Use articles on issues raised as to the importance of circumcision today for Jews. Suggest to the class that circumcision is a cruel practice that is not necessary in a modern Jewish society – do you agree? Break the class up into groups to argue for and against this and provide texts to consider and ask students to also research this on the internet if this is possible. Have available rabbinic commentary as well to determine how important it is to follow mitzvahs to the letter. For example, here's Rabbi Hillel on Torah: 'What is hateful to you do not do to your neighbour . . . all the rest is commentary'. Encourage students to recognise the bases of different attitudes and interpretations of mitzvah promoted by different Jewish authorities in coming to an informed decision.

Finally, ask students how the key concepts of Covenant and mitvah can be related and whether or not this relationship changes over time for Jews.

# Humanism

This unit of work was produced by Rebecca Costambeys, Advanced Skills Teacher in RE and Head of RE at Costello Technology College, Winchester (see Costambeys 2007: 15–24).

Here I shall focus on two of the six conceptual cycles included – Utilitarianism and Kantian Ethics – as two main ethical positions that underpin Humanism. The unit is intended for Year 9 students (level 5 upwards). These cycles are focused on ethical enquiry.

## Utilitarianism

*Enquire*

Information on Jeremy Bentham and the main principles of Unitarianism are introduced using text from Philip Stokes' (2006) *Philosophy: 100 Essential Thinkers*. Students précis from this the tenets of Utilitarianism and how this differs from (one or more) other ethical philosophies of which they are aware or moral positions that it challenges.

*Contextualise*

Students use the moral questionnaire in Jeremy Hayward, Gerald Jones and Marilyn Mason's *Exploring Ethics* (Hayward *et al.* 2000: 35) and respond to four of the nine dilemmas from a utilitarian perspective.

*Evaluate*

*Key question: Is Utilitarianism a sufficient ethical theory?*

Students report on the issues raised by Utilitarian responses to the moral dilemmas investigated and the positive or negative values of this ethical theory.

*Communicate*

Students communicate ways in which Utilitarianism endorses or disputes particular ethical principles they hold and justify the distinctions or compatibilities involved.

*Apply*

Students consider contemporary moral dilemmas. Here stimuli based on current topical issues could be provided. They need to decide on the extent to which applying a Utilitarian perspective would or would not be effective.

## Kantian Ethics

*Enquire*

Information on Immanuel Kant and the main principles of Kantian Ethics are introduced using text from Philip Stokes (2006). Students précis from this the tenets of Kantian Ethics and how this differs from the Utilitarian perspective and other ethical positions.

*Contextualise*

Students again use the moral questionnaire in Hayward *et al.*'s *Exploring Ethics* (Hayward *et al.* 2000: 35) and respond to four of the nine dilemmas from a Kantian perspective. They then distinguish how this perspective results in differing moral outlooks from others in terms of cause and consequences.

*Evaluate*

*Key question: Does Kantian Ethics present us with a sufficient response to our moral dilemmas?*

Here students compare and contrast Kantian Ethics with Utilitarianism and weigh their respective merits.

*Communicate*

Students communicate ways in which Kantian Ethics endorses or disputes particular ethical principles they hold and justify the distinctions or compatibilities involved.

*Apply*

Students consider contemporary moral dilemmas, as previously. Here stimuli based on current topical issues could be provided. They need to decide on the extent to which applying a Kantian perspective would or would not be effective.

Finally students have to decide to what extent a Utilitarian or Kantian perspective on Humanistic ethics is sufficient and how they can be connected or contrasted. Also, to what extent is a Humanist position, based on these differing ethical principles, sufficient in relation to, or compatible with, other religiously based ethical positions?

## Assessing units of work on religious worldviews

The capacity to interpret worldviews depends on students being able to see the connection between the key concepts on which they are based. Therefore assessment of any unit of work based on a specific worldview needs to determine the extent to which students are able to do this. At the same time you want assessment to be creative and based on the utilisation of skills and focus on students' religious literacy. Here are two examples of ways in which you might do this. One is based on Christianity, the other on Islam.

## Crucifixion gallery

At the end of a unit of work on Christianity students should have engaged with concepts such as atonement, redemption, sin, grace, agape and incarnation. A crucifixion gallery involves presenting students with artistic depictions of the crucifixion to which they can bring their understanding of these concepts and show which concept(s) relate to the depictions of the artists and how they do so. In this way they will be exploring how these artists have interpreted the crucifixion event and can deliberate on why.

Images you might use are available in various packs but many are also on the web. Ones I have used are: 'Crucifixion No. 5' by Marcus Reichert (1991), www.marcusreichert.com; Pieta by Fenwick Lawson, www.fenwicklawson.co.uk; 'Crucifixion' by Cecil Collins (1952), the British Museum; 'Reconciliation' by Keiji Kosaka. For depictions of these and a related article, see Erricker 2007: 20–22.

# Zone of relevance

Zone of relevance was originally introduced as a Key Stage 3 strategy for enhancing learning. The idea is to create a box shape on a sheet of paper and list a number of ideas that might or might not be placed in the box according to their relevance to a particular topic or question. This is then justified by students. After completing a unit of work on Islam students can be given a number of terms related to Muslim vocabulary that they will have covered; some will have been key concepts, such as tawheed, shirk, jihad, umma, yawmuddin, others might relate more specifically to practice, such as salat, prayer mats, wudu, qibla, etc. Pose the question: 'Which of these terms do you think it is most important to understand in order to understand Islam?' Ask them to put the ones they choose in the box (zone of relevance) and the others round it. They now have to justify their choices. An extension of this is to create a concept map. Ask them to link up the terms they have put in the zone of relevance by creating sentences between them to explain the connection. Students who perform best will have a web of sentence connections between differing concepts. Those who perform less well will have simple sentence connections of a linear kind between just two different terms. This can be extended again by asking them to write a commentary on Islam, in the form of a paragraph that uses the sentence connections they were able to make. Finally, students can judge which is the best commentary on Islam. This could be connected to the idea of an encyclopaedia entry.

## Conclusion

This chapter has explored how interpreting worldviews builds on religious literacy by creating cycles of enquiry and then a unit of work on a worldview that enables students to enquire into the distinctive features that characterise a tradition based on its (type C) key concepts. Two ways of creating assessments were then presented to show how student learning could be evaluated. As a result you may wish to identify a tradition, two or three of its distinctive concepts, and create cycles based on those. Then devise an appropriate assessment.

# The future for education and religious education

CHAPTER

# 8

# Worldview analysis and the future of religious education

## Introduction

This chapter will involve us in returning to some of the debates presented at the beginning of this book, in Chapters 1–3, and taking them further. It will also lead us to ask how religious education can broaden its horizons whilst retaining its integrity as a discipline and contribute to the values debate that lies beyond the curriculum subject itself but with which the discipline of RE needs to engage. First, we shall engage with the idea of worldview analysis as the promotion of religion as a means to cultivate liberal non-ideological values. This will then be contested by investigating how liberalism itself can be understood as an ideological worldview. Next we shall investigate the politics of worldview analysis as a way of recognising that it has to include an examination of concepts that are interpreted differently by religious and other worldviews, and the complexity involved in such enquiries. Here specific practical examples will be introduced. Finally, in the summary to this chapter (pp. 193–194), I shall present some pedagogic principles that underpin worldview analysis as a way of approaching it in the classroom.

By worldview analysis I mean the need to enquire into not just the concepts that underpin particular religious worldviews, as was the subject of Chapter 7 (interpreting worldviews), but how worldviews impact on us due to the differing interpretations of concepts and how they are contextualised in world events and changes over time, and the complexity that involves; also the way in which behaviours change as a result and the way that impacts on the world and its societies. This involves understanding why the politics of the world, its values, and its conflicts and tensions arise, which may involve religious issues or other ones. For students it is about gaining a grasp on how events occur due to the changing circumstances that bring about the impact of and differing interpretations of particular ideas. This, of course, often invites inter-disciplinary collaboration and demands, and extends, religious literacy.

## Worldview analysis and the promotion of religion

Worldview analysis is a term most closely associated with Ninian Smart. His intention in using it we can link to his desideratum, quoted in Chapter 3 (p. 46). Smart's larger purpose was to ask how religions, and non-religious worldviews, their values and aspirations, could be harnessed to the creation of a liberal democratic society beyond ideology. In effect, this was a particular type of worldview which Smart saw religions as contributing to significantly. For John Bowker, contrastingly, religions were identified as ideologies that would destroy the world (see the quotation from him in Chapter 1, p. 4). We explored how Philip Pullman characterised theocracies as ideologies that worked against the democratic spirit and its educational values and he did not draw a distinction between religious ideologies and others, such as Stalinism (see the quotation in Chapter 1, p. 11). We noted Regis Debray's pharmakonic view that religion is both cure and poison and there is 'no need to break swords' over this (see, again, Chapter 1, p. 8). This debate suggests that we cannot simply talk of religion as one thing. Religion manifests itself in different ways. Smart exhorts us to think of religion as about faith and values. But Bowker was concerned with the ideological expressions of religion and the need to curb the influence of those. Debray recognised both faces of religion as making up their Janus-like quality. Pullman's point is that the significant categorisation is not between religion and secularity but between ideology and liberal democratic values. This suggests that when analysing worldviews there is more complexity to attend to beyond whether they are religious or not.

Scientific secularists, such as Dawkins and Hitchens, wish to retain the binary divide between science/secularism and religion as the fundamental category distinction on the basis that the latter is irrational and ideological, the cause of conflict and the agent of repression. Their examples pay no attention to the faith and values aspects prized by Smart. Terry Eagleton's polemic (Eagleton 2009) against both Dawkins and Christopher Hitchens (he often conflates their names and refers to them as 'Ditchkins') is worth reviewing at this point; in part because Eagleton still recognises himself as a Marxist and therefore not a priori likely to be a supporter of religion.

Eagleton's riposte to 'Ditchkins' alerts us to how different takes on religion result in different interpretations of a phenomenon that is multifaceted and none too well defined. Whereas Dawkins' and Hitchens' ire is focused on the way in which religious adherents and institutions, in their panoply of expressions, oppose science and reason, Eagleton's approach is to speak of the abstruse and sophisticated nature of theological reflection (especially that of Aquinas) and the social and ethical zeal of Jesus. These, he contends, point to a different, positive, assessment of the contribution of religion to the enrichment of humanity.

Eagleton, in his first sentence, acknowledges the harm religion has done over time but seeks to construct a fuller picture of what religion is in relation to its philosophical reflection on metaphysical and meta-ethical questions. These differing approaches mirror not only the problems in the debate on the value of that ambiguous phenomenon called religion but also require a debate over the way religious education has been approached over the last three decades (in the UK at least). Built into each approach is a particular desire to present religion according to a different a priori characterisation. Eagleton is in Smart's camp in defending religious faith and values whilst acknowledging the pharmakonic quality presented by Debray. Dawkins and Hitchens side with Bowker. Eagleton's approach is most succinctly demonstrated in the following passage:

> Because God is transcendent — that's to say, because he doesn't need humanity, having fashioned us for the fun of it — he is not neurotically possessive of us . . . He is therefore able to let us be; and the word for this is freedom, which is where for Christian theology we belong to him most deeply.
>
> (Eagleton 2009: 15)

This is a strange statement from a Marxist but the nub of it is Eagleton's concern with freedom. Freedom is the quality to be prized and if the Christian God is in favour of freedom the Christian God is a good God, or, at least, Christians who value freedom and whose theology advocates this are valued fellow travellers. Here liberation theology springs to mind.

Eagleton, perhaps unwittingly, puts his finger on the spot. It is about faith, in its larger than religious sense, and specific values that liberate us from ideologies, whether religious or not, including scientism, which are repressive and exclusivist.

This is a particular type of theological stance that Eagleton is advocating and, as he acknowledges, the idea of freedom is central to many writers who are not inclined to religion or theology: Hume, Nietzsche, Sartre, Lyotard and Foucault, to name a few. If we ask the question whether theology and religion have a contribution to make to debates over human freedom the answer might well be yes. If we ask what role religion has had in promoting human freedom the answer might well be more ambiguous. In pursuing religious education we would need to take account of both possible answers in constructing an enquiry into the role of both theology and religion and in relation to the concept of and the praxis of freedom. As witty and intellectually deft as Eagleton is in his critique he does not answer the question as to the value of religion (as opposed to just faith and freedom) in human affairs. He contributes to an ongoing debate, which is also the purpose of religious education and concerns worldview analysis.

What we have to wrestle with is whether God is to be understood as an immutable doctrinal concept or as a malleable, shifting conception in the world of human designs, even as an ineffable and therefore indefinable but somehow present reality, or as (amongst others perhaps) an instrumental force for achieving specific ethical designs that enhance humanity.

What Eagleton does is present a form of liberation theology, and its antecedents, as mainstream Christian theology and ethics. In doing so he is actually presenting an idealised Christian agenda as the norm. I have no objection to this approach, nor to his attack on Dawkins' argument against theism or, in Hitchens' case, all religion. However, presenting forms of liberation theology as the mainstream position in the spectrum of Christian religion is disingenuous. It is Marxism without its ideological consequences in Stalinism. As an apologia for a representation of social and ethical values of the left it is fine. As a way of critiquing criticisms of religion it is inadequate. With regard to RE and its representation of religion, and in particular Christianity, its partiality impoverishes it. It is religion focused on faith and social justice. It is not religion as ideology. If we are to analyse worldviews we must take account of both the way they oppose power and the way they use it.

Similar apologetic positions have been presented by others for religious education, as in the fairly recent volume *Peace or Violence: The Ends of Religion and Education?* (Astley *et al.* 2007). Here I refer to two articles contained in this. First, Jack Priestley's essay; in this he states:

> Peace, I am suggesting, is the agreed aim of all our religious quests and it seems to me, is the stuff of religious education. If the core aim of all religion is that of trying to arrive at a state of peace, then it surely follows that religious education should be primarily focused on what makes for that.
>
> (Priestley 2007: 32–33)

Whereas, for Eagleton, religion is to be valued in the service of freedom, for Priestley it is to be valued in the service of peace. Priestley also states:

> It is all too easy for us to convince ourselves as scholars that we can somehow stand outside the drama of the real world.
>
> (Priestley 2007: 33)

Jack Priestley's aim is, of course, laudable. Priestley's further point is also that peace is a peripheral issue in Agreed Syllabi. This seems to imply that they do not engage with real issues, just descriptive content. Again I agree this is the tendency. But to engage with issues, such as peace, is not the same as suggesting that the aim should be to promote peace as 'the agreed aim of the religious quest'. And it is contestable that arriving at a state of peace is the core aim of all religion, though it may well be said to be a concern of much religious faith and secular hope.

When, later, he argues that the major acts of genocide of the last eighty years have all been driven by secularists and that it is all too easy to assume that religion has been a major cause of conflict (Priestley 2007: 34–35), he moves into an apologetic mode for religion. It is a disingenuous argument. Why defend religion rather than the promotion of peace against all those who oppose it? Surely, you only do this if you want to be partisan toward religion in the prospects of promoting peace. If we are genuinely concerned with worldview analysis there shouldn't be a prior determination to defend religion.

Later, again, he asks the question 'Have we the courage to take on, not the people, but the distortions that are being presented to the world as "real" religion, under the guise of which conflict and violence are breaking out all over the world?' (Priestley 2007: 38). But what does he mean by 'real'? Does he mean the idealised peace-promoting messages we can selectively extract from its scriptures? And should we denounce as distortions any manifestations of religion that, whether scriptural or otherwise, promote conflict? So it would seem.

For Priestley fundamentalisms are false (Priestley 2007: 44) and we should follow the teachings of the Buddha, Christ, the prophets and *the* Prophet and 'their modern exponents like Gandhi or Martin Luther King with their non-violent action' (Priestley 2007: 45).

There is much to admire in Jack Priestley's approach but he leaves no room for students to carry out their own enquiry, arrive at their own conclusions and deliberate on their own values. Students are to know that the great religious leaders and prophets and exponents of non-violence are right, others are wrong . Yet, was *the* Prophet always an exponent of non-violence? Consider the differences between the Medinan and Meccan suras. Gandhi was inspirational to many but he was also controversial. His assassination was carried out by an unrepentant advocate of Indian progress. Are we to make no balanced assessment of his worth? Priestley re-presents the desideratum of Smart. In doing so he pre-empts any evaluative enquiry into the phenomenon of religion, and its non-violent protagonists, and any broader study of worldview analysis and its complexity. If today someone tried to present a similar argument for communism would it be regarded as credible?

Included in the same volume is Andrew Wright's essay 'Hospitality and the Voice of the Other: Confronting the Economy of Violence through Religious Education'. Wright refers to John Locke's vision of a commonwealth of nations in which he argues that the privatisation of religious belief is necessary to neutralise a key source of violence in society (Wright 2007a: 65). He also cites John Hull's use of the term 'religionist' as the root of this fragmentation and dissent and Hull's call for anti-religionist training in the classroom (Wright 2007a: 66–67). Thus, Locke's thesis is attributed not so much to antagonism towards religion as to a type of anti-religionist stance, since it is 'religionists' who are responsible for such violence.

Wright, however, departs from liberalism on the basis of its universalising tendencies (those of 'liberalists'?), which fail to 'appreciate the distinctiveness of religious traditions' and lead to 'the imposition of a normalistic liberal metanarrative' (Wright 2007a: 67). His alternative is 'an economy of alterity rather than an economy of sameness' (Wright 2007a: 71), by which we recognise competing versions of religious truth, which sounds promising but is seen as a way of serving the 'pedagogical task of utilizing religious education as a tool for combating violence' (Wright 2007a: 71) by turning to the 'resources offered by the world's religions themselves as a means of opening up the possibility of alternative paths to salvation, enlightenment and the cessation of violence and suffering' (Wright 2007a: 78). Without further elucidation Wright's point escapes me here. The idea of salvation has produced violence as well as opposed it.

Wright, as with Priestley, wishes to present the teachings of religion as non-violent but the violence of religion as an aberrant and disassociated manifestation. These approaches act as a validation of a particular kind of theology that argues for the good in religion and rejects the bad as not the real thing. But, for an analysis of worldviews, surely we have to take account of the good, the bad and the ugly.

It seems that the relationship between those who are scholars of religious education and their subject is somewhat different from other subjects; the relationship is closer between the scholar and the subject in certain respects, in that they are often theological insiders as well as academic commentators. With regard to all three authors cited above – Priestley, Hull and Wright – this is true to some degree. It seems to result in a defence of religion against those who represent religion's negative side such that the subject is viewed positively in values terms. In other words, we get the 'othering' of fundamentalists, 'fanatics' and those regarded as religious 'terrorists'. Whilst this is understandable it is not necessarily acceptable if we are to regard religious education as a discipline that presumes a certain level of objectivity in relation to the phenomenon of religion. Wright may well wish to oppose the hegemony of liberalist imperialism in relation to the representation of religion but he still wishes to invoke religions in decrying violence and suffering on the basis of its differing salvific possibilities.

I suggest we need greater distance from the phenomenon itself. This presentation of it gives a certain uncritical and preferential treatment to the representation of the religion in order to affirm its value within a curriculum dedicated to the development of students in a democratic society. This also indicates how entwined RE is with a form of values education as its extrinsic rationale, almost a form of values instruction. I do not think any other discipline within the curriculum finds itself in this uncomfortable position. It suggests that the original rationale for religious education as a form of faith nurture is still with us but simply broadened to a form of nurture in values based on religious belief. This falls somewhat short of an enquiry into religion in which students are expected to form their own judgements. It also omits to examine the somewhat revolutionary nature, in one way or another, of the genesis of a number of religious traditions and the tensions that ensued in both the development and schisms of these traditions. With regard to this we need to be sensitive to the way in which religions have changed their values over time.

For example, the message of Guru Nanak on equality was changed with the establishment of the Khalsa by Guru Gobind Singh and has been compromised by caste, not just on the Indian sub-continent but also in its diaspora in Britain and elsewhere, as Sanjay Suri observes in *Brideless in Wembley* (Suri 2007: 307–332), where he recounts the case of the Ravidassias in Southall. The history of Christianity reveals similar complexities. When Romanised Christianity entered Britain with the Roman invasion, having already affirmed the doctrines of the Trinity and Grace, it met with a Celtic Christianity informed by the theology of Pelagius, which it ultimately defeated. With the assistance of the history composed by the Venerable Bede, Pelagian Christianity was erased and Trinitarianism triumphed. It could be argued that the vision of Pelagianism was much stronger on the liberatory possibilities of Christian teachings, in this life, than the Romanised form, which stressed sin and salvation in the afterlife, by way of judgement. We now have an orthodoxy of Trinitarianism in Christianity that is largely undisputed. Do we ignore the means by which it came to this undisputed representation or uncover its doctrinal fault lines and ask new questions about its veracity? We have to ensure we do not present a normative and erroneous representation of religion based on idealisation or conquest.

It is, at least, a deficient form of pedagogic nurture that emphasises the goodness of religion (selectively illustrated) and ignores its negative contributions. It is religion presented in the service of liberal values rather than an enquiry into religion per se. Michael Hand makes a distinction in this respect between 'positive regard for religious traditions other than one's own' as a 'defensible aim of RE' but warns of the dangers that can accompany it. He states:

> Cultivating in pupils a positive regard for religious traditions is, at best, a secondary aim of RE. It is crucial that we do not eclipse or obscure the primary aim of subjecting religious beliefs and ideas to careful and critical scrutiny. The basic reason for teaching RE . . . is that children have a right to be exposed to religious truth claims and be equipped with the wherewithal to evaluate them. It would be disastrous for the integrity and credibility of RE as a serious domain of theoretical enquiry if the aim of fostering positive regard were to overshadow this primary aim.
>
> (Hand 2006: 32)

It makes sense that, by using the term worldviews, rather than just religion, and by broadening the studies we conduct, as a result, we do away with the idea of just showing a positive regard for religious traditions. At worst, we have to avoid the Hollywoodisation of RE: religious goodies against various ideological baddies, based on empathy. The a priori expectation that students should empathise with religion and the consequent disassociation of forms of religious expression and behaviour that are ideologically motivated pre-empts the possibility of analysis of the value of religious worldviews. The approaches we have reviewed in this section exhibit the promotion of religion in the service of a form of religiously based values education. Next we have to examine further whose values we are talking about.

# Humanism, values and myth: worldview analysis and two kinds of liberalism

Our values position in education in the West generally has emerged from the thinking of the European Enlightenment. On this the political philosopher John Gray has written:

> Of course the Enlightenment was a highly contradictory movement. It contained thinkers such as Spinoza, who despite his faith in reason knew that humans would always live by illusions; sceptics such as David Hume, for whom history was the working out of chance events; Schopenhauer, who used the work of Kant . . . to argue that history is a kind of dream; and Freud . . . who showed the humans could only ever be partially sane. But it was the Enlightenment belief in progress that had mass appeal, and here religion comes into the picture. Like much else in secular thought the idea of progress is a legacy of Christianity.

> (Gray 2009: 12)

Out of the Enlightenment came the movement now known as Humanism. Humanism was the antidote to religious belief. Humanism, based on rationalism and scientific thinking, sought to create the moral basis of a society that had outgrown religious belief. In its fundamental form it is a Promethean venture into a new age, devoid of superstition, that can fulfil human potential. Secularity was a defining feature of Humanism but so was its belief in human progress, rationality and knowledge.

Gray further comments that 'the belief that knowledge is intrinsically benign is perhaps the definitive modern myth' and that 'contemporary humanism is a religion that lacks the insight into human frailty of traditional faiths' (Gray 2009: 15). Gray opposes the Humanist project on the basis that humans are not supremely rational by nature but, rather, desire to see themselves as such and that this in itself is a fallacy that places Humanism amongst its religious counterparts.

He states:

> The myth-free civilization of secular rationalism is itself the stuff of myth. Myths are fictions, which cannot be true or false; but fictions can be more or less truthful depending on how they capture human experience. No traditional myth is as untruthful as the modern myth of progress. All prevailing philosophies embody the fiction that human life can be altered at will. Better aim for the impossible, they say, than submit to fate. Invariably, the result is a cult of human self-assertion that soon ends in farce.

> (Gray 2009: 16)

Here we might be forced to reflect further on the ideas presented by Priestley, Hull and Wright on the idealisation of religious education and on the relationship between religious truths, values and myth.

With religions there is a contradiction, which is that they claim truth which is exclusive and yet, unless fundamentalist, they have to live in co-existence with other truth-systems and, at least, with tolerance. For example, with Christianity the truth is that Christ died for our sins. For Christians that has to be true, not just for Christians but for everybody; it is the explanation of the human condition and the prerequisite for salvation. Similarly for all religions there is a defining truth and it is not just the mark of the religion but the truth expressed as to the human condition and its means to a particular soteriology that applies universally. This is what doctrine is. Doctrine cannot be translated into myth without losing its force as truth. Exclusivity is the mark of the distinctiveness of a religion. Truth is its power and rationale. If we reduce religious truth to myth, then its truth becomes 'a' truth for the believer. Without the definite article the universality of the claim of each religion is neutered, in effect a faith and a values position. To put it another way, it ceases to be an ideology. It is the transmutation of pre-modern religion into modernism.

There are other reasons for belonging to a religious group. One is enculturation into that group, which may become a source of belonging, security and empowerment; another, concomitant reason is that a religion provides a source of values. However, on neither of these grounds can any religion claim exclusivity and thus religions become party to a project greater than themselves; for example a project on shared identity or shared values or one that is anti-secularist or anti-materialist. In other words, for pragmatic reasons, religions then seek to identify shared grounds on which to oppose an alternative ideology based on premises that endanger their own, such as secularism. The sometimes internecine warfare of the past, predicated on exclusive truth and the resultant heresy of others, mutates into the more prag-matic manoeuvres carried out in late modern society. Again, religious education is susceptible to such manoeuvres on the grounds of common interest: we all want peace, religions proclaim peace, so shouldn't religious sources be those we should turn to for procuring peace? But why just turn to religions?

The fissures in Christianity and Islam in the late twentieth and twenty-first centuries can be explained by asking to what extent groups in the religion have accommodated themselves to this modernist age or still act in defiance of its liberal character. Obvious examples arise concerning authority in the Episcopal Church connected to the schism over homosexuality, and with the Roman Catholic Church's pontifical response to AIDS and condoms in Africa. When the 'modernisation' of religion is spoken of, as it was by the New Labour government under Tony Blair, it effectively meant that within the public space of society religions should operate as myths with pragmatic aims that value tolerance and progress. It is still possible to speak of the 'truths' to be found in religions but these are shared 'truths' (pragmatic truths, we might say) and therefore amount to a shared basis for religious and political policy making. There is no place for the exclusive, universalist, salvific truths that are necessarily conflictual. This changes the whole pedagogy of public discourse over religion. Truth (with a capital T and definite article) changes to truth or truths to which religions speak and which are understood to pertain to and be affirmed by modernist society as a whole whether one is religious or not. Peace acts as a good example of the rhetoric of this sort of venture, and violence its contrary.

This mutation in turn changes the project of education, or the predicates upon which pedagogy in education is based. If we remind ourselves of the positions of those writers and projects in religious education discussed in Chapter 3 and those mentioned above, then we can identify different responses to this situation. Before we do that a further consideration ensues. This is the exclusion of pre-modernist and affirmation of modernist understandings into one pragmatic project. We can place this under the heading of community cohesion (see the section on this on pp. 186–192), since that is the name it has been given. It is the toleration and acceptance of different narratives. It requires the renunciation of exclusivist truths, in the public space, as defined by ideologies that participate, whether religious or scientific. It does not require that those truths cannot be adhered to by the communities of believers privately. In effect, what is at play within the rules of this game is a bilinguality. One language can be used within the private spaces of differing (epistemologically faith-based) communities, but another, a sort of Esperanto of public values, within the larger public space. Necessarily, the latter has to take precedence over the former as a means to 'progress' in the social sphere. Necessarily again, epistemological truths that are incommensurable give way to pragmatic values which are livable in concert with others.

For Gray this is a *modus vivendi* within which different ways of life can be acknowledged without the overarching master narrative of a liberal universalism (Gray 2009: 40) or the religious ideologies it has sought to replace. This relates closely to Andrew Wright's distinction, in Chapter 3 and on pp. 56–57, between comprehensive and political liberalism, or liberalism and imperialist liberalist tendencies. Here Gray and Wright seem to agree but I do not think this leaves either of them free from criticism. According to their critique, liberal universalism has become the new imperialism, replacing the previous hegemonies of pre-modern religious truths. To what extent has liberalism replaced religious truths? Is it possible to agree on different ways of life but still acknowledge common values, as Gray maintains?

Gray wishes to acknowledge universal human rights (Gray 2009: 40) in the same way as Wright promotes agreement on the four basic liberal virtues of respect, freedom, tolerance and equality without affirming them as '*constitutive* of the good life itself' (Wright 2007a). But it is unclear how promoting these rights and virtues falls short of a liberal universalism. These virtues are derived from the values position of liberalism with the ethical conviction that universalising them should be promoted and opposition to them should be challenged. This is, surely, a universalist position. Are we really saying that all religiously influenced culture's ways of life conform to or wish to aspire to such an ambition? We know this is not the case as a matter of documented evidence, and Ayan Hirsi Ali's (2007) *Infidel: My Life* provides us with a suitable case study in this respect. The pathological tendency to suggest that branches of religions that do not respect these virtues are not the true religion (Islam being the common contemporary example) is the normal liberal response, whether pluralist or universalist. Therefore pleas for liberal pluralism, within which differing *modus vivendi* or ways of life that differ from liberalist values are to be affirmed, either tend to founder on the lack of any defining standard by which ways of life can be deemed acceptable or unacceptable or seek to use the democratic process as a means of asserting the importance of the credentials of these virtues, but recognising that others may differ and that is to be tolerated, if not positively affirmed. This is the multiculturalist dilemma. How can liberal pluralism ignore the substantive moral issues at stake whilst affirming differing *modus vivendi*? Perhaps the most significant difference between pluralist and universalist liberalism is that the stance of the former tends to be apologetic and the stance of the latter dogmatic. Thus, for example, liberal pluralists tend not to be in favour of invading other countries to create 'regime change'; nor do they tend to support laws based on secular principles with regard to public dress, but they do protest against human rights violations.

This relates back to our discussions of multiculturalism in Chapters 1 and 2 and the comments by Wright in Chapter 3, as well as the other writers in that chapter and this chapter.

It can be argued that the dilemma this tension raises is one that is more significant for religious education than for any other subject in the curriculum. It can also be argued that this is one reason why religious education becomes a significant and important subject within the curriculum. No other subject has to attend to these values dilemmas as a means to its justification. Is the subject intrinsically a vehicle for the attestation or contestation of religious truths, values and practices? Is this the position of Wright to some degree? Does it stand for the values that religions promote when seen through a liberal lens; a means of contributing to community cohesion through promoting toleration, and even respect, for the ways of life of others? Is this the position of Jackson? It is arguable that the subject is confused, caught on the horns of its own ideological dilemma.

In this way we can see how the differing approaches represented in Chapter 3, and this chapter, deal with this dilemma differently. Whilst Jackson wishes to deal with religion as a cultural phenomenon, Wright wishes to present it as a theological reality. Hay wishes to present it as an inherent aspect of humanity, which can be described as spirituality. As a result Jackson's approach is essentially modernist but Wright, Copley and Hay in different ways occupy positions that contain pre-modernist stances, because they are making claims as to the religious or spiritual truth in what religions say and this translates into their advocacy of pedagogies that call for the recognition of that truth (either the truth of a religion's claim or the truth of religions in general).

The relevance of this for worldview analysis should be clear. We are now in a position to take stock of the complexity of religious education as a curriculum discipline overtly concerned with values questions, clarify its intrinsic and extrinsic aims and determine what pedagogic methodology would best serve it, as a result, as it mutates into worldview analysis. But the values issue now predominates. Gray again, on John Stuart Mill:

> His [John Stuart Mill's] mistake was to suppose that liberalism must be understood as a system of principles, and to seek to replace reference to principle by the guidance of tradition – as if any late modern society, least of all his own, contained only one tradition. If contemporary societies contain several traditions, with many people belonging to more than one, politics cannot be conducted by following any one tradition. It must try to reconcile the intimations of rival traditions. As Hobbes understood, it must seek *modus vivendi*.
>
> (Gray 2009: 50–51)

In conclusion, he states:

> Because *modus vivendi* rejects the claims of liberal values to universal authority, it is bound to be at odds with the prevailing philosophy of liberal toleration. Yet *modus vivendi* can still claim to be a renewal of the liberal project. For it constitutes the search for peace that liberal toleration began.
>
> (Gray 2009: 51)

We have to ask to what extent *modus vivendi* or different ways of life are possible and acceptable, as Gray claims, in a search for peace that goes beyond liberal toleration. And, as Gray rightly states, this is an ongoing project. Therefore, it is not just a matter of academic debate but an enquiry in which we should involve our students.

If we consider, for example, what principles might not be exchangeable for peace we might return to Wright's comment in Chapter 3 in which he used the example of acknowledging the anti-gay rights position of Rocco Butiglione, Italian European Affairs Minister, as an appropriate way of demonstrating why liberal values should not be hegemonic (see pp. 56–57). However, it would be appropriate to consider that striving for gay rights is a principled issue, in the same way as women's suffrage was at the beginning of the twentieth century. Also, this right is now enshrined in the United Nations Declaration of Human Rights. Would we regard women's suffrage as a disputable right today and somehow negotiable? Would gay rights come in the same category? If not, what is the relationship between liberal values, toleration and reconciling the intimations of rival traditions (Butiglione's position is based on his Roman Catholic beliefs)? And, to what extent is peace, or tolerance, or respect, to be prosecuted as a desired condition when put against the compromises that might be entailed in rights and freedoms? Other issues also face us contemporaneously, for example hijab and wearing religious symbols within public spaces, on which French and English law differ. Enquiries into these issues with students engage them with the questions that we face and which they as future adults will inherit. The learning of students and the challenge for them to determine their values positions is part of the project. This brings us to the politicisation of worldview analysis.

## The politics of worldview analysis

This section specifically focuses on the way in which we need to engage students with the fact that worldviews have political dimensions by virtue of which, if we ignore them, our understanding of worldviews is impoverished and incomplete and can, actually, be distorted by prevailing moral, social and cultural pedagogic discourse: a domestication of worldviews.

Eagleton states:

> There is good reason to believe the outrageous violence of Islamist terrorism is among other causes a reaction to this [western and latterly specifically United States] imperial history.
>
> (Eagleton 2009: 101)

He presents Aijaz Ahmad's argument that Islamicist dissenters in the Arab world have seen their rulers 'mortgaging their natural resources to the West; squandering their rentier wealth on luxury for themselves and their ilk; and building armies that may fight one another but never the invader or occupier' and '[t]hey have seen so many countless civilians getting killed by the Americans and Israelis that they do not deem their own killing of civilians as terrorism, or even comparable to what their own people have suffered. If anything, they would consider themselves *counter*-terrorists' (Ahmad 2008: 12, 14; quoted in Eagleton 2009: 101–2).

In Iran, as Ahmad points out, the institution of Khomeini's regime as a hard-line Islamic state developed as a result of a revolution predicated on Western support for the autocracy of the Shah's regime, which, with the support of the CIA, eliminated the influence of communists and social democrats, in order to ensure the imposition of the monarchy. As a result it was a radical form of Shia Islam that eventually came to power. Thus, the West is complicit in the outcome it now opposes. Of course there are other examples, including the support for the mujahedeen in Afghanistan against the Soviets that eventually led to Taliban rule in Afghanistan, and the way in which this influenced Pakistan's foreign policy and made it vulnerable to such an outcome.

If we are to recognise that religions are both faith-based traditions and ideologies (in the same way as non-religious worldviews can be), then we need to pay attention not only to their ideals, enshrined in their foundational documents, but also to the way in which they act politically and morally within the world, as a result. In short, we must pay attention to the way in which these worldviews impact upon affairs in a situated, or contextualised, manner.

Concepts and states of affairs that we prize are not always complementary to one another. We may prize peace but we also prize freedom. We may prize freedom but we also prize security. We may oppose violence, but, for most of us, not on all occasions when other things are at stake. This unresolved debate and complex state of affairs are something our students should engage with. If imperialist liberal activity produces violent responses to preserve other ways of life, to what extent should we acknowledge the value of other ways of life and respect them? Or, to what extent should we oppose them if they infringe on what we understand to be important rights and virtues? Politically these are complicated questions, and ones that do not only have ethical dimensions, but ones we should not refrain from asking.

## Worldview analysis and conceptual enquiry

### Islam

Rebecca Costambeys has produced two enquiries that exemplify how we might examine facets of worldviews in the classroom. In the first, in a unit of work on Islam, she focuses on the concept of Islam itself, as obedience leading to peace, and contextualises it in two of its main beliefs and practices: salat and jihad. For salat an image of Muslims at communal prayer is used. For jihad, one of the attack on the Twin Towers on 9/11. What might the link to Islam in both images be? This is enriched by resource material, including an interview with a female Muslim plane hijacker, Leila Khaled, a resource on how party politics in the USA affects support for Israel, and a resource explaining the importance of salat.

In the Evaluate element of the cycle she asks the following questions: in what ways do these represent differing forms of obedience, levels of obedience and interpretations of obedience leading to peace (Islam)? Why do you think different Muslims express this obedience differently? Are they compatible and what is their aim? (Costambeys 2006). Another way of approaching these issues is by using jihad as the key concept, with salat and the attack on the Twin Towers being seen as two different interpretations of jihad. This would then provide an enquiry into different interpretations of jihad, differing motivations and interpretations behind the concept, and the need to determine the relationships formed between greater and lesser jihad.

### Freedom

In a second, separate, enquiry she focuses on the key concept of freedom with the key evaluative question: 'What is freedom? Is it a price worth paying for?' First students are asked to complete the statement: 'To me freedom means . . .' (Communicate). Then they are asked to note down any similarities and differences in the expressions of freedom they have given (Apply). Enquire focuses on the Statue of Liberty and what idea of freedom that stands for, with an analysis of its symbolism and its reference to immigrants. They are also encouraged to think of how freedom can be understood differently when it is understood as freedom from . . . as well as freedom to . . . Contextualise focuses on different quotations on freedom from the American Constitution, Martin Luther King, Osama Bin Laden and John Lennon in *Imagine*, and an image of Ground Zero in New York. What are the issues raised? Evaluate begins with students making their own statement about freedom that they would place in a national constitution. They then have to reflect on what the cost of defending this inter-pretation of freedom might be, drawing on the previous resources from the Statue of Liberty, the American Constitution, Martin Luther King, Osama Bin Laden and John Lennon as differing interpretations of freedom (Costambeys 2008).

Following on from Rebecca's work are two enquiries I have written on El Salvador and Che Guevara.

## El Salvador and the concept of discipleship

This article was originally published in *Hampshire RE Secondary News* (Erricker 2003) and has been adapted here. The enquiry focuses on the concept of discipleship. El Salvador at the time of the assassination of Archbishop Oscar Romero is the context. Starting with Enquire, the concept of discipleship in Christianity is introduced using the teachings of Jesus. The task is to examine these texts to determine what is entailed in discipleship and its demands.

Contextualise introduces background information on El Salvador at the time:

■ The country's government is supported by the United States.

■ 14 families in the country own 90 per cent of the wealth.

■ The Roman Catholic Church is divided in its allegiance: most priests do not speak out against the government but some, such as Oscar Romero, have started to do so because of the inequality and intimidation of the people by the government and army.

■ Most people live in rural villages and are illiterate.

The class is divided into groups, each group represents a village and one student acts as the priest, who is literate.

The groups each receive the same information on information sheets. These are based on reports at the time. They then receive instruction sheets, which ask them to respond to the event that happened in the information sheet and require them to make a decision, with the concept of discipleship in mind. The teacher does not wait for them to have made up their minds about each situation in the information and instruction sheets before moving on to the next because that is not how things would happen in real life. The groups have to respond as things happen according to each new piece of information they receive. Each information sheet makes more pressing demands on them.

First, they have to decide whether they will shelter a woman and her two children running from government troops who have burned down her village and killed her husband, who was suspected of supporting rebels.

Second, they have to decide how to respond to a pastoral letter from the archbishop urging them to stand up for the Church's teachings and speak out against the government. They then discover he has been assassinated.

Third, they receive information about a Christian nun who is supporting the guerrillas and is asking for whatever help they can give.

Fourth, a rebel arrives, bringing information on the death of a young Christian who died of starvation whilst fighting beside him. At this point analysing text itself can be helpful. It is a diary entry written as a prayer:

> You know, God, that I have tried by all means to be faithful to you . . . This is why I am here. I see love as the urgency to solve the problem of the other person, in whom you meet me. I left everything I had and came here. Today is perhaps my Thursday and this night is my Friday. I lay everything I am in your hands with a trust that has no limits because I love you . . . because you are my Father. No death is useless if the life has been heavy with meaning, and I think this is true of us. Goodbye, Lord; until that Heaven of yours, that new world we desire so much!

For students to make a decision in role as to how they respond to this text they need to recognise the worldview it presents and how it does that. In the context of the role play they have little time, but beyond it, in discussing their response, attention can be focused on the effect it had on them and, beyond that, attention given to an analysis of it. What are the constitutive aspects of it that characterise the worldview presented? For example, faith and the way that is expressed with the individual narrative contextualised in a 'master' narrative (the reference to Thursday and Friday); the belief that violent means can achieve salvific ends (the Kingdom of God is not explicitly mentioned but lies behind this); the imperative of loving others and the sacrifice and martyrdom that may entail; the primary ethic of obedience that all the previous entails; the sublimation of individual aspiration, even personal survival, to that ethic, but with the expectation of reward. In carrying out a textual analysis of this kind students not only come to some evaluation of the constituents of worldviews but also, in this case, some appreciation of what might be the purpose of prayer.

Fifth, their priest himself informs them of his decision to leave them and fight with the rebels (as did the Colombian priest Camillo Torres).

Evaluate consists of reflecting on the experience of going through the role play and the issues arising in relation to discipleship. What did this experience tell them and how did that affect their ability to act as disciples? What would discipleship mean for these people in this situation? To what extent is discipleship possible in this situation? Is discipleship compatible with a violent response to injustice?

Communicate and Apply then ask the students to place the idea of resistance to injustice (their response to discipleship) in the context of their own lives and issues of these kinds that are prevalent today. In what sense and to what degree do they think they share a responsibility to act, and if so how?

The point about the learning in the enquiry is to recognise the demands of discipleship (from a Christian perspective) and how Christians might interpret and respond to those demands differently (or at all); then to place the idea of taking on responsibility for similar issues in their contemporary situation as a question considering the sort of social justice that Christian discipleship, according to Gospel texts, requires. This is not an exercise in telling students, or getting them to realise, the importance of discipleship and it is not expected that they are meant to value it themselves at the end – they are enquiring into it and responding from their point of view, on the basis of the learning undertaken and the questions they have had to engage with (for a version of this cycle, see Erricker 2005).

## Che Guevara and the concept of liberation

Starting with Enquire, give students a number of texts in which 'liberation' and 'liberate(d)' are used. These can range from adverts and TV commercials to news reports involving, for example 'the liberation of . . .' or 'being liberated from . . .' Students discuss the different meanings and connotations of the way the concept is used, in relation to liberation for what and as liberation from what. Students can then compile a set of meanings of the concept, then also discuss what its opposites might be (desire, repression, etc.) and how other terms might be associated with the idea of liberation in a positive or negative way.

In Contextualise Che Guevara is introduced with the question: 'Was Che Guevara a liberator?' An information sheet on main events in his life can be introduced, some of the statements he made and quotations from his diaries and excerpts from DVDs that have been produced from recent films made about him. Start with this quotation:

> No soy un libertador
> Los liberators no existen
> Son los pueblos quienes
> Se liberan a si mismo.
> I am not a liberator
> Liberators do not exist
> Only the people
> Can liberate themselves.

Using the diverse texts with the question 'Was Che Guevara a liberator?' in mind, students work toward a press interview with him (here one student, or the teacher, prepares to be Guevara and others are journalists). The student or teacher 'hot seated' as Guevara has to answer the questions devised by the other students and put his or her own point of view. Then students record the extent to which the interview did or did not reflect evidence of him being a liberator.

Evaluate can start with a photograph of the dead Che Guevara. Underneath write: liberator or terrorist? Present some posthumous comments, for example Regis Debray's tribute: 'Che is not one of those who can die – an example and a guide, he is immortal – because he will live on in the heart of each revolutionary'.

As a contrast, get students to read this email on a Che Guevara website:

I was just wondering . . . Is it possible to honour a man as Che Guevara, who has killed so many people? I myself am very non-violent, so how can what he did be fair? What right did he have to take another person's life?

(www.voy.com, 26 May 2006).

Ask students to discuss and decide on judgements for their decision and present these and vote in a plenary session.

To create a simpler cycle the concept of freedom can be used with the key evaluative question: 'Freedom fighter or terrorist?' To extend the evaluation ask students to write an obituary on Che Guevara using the key concept as the thread. (This is a revised version of Erricker 2003: 6–13.)

These conceptual cycles raise some of the issues discussed previously and seek to address the complexities involved in determining how different political and values responses can be evaluated by students.

## Worldview analysis and community cohesion

Earlier in this chapter I made reference to community cohesion in relation to its contribution to worldview analysis and values education. I suggested that there was some confusion as to how this should be approached due to the liberal and liberalist agendas at play and the modernising political ideology that invites religions to contribute to this venture and schools to promote it. There needs to be some resistance to these influences, otherwise students will simply be taught values that are sympathetic to it rather than engage with the issues that this initiative confronts. Simply put, if there is a need to promote community cohesion, then there must already be a problem, or set of problems, that makes community cohesion difficult to achieve. What are those problems and how can we respond to them effectively?

Below I have presented selected extracts and the findings of an initial project carried out by a number of selected Hampshire and Southampton schools to investigate what issues community cohesion raised locally and what recommendations students could make, as a result. This was constructed as an enquiry into the concept of difference, with the key question being what differences do we celebrate, which do we tolerate and which do we find difficult?

## Is difference good for us? A report on Hampshire's and its neighbours' community cohesion project

### Introduction

This is a report on Hampshire and its neighbours' pilot project on community cohesion conducted between March 2007 and March 2008. It was financed by Hampshire County Council and NASACRE (National Association of Standing Advisory Councils for Religious Education), with the Westhill Trust and Aim Higher. It involved six schools, secondary and primary, in Hampshire and Southampton. The purpose of the project was to conduct a pupil-led enquiry into the concept of difference and determine to what extent and in what ways forms of difference impacted on these pupils' experiences and attitudes as they pursued the project. At the end of the project pupils presented their findings and recommendations at a conference held at the University of Winchester on 27 March 2008. These findings and recommendations suggest that pupils were significantly affected by the experience of undertaking the project, that their attitudes were affected by participating with pupils in schools other than their own, and that their perceptions of difference and awareness of the significance of community cohesion were appreciably altered.

## Background

Following events of recent years, most obviously the attack on the Twin Towers in New York, the London bombings, the activity of Al Qaeda, the wars in Iraq and Afghanistan and the recognition that suicide bombers were often 'home grown', there has been an increasing concern about the cohesiveness of British society, on the one hand, and 'homeland security', on the other (for relevant recent literature on this subject, see, for example, Ali 2007; Husain 2007; Omaar 2007; Spencer 2006). Because recourse to religion has been a significant feature of these events it has impacted locally in Hampshire on some attitudes to what, previously, would have been seen as positive, or at least unobjectionable, multicultural educational provision; most obviously visits to places of worship by schools.

Headteachers began to notice and report increasing parental withdrawal of consent for their children's participation in these events, especially in 2006–2007. This withdrawal was especially related to visits to a local mosque in Southampton but also applied elsewhere, Sikh Gurdwaras and Hindu Mandirs. One primary school headteacher reported a 10 per cent withdrawal rate by parents when she had previously run the visit to the mosque for several years with no parents withdrawing their children. Reasons for withdrawal could be varied but one given was that a parent was afraid of her child being bombed (there had been a recent bombing of a mosque in France). Therefore it would be wrong to conclude that it was just attitudes to Islam that were changing when the safety of offspring was also an issue.

## Approach

The approach to the project was particularly influenced by two publications, *Brideless in Wembley* by Sanjay Suri (2007) and *Guidance on the Duty to Promote Community Cohesion: Draft Guidance for Schools and Consultation Response Form* (DfES 2007).

In one of his studies for his book *Brideless in Wembley* (Suri 2007), Sanjay Suri parked himself on a bench in Leicester's largest shopping centre, the Shires, to conduct a study, between 12 p.m. and 5 p.m., concerning 'what I dared to call myself a rough quantitative survey . . . I wanted to see how many came to The Shires with their ethnic own, and how many with others . . . the mall seemed a random enough place to see who might step out in mixed ethnic company' (Suri 2007: 23). After five hours he reports:

> I scanned perhaps 12,000 to 15,000 people. Through this I counted only 44 people in 12 mixed groups . . . Most of these mixed groups were clearly university students . . . If this observation was

valid we were talking zero point zero zero something by way of multicultural Leicester . . . Leicester did not appear a multicultural city, only a city of adjacent cultures. Perhaps not even that; just variously monocultural.

(Suri 2007: 25)

In *Guidance on the Duty to Promote Community Cohesion: Draft Guidance for Schools and Consultation Response Form* we read:

[W]e passionately believe that it is the duty of all schools to address issues of 'how we live together' and 'dealing with difference' however controversial and difficult they might sometimes seem.

(DfES 2007: 1)

The project's approach sought to address ways in which pupils from different backgrounds could work together and ways in which issues related to 'difference' could be addressed.

## Method

In February 2007 the Executive Member for Education endorsed this two-year project on community cohesion. The project has now been running for one year with pilot schools in Hampshire and Southampton. This report is a commentary on its progress and presents the findings and recommendations made by pupils involved at the conference held on 27 March at the University of Winchester. This conference was attended by sixty-four guests, including headteachers, faith representatives, education officers and Council and SACRE members.

Six schools have been involved to date: four Hampshire and two Southampton schools, comprising three primary (Year 6 students) and three secondary schools. The schools were paired in order to construct joint enquiries into the concept of difference as they experienced it in their lives and in relation to those differences they celebrated, were comfortable with or found challenging. Selected students from these schools met to carry out this enquiry, which involved creating cultural maps, questionnaires, learning walks and research training. Attention was paid to ensuring that these pairings took account of diversity, especially in terms of social and cultural background and ethnicity. Sixty students presented at the Winchester conference.

The students' enquiries in the twinned schools developed different foci. In the Fairfields Primary and Costello Secondary enquiry the main focus was the admission of new Nepalese students into Costello Technology College and the need for them to be socially accommodated within the school population. Pupils already in the school needed to be prepared for the arrival of the new Nepalese students. Since Fairfields is a multilingual school its Year 6 students were able to work with Costello students in determining how best to address these issues.

In the Wildern and Cantell enquiry the main issues were media misrepresentation of minority groups and the connected issue of parental attitudes. Since the schools had very different catchment areas, resulting in a diverse ethnic population in Cantell and a mainly white population in Wildern, they explored how this affected perceptions of difference within their own schools and through meeting together with named partners for each pair of pupils.

In the Mount Pleasant Junior School and Kings Copse Primary School enquiry issues concerning meeting students from different socio-economic and ethnic backgrounds emerged and the impact of those on perceptions of identity and on pupil confidence and preparation for later life. For example, one pupil wrote: 'When I was back at [my] school I felt safe and at home' and another wrote: 'We may have differences but it doesn't mean we can't be friends'. A strong feature of this partnership was the way in which students were paired up across schools and the preparation for meeting up done through photographs and email communication. When the students at Mount Pleasant initially received a photograph of the Kings Copse students there was some apprehension. One student observed they were all white and asked whether they were all posh and Christian.

In all schools they initially produced 'cultural maps' before meeting the students of their twin school. These consisted of mapping their important weekly and annual movements: whom they met with and why. This could be in relation to their family, friends, in school, out of school. These were then compared and commented on to get a sense of how their cultural lives were similar or different. These cultural maps were then compared, subsequently, with those of students at different schools, using a 'buddy' system of support.

The project was supported by Hampshire services, especially the RE inspectorate, the Intercultural Inspector, the Hampshire Archive and Local Studies, as well as other members of the Hampshire Inspectorate and Advisory Service (HIAS). This brought together varied expertise and ensured that the Hampshire initiatives already in place, Rights, Respect and Responsibility and the conceptual enquiry methodology in the Agreed Syllabus Living Difference (Hampshire, Portsmouth and Southampton Councils 2004), were used to maximum combined effect to give direction to the project.

Outside funding was made available through the National Association of SACREs (NASACRE) and the Westhill Trust, Aim Higher and the University of Winchester and through the Hampshire Archive and Local Studies. Additional funding was provided from the Rights, Respect and Responsibilities budget and the Hampshire Interfaith budget. The RE inspectorate received £18,000 from the education budget to lead and support the project.

The project also involved providing training for faith representatives to inform them of the role they might be invited to play in progressing the community cohesion enquiry by pupils in schools. To date two separate training days have been delivered to a total of seventeen representatives. It is intended that these training opportunities were also made available in 2008–2009 as the project undertook its second year.

## Findings and recommendations

The schools involved presented their findings and recommendations at the conference on 27 March 2008. The main findings and recommendations are summarised below.

*Findings*

- Parental involvement in community cohesion would be beneficial.
- Media representation of schools and of religions can prevent cohesion amongst children and misperceptions of religion.
- A felt lack of national identity prevents cohesion.

■ It is very easy for students from different schools to see each other as rivals and to initially be uncomfortable working together and make judgements based on 'race' and class. They need opportunities to share activities and experiences and to develop a project dependent on shared responsibilities and outcomes in order to enable friendships and respect to develop, for example shared whole school days would allow for mixed team sporting and cultural activities. Working toward a shared presentation on this project increased commitment to one another.

■ The admission of new pupils of different ethnicity and mother tongue can result in tensions if students in the school are not prepared for this by the school.

*Recommendations*

The recommendations below were agreed by the students of the schools involved and presented for consideration by Hampshire County Council and the management and governors of their own schools:

■ Prepare students for intake of new student admissions of minority cultural and ethnic backgrounds by educating pupils into the cultural heritage of new pupils.

■ Provide a buddy system for new students.

■ Ensure space is available for minority groups to meet together and use strategies to ensure that mixing together occurs more readily within school and class time, for example by using teamwork strategies in classroom learning.

■ Support and monitor the integration of new students and provide opportunities for them to speak with other students about their cultural identity and experiences.

■ Teach cohesion in and out of school.

■ Address community cohesion with Years 6 and 7 as students transfer to a new school.

■ Introduce the Rights, Respect and Responsibility initiative in all schools.

■ Link schools with different catchments in Key Stage 2 and Key Stage 3.

■ Involve parents through parent conferences/culture days.

■ Provide greater financial resources to enable schools to address community cohesion effectively.

## Summary and future action

The above recommendations will now be considered by Hampshire County Council and the management and governors of the schools involved to determine how they might result in improved provision for social cohesion.

The completion of this one-year pilot project is intended to provide the basis for schools in Hampshire and Southampton to respond effectively to the duty to promote community cohesion.

# Community cohesion: a further analysis and the broader issues

Community cohesion is an extension of multiculturalist policy, but with a new accent. Difference was mentioned, rather than diversity, in the DfES guidance quoted on p. 188. There was still a desire amongst teachers involved in the project to celebrate diversity rather than address difference. Since the duty to promote community cohesion was introduced, a Prevent Strategy has been promoted which actively seeks to identify any Muslim activity that might be subversive. The Hampshire project, over its second and third years, focused more specifically on an increasing number of Nepalese students enrolling in schools in the north of the county, close to Aldershot and the Gurkha barracks. The issue as to whether Gurkha veterans could claim British nationality was in the news in 2009. Support for this was championed by the actor Joanna Lumley. The significance of the community cohesion initiative is linked to the liberalism and liberalist agenda discussed earlier. Is it to be understood as a further multiculturalist initiative or is it something more hard-edged in identifying issues and solving problems that multiculturalism has failed to address? Could it be construed as more liberalist than liberal?

The project initially undertaken by Hampshire was based on conceptual enquiry. This meant that the students themselves had to identify issues and report findings and recommendations based on their experience of undertaking the project. This ensured, as far as was possible, that students would report their own views, as was the case with the Children and Worldviews Project (see Chapter 4). This involved them in some uncomfortable experiences as they stepped outside their usual cultural and relational boundaries. They encountered aspects of worldviews and socio-cultural circumstances other than their own and this influenced the sorts of categorisations they habitually made. For example, in one secondary school I conducted a seminar with the twelve students in which we focused on the question 'Within this group what differences do you notice that are most significant?' One Year 11 boy stated that the answer was self-evident. There was one black girl in the group and that identified her as significantly different. She responded to this with vigour. Nevertheless, he wasn't being racist, just honest in relation to his enculturated response to the question asked. In another secondary school, twinned with the first, I asked the same question of a further group of twelve students. The answer was wholly different, since it would not have been possible to distinguish difference by skin colour. Here the consensus was personality. When students from the two schools met in the second school this was an uncomfortable experience for the Year 11 student from the first school, simply because a cultural truism no longer applied.

Similarly, with two of the primary schools involved there was anxiety over 'colour'. One school was an inner-city school with a diverse but mainly non-white intake. The other was a preponderantly middle class, 'white' school in a suburban area. By car they were just fifteen minutes from each other but also worlds apart. When group photos were emailed in advance of meeting up the students from the latter school asked whether those at the former school were all Christian and posh. From the perspective of worldview analysis this gives us a sense of how classifications are formed based on specific types of enculturation, social groups, class identity, geographical location and belief systems. If community cohesion is to be an effective educational initiative it has to operate at a level of discomfort, seeking to disturb students' worldviews and promote collaboration across difference. This, of course, goes beyond the remit of religious education and invites interdisciplinary collaboration as well, to which we turn in Chapter 9.

## Worldview analysis as a critical endeavour: a summary

Consider Figure 8.1. The two axes are from religious to secular and faith to ideology. In order to begin to determine the characteristics of a worldview we might plot them against this chart, with its four quartiles. This would at least give us reference points for how worldviews differ in relation to significant definitions or characteristics. To what extent is a particular worldview faith based or ideologically driven? To what extent is it overtly religious or secular?

You can start by thinking about specific religions. Can they, as a whole, be put in one place? In Christian terms where would the Society of Friends be situated? Where would the Roman Catholic Church be situated? Are those categories still too broad to situate religions with reasonable accuracy? Liberation theology? Where would the secular society or Richard Dawkins go? What about Wahabbi Islam? Sufi Islam? Or corporate free-market capitalism? The Church of England? Unitarianism? Theravada Buddhism? Humanism? Jehovah's Witnesses, Strict Brethren and the evangelical Christian right? Where would you put the terms fundamentalist or literalist? Authoritarianism? Where would you put liberalism? Where would you put liberalist? Inclusivist and exclusivist? You can create your own map of quadrants and continuum on each axis. What

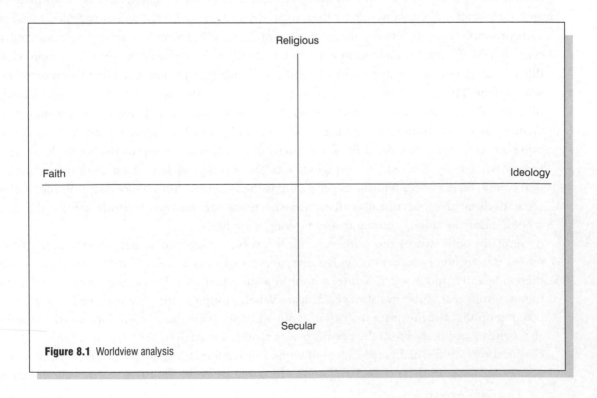

**Figure 8.1** Worldview analysis

may turn out to be surprising is what you put where. This can revise our taxonomies of worldviews into something more subtle than just religions. Movements that may, in traditional and conventional terms, be linked together under a larger religious or non-religious or denominational category can end up in surprisingly different places to other movements in the same conventional category and can be surprisingly closer to other movements thought to belong in a very separate one. The object is to see the complexity involved in worldview analysis.

Additionally, the question can be asked: 'Where would you position yourself, your own worldview and its values?' One aspect of this to consider is that we may, because of the characteristics and values of our own worldview be predisposed toward and against certain others, but if we are to regard the analysis of worldviews as an academic and disciplinary exercise we can't, as a result, teach in favour of some and not others. The point is to recognise the characteristics of particular worldviews and engage with them seeking to understand why they are as they are, what motivations underlie them and what the contexts are in which they are situated, before we come to an evaluative judgement about them which challenges them and also challenges ourselves.

For students, we have to ask what concepts they need to enquire into for them to be able to conduct worldview analysis with a sufficient form of literacy. This then presents us with an idea of progression commensurate with the ultimate aim of our task.

## Conclusion

Worldview analysis involves recognising how ideas shape the world we live in and inform its events and changes. Understanding this and responding to it is a prerequisite of mature participation in democratic society. It is what we should challenge our students to aspire to within their learning and our teaching. It relies upon religious literacy and the capacity to interpret worldviews, within religious education, and complementary abilities within other disciplines.

Worldview analysis as a critical endeavour that we lead our students toward should not reflect an uncritical acceptance of:

- religious teachings as idealised expectations;
- culturally informed values;
- religious beliefs and practices as inherently good and appropriate.

Worldview analysis should promote:

- a curiosity to evaluate contemporary issues;
- a willingness to take insights from religious sources seriously;
- a resistance to being told how to think and to embrace the Kantian imperative to have the courage to think for oneself;
- the idea that enquiry is the prerequisite to making informed judgements and finding one's own voice;

■ the recognition that worldview analysis may be best undertaken through interdisciplinary investigation.

Before we enter the classroom we need to ask ourselves whether what we intend to do reflects progressing students' abilities in this way.

# 9

# Interdisciplinary education

## Introduction

The idea of interdisciplinary education is a fascinating one. Not only does it promote the proposition that learning in isolated disciplines is not the most effective means of learning but it also opens up new principles on which learning can be based. To explore these, first I want to distinguish interdisciplinarity from the more familiar term 'cross-curricular' learning. They are wholly distinct in conception.

Cross-curricular learning implies that subjects will contribute to an overall theme that draws together the learning. It is most prevalent in primary schools but is now also advocated by QCDA in the secondary curriculum. Of itself, this provides no rigour and does not pay specific attention either to enquiry-based learning or the need to attend to disciplinary requirements of skills progression, specific to subject disciplines, or a conceptual focus or foci on which to base the enquiries.

By contrast, interdisciplinary education demands that the integrity of the discipline is maintained and that skills and conceptual focus are paramount. These are the principles that determine how following more than one discipline in an enquiry can, potentially, be more educationally enriching than learning through separate and discrete disciplines. It follows that interdisciplinary enquiry is only worthwhile if the enquiry itself demands more than one discipline in order to be sufficient and meaningful and relevant for students. Therefore, when conceiving interdisciplinary enquiry it may be that certain obvious areas of the curriculum as it stands obviously lend themselves to it or that new, relevant areas for enquiry suggest themselves.

The examples given below offer ways in which interdisciplinary enquiry can be undertaken and subjects on the curriculum that it could involve. These are primarily illustrative of ways in which RE can be involved in effective interdisciplinary enquiry in collaborating with other subject disciplines. The possibilities for interdisciplinary education are much broader and richer than my suggestions, but having grasped the principles on which these are based RE teachers should be able to make a rich contribution to interdisciplinary development.

## Example 1: The Holocaust

A simple and useful example is the study of the Holocaust. The Holocaust is studied in both history and RE at Key Stage 3. Historians tend to focus on the rise of the Nazi party and the impact of that on changes in Germany during the early 1930s and the Second World War in relation to Jewish persecution, sometimes including other persecuted minorities: Poles, Romanies, communists and homosexuals. RE tends to focus on the Jewish Holocaust from the point of view of empathy for Jews, often (and sometimes exclusively) using Anne Frank as a particular case study. There is also a tendency in RE to use the Holocaust instrumentally as a moral lesson on persecution, with the 'this should never happen again' strapline. Whilst it is appropriate that RE focuses on the Jewish experience, overt moralising is not, because this undermines student enquiry and fails to take account of the genocides that have happened since that time, which suggest we have not learned much from it.

If we regarded the Holocaust as an interdisciplinary enquiry how might this be undertaken? From a history perspective the evaluative question might be: who did the Nazis persecute and why? From an RE perspective, if we want to concentrate on the Jewish experience of the Holocaust, the evaluative question might be: what was the effect of the persecution Jews experienced during the Holocaust? In both cases the key concept to be engaged with is persecution: what does it entail, why is it undertaken and what are its effects?

The historical enquiry and the RE enquiry are complementary; they inform one another and enrich the overall complexity of the learning. From a history perspective students will come to understand and respond to causes, effects and interpretations of persecution based on evidence provided by sources. This will fit into material already covered within the history curriculum on the rise of Hitler and the Third Reich. In the way it approaches persecution it may well range wider than an RE focus on Jewish experience. From an RE perspective the experience and responses of Jews to persecution can focus on Jewish interpretations of experience, with Jewish concepts, especially that of Covenant, as understood in Judaism, at their heart, and examining the writings of survivors in relation to that. By this I do not mean that all Jews were religious and adhered to this idea but that it was a defining concept for religious Jews, and this is reflected in the memoirs of survivors, whose faith was both strengthened and lost accordingly. In this way the RE enquiry is distinctively different from the history enquiry because it is specifically attending to the particularity of Jewish perspectives (which falls within the discipline of RE but not that of history). The complementarity of learning in the two enquiries is crucial since you want the students to bring their learning together so that this becomes one area of study. The key question to ask is whether persecution is an important concept for the students to focus on: will it enrich their understanding of human affairs, society and world events both in an historical and, by transfer, a contemporary fashion in relation to diversity and difference, identity and political affairs? If the answer to this is yes, then that is the most important reason for carrying out this interdisciplinary study and the reason why the whole is more than the sum of its parts. In this sense, the purpose of interdisciplinary enquiry transforms the aims of education: the focus is on the development of the learner not just the contribution it makes to the discipline of being an historian or the study of religions, though it does that as well. The complementarity of this approach, in relation to both preserving the integrity of the disciplines and identifying their contribution to the development of mature individuals, is its fundamental rationale.

## Example 2: Values education

This example directly relates to the problems often encountered with RE at Key Stage 4. Many schools encounter difficulties with the compulsory nature of RE at Key Stage 4 for all students. This is the case because students are reluctant to study RE when they have not chosen to do so and where the teaching of the subject does not engage them. In some schools this results in something of a crisis; the subject becomes anti-educational on the grounds that its compulsory nature is not reflected in an equivalent meaningfulness in what is learned. Within some schools the recourse to a short course GCSE provides a qualification, which can ameliorate the problem but still does not provide sufficient educational grounds for the compulsory legal requirement; relevance is not obvious because religion is still the compulsory factor even if syllabuses reflect ethical and philosophical emphases. A form of values education (though it may take differing titles) can overcome this problem if well conceived and planned to a sufficient methodological purpose. In order for this to work the starting point should be the value of what is studied for the students' development, not how do we cover more than one subject at the same time, or the idea that this is just another name for RE.

Here I present two case studies, from Park Community College and Wildern College, both in Hampshire and both with performing arts specialisms.

## Park Community College

Park Community is on Leigh Park estate, outside Portsmouth, which was at one time the largest housing estate in Europe. Its catchment is white working class, among whom the role of education is not highly valued by all parents. In 2009 it was placed first in the country in terms of value added. Its RE at Key Stage 4 was previously counter-productive and, as a result, it was removed from the timetable. But what was required was something more drastic because the students had an insular mentality, with a sense of territory and belonging that often only extended to the parameters of the estate. For example, it was very difficult to fill any work-experience placements off the estate, whilst those on it were oversubscribed. What was required was to extend the boundaries of both student confidence and curiosity, in effect their spiritual, moral, social and cultural horizons. In the words of the present headteacher, it was about contributing to students becoming adults who were both resilient and lived authentic lives. A first step toward this was to create a values education programme from Year 7 to Year 11 so that this could be systematically addressed. Incorporated within this programme were RE, Citizenship, PSHE (Personal, Social and Health Education) and careers education. This would not have been effective if the process of learning had not been attended to in detail; this was based on the conceptual enquiry methodology explained in previous chapters. Approached in this way the focus for development and progression is based on the concepts studied and the context provided. This ensures that students come to understand the relevance of the concepts in their own lives and take ownership of their learning, applying it to their own lives, whilst recognising the significance of the concept for others in society and how it applies in national and global contexts. They also stop thinking in terms of different subjects being studied, since learning across what were previously understood as discrete and different parts of the curriculum is integrated. Here are two examples of conceptual cycles of learning that have been developed, which have an obvious RE basis, but go beyond that. Santina Cavanagh is the teacher in charge of the Values Education Programme and is responsible for the planning I have included below. She is a geography rather than RE specialist. She has remarked that the enquiry process approach used has had a dramatic effect on the way she now teaches and that many of the students now regard Values Education as their favourite subject.

## Cycle 1

*Key concept: goodness*
*Key question: Is being good the path to a better life?*

*Communicate and Apply*

First consider the meanings of the term 'good' in relation to sport, TV programmes and being a teacher. This draws out the criteria for 'goodness' that we use for different examples.

Next consider what 'good' means when we think about being 'a good person'. This introduces the distinctively moral dimension of 'goodness' in contrast to the above.

Next pose the question 'How do you know you are being good?' Here three categories are introduced: good at home; good at school; good in the community. This explores the idea of what 'being good' means in different contexts.

Next pose the question 'Why do we choose to be good or not?' This draws out the question of agency and choice and how we exercise that: motivations, attitudes and incentives.

*Enquire*

A modern version of the Good Samaritan story is introduced based on local rivalry between Portsmouth and Southampton football fans. Who will help whom? Here the inclination to do good is tested and the question of what 'goodness' means in the context of this Christian teaching is raised.

*Contextualise*

The contextualisation focuses on the Hindu idea of karma in relation to the consequences of good and bad acts (in this life and beyond) and what makes those acts good or bad. This raises further issues concerning differing understandings of 'goodness' and its effects. By now students have become aware of the varying understandings of, standards of and effects related to 'being good' in differing contexts – religious, cultural and ethical – and how these are variously inter-twined.

*Evaluate*

Within: The question is posed 'How does being good help someone in the Hindu faith?'
Without: We return to the initial key question posed 'Is being good the path to a better life?' (Cavanagh 2008).

Points to note:

1 In going through the above cycle differing learning techniques for collaboration, decision making and enquiry are used, with which the students become familiar over time. At Park, Kagan structures, Community of Enquiry and philosophy for children techniques are often employed.

2 PowerPoint slideshows are used to present information, stimuli and tasks throughout the cycle.

3 The point of the enquiry is for students to grapple with the concept of goodness and the key question is focused on their decision making. The material introduced both contributes to this process and gives them understandings of goodness from differing faith perspectives, but not with the prime aim of investigating those perspectives as part of understanding an overall worldview, as might be the purpose within an RE-focused set of cycles.

4 Addressing values education is the context for the cycle, and in doing this it also addresses aspects of RE, Citizenship and PSHE in an integrated fashion.

## Cycle 2

*Key concept: mistakes*
*Key question: Is making mistakes part of the journey?*

*Communicate and Apply:*

First the song 'The Circle of Life' is introduced from the Disney film *The Lion King* and students are asked to consider what is meant by the circle of life and what messages the song gives in relation to the idea of making mistakes. The following refrain, in particular, is analysed and students are asked to relate it to their experience of the emotions and qualities cited:

> It's the Circle of Life and it moves us all through despair and hope
> Through faith and love till we find our place on the path unwinding in the Circle the Circle of Life.

Next, the teacher poses her own experience of mistake making in the context of her driving test, which she had to take four times. Under the heading of 'Learning from my mistakes' she cites the reasons why she failed.

Students then have to respond to the question 'Why was it important that Mrs Cavanagh learned from her mistakes?'

Next, students are asked to reflect on their own mistakes and then answer the following question, in groups: would you take a pill that allowed you to forget your mistakes in life?

*Enquire*

Scenes from the film *Groundhog Day* are introduced as a stimulus. The main character Phil keeps making mistakes and can only move on to his 'next day' by rectifying his mistakes. By analysing the scenes students are asked to determine whether a consequence of Phil changing was him being allowed to move to the next day. Students complete the sentence 'I think Phil was allowed to move to the next day because . . .' or the sentence 'I believe that Phil did/did not learn from his mistakes because . . .'.

*Contextualise*

In Contextualise the cycle introduces change and mistake making on a grand scale through the Hindu ideas of time and reincarnation (relating back to but progressing the 'circle of time' idea introduced previously).

> Just as a person puts on new garments, giving up old ones, similarly the soul accepts new material bodies, giving up the old and useless ones.
>
> (Bhagavad Gita 2.22)

And:

> The soul is never born nor dies; even if the body is slain the soul is not.
>
> (Bhagavad Gita 2.20)

Here students discuss the impact of the idea of reincarnation and the soul on the ideas of change and making mistakes. How does this affect our understanding?

*Evaluate*

Two questions are then discussed:
Within: If you are Hindu and you believe in reincarnation does it have a positive or negative outcome on your life in relation to making mistakes?
Without: We return to the initial key questions posed: Is making mistakes part of the journey? And does it ultimately become frustrating if you don't learn from your mistakes? (Cavanagh 2008a)

Points to note

1 The contextualising material based on Hindu ideas of change and reincarnation is used instrumentally to broaden students' horizons as to the way in which mistakes are conceived and understood at the same time as introducing ideas from a different worldview in a relevant way.

2  The use of the circle of life material from *The Lion King* in Communicate and the *Groundhog Day* material in Enquire foreshadows the Hindu material and ideas introduced so that they are not incongruous and represent a further challenge to students' thinking.

3  The cycle on mistakes directly addresses the school's vision for preparing students to be resilient adults.

4  Again, addressing values education is the context for the cycle and in doing this it also addresses aspects of RE, Citizenship and PSHE in an integrated fashion.

# Wildern College

Wildern was an underachieving school with a 24 per cent A*–C GCSE success rate. This was improved to 86 per cent in 2008. In 2009 the RE department decided that, despite offering two short-course GCSEs with high success rates for all students, it was not offering the sort of course that was relevant to all students at Key Stage 4. As a result it changed to a full-course option for those who decided to continue with RE/RS and a broader course for all students to satisfy legal requirements for RE but inclusive of Citizenship and other elements that befitted learning for adult life. It introduced its Culture, Society and Identity (CSI) provision, which would be internally assessed according to its own mark scheme based on the levels in the Living Difference Agreed Syllabus, with additional components relevant to the material introduced covering local, national and global components. Wildern is a rights-respecting school, identified as such by UNICEF through the Charter on Universal Rights, Respect and Responsibility and the Charter on Children's Rights. Therefore this new syllabus reflects these characteristics and obligations.

Wildern begins its Key Stage 4 programme in Year 9, having reduced Key Stage 3 to two years. In Year 9 the CSI provision begins with cycles based on the five key concepts of Humanity, Community, Free Expression, Media and Islamophobia. The overall title is Being Human and the overall question asked is 'What does it mean to be human in relation to the way we treat others who are humans?'

The cycle on the key concept of Humanity examines the key question of 'If we don't show humanity to one group of people should we claim to show it to all?'

In Communicate and Apply it examines the extent to which our sense of humanity depends on sharing similar views in our class. In Enquire it examines the extent to which views of Britishness equate with our understandings of humanness and the extent to which we regard Britishness as exclusive of others who are human. In contextualise it examines two different case studies of immigration and contrasts the way in which attitudes have been applied to them in terms of their humanity based on ideas of Britishness. Evaluate then asks students to determine what our idea of humanity entails if we don't treat all humans equally and the extent to which our idea of Britishness influences our idea of humanity.

The second cycle on the key concept of Community examines the key question of 'How do we decide who belongs to a community and who does not?' In particular, the cycle focuses on the issues associated with the European Union as an example of a community beyond the idea of Britishness as defining community belonging in the spirit of nationhood.

In Communicate and Apply students are asked to define and exemplify what constitutes being part of a community and then determine examples of what stops a community being a community: what issues prevent this. In Enquire the European Union is introduced and students have to determine what sort of community this is; its values and economic base and the positive and negative implications involved, for example economic migration. In Contextualise students are asked to consider case studies of change brought about by legislation of the European Union and whether this contributes to the EU being understood as a good example of community or not. What are the issues involved and how are they overcome? Evaluate asks the question whether there can ever be a sense of global community proceeding from the above, and if so how? Students, from their prior learning, have to determine the values and economic principles that might need to be evoked if this is to be possible.

The third cycle on Free Expression asks 'Do we all have a right to freedom of expression?'

In Communicate and Apply students are first given a set of symbols and asked how they can be interpreted – for example the swastika and its interpretation within our own culture given its Nazi significance, but not the only way in which it can be interpreted given its more ancient symbolic value within Jain culture. They are then asked to decide what examples of symbolism can be deemed acceptable or unacceptable, given their various definitions, within our own culture. In Enquire the different notions of authority are linked to freedom of expression through the fatwah on Salman Rushdie's *Satanic Verses* and the limits on freedom of expression entailed in that. How does the locus of authority impinge on freedom of expression and why? In Contextualise the tension between freedom of speech and censorship is explored with a case study on the incident of the teddy bear called Muhammad in Sudan, for which a British teacher was imprisoned, but later released. What does this say about the problems inherent in bases of authority, freedom of expression and sensitivity to other cultures? Evaluate: should expression be wholly free? Consider this in relation to the work done so far on humanity, community and free expression.

The fourth cycle on media asks 'Why do we have media freedom?' This, of course, links directly to the last cycle on freedom of expression and the issues that raises in democratic countries.

In Communicate and Apply students are first asked what 'media' means and what the media's role is. Then students, in groups, are asked to create a media story that will gain attention and to consider the stories they have devised and which will gain most attention and why. Enquire shows a series of media items which gained the most attention and least. Students have to identify why. Contextualise presents a case study of smaller Muslim protests gaining more media attention than IRA protests that were much larger. Why is this the case? What does it say about media influence? Evaluate: do we shape media views or does the media shape our views?

The fifth cycle on Islamophobia narrows down the focus and relates it to a significant community cohesion issue. It asks the key question 'Should we engage with Islam or oppose it?'

This cycle starts with Enquire. Therefore it directly engages with the idea of Islamophobia. Here various quotations are introduced from the media and other sources on the nature and influence of Islam. Students are asked to consider to what extent such a thing as Islamophobia exists and, if it does, what are its distinctive characteristics. Here the question pursued is 'Is Islam a threat to our society or not?' Students determine their responses. Contextualise probes deeper into case studies of Muslim activity in society through analysing instances of discrimination against Muslims, e.g. in relation to ordinary Muslims being discriminated against, by reading articles such as that of the girl who was refused service in a shop in the UK. Students then discuss the articles and then identify how we have come to this situation in Britain today. Then they read about examples of Muslims who have acted in a subversive role in relation to British democratic interests. How does this influence our view of Muslims and whether all members of a group can be treated the same? Evaluate starts with the question 'Does Islamophobia mean Muslims are the new Jews?' Here previous work on the Holocaust will be drawn upon, but the emphasis of the question is on whether we need to Other Muslims or not. This is related to the idea of tolerance and related issues introduced earlier in this cycle and within the overall unit of work. The Evaluate element then raises the key evaluative question 'Should we engage with Islam or oppose it?' The question is linked to the concept of Islamophobia and any evidence of its manifestations. Communicate and Apply focus on whether Islamophobia is a new form of intolerance or not. Students are asked to what extent tolerance can be extended, in their view, in the light of Islamophobia, and to whom: to Muslims, to Islamophobes? Would that require a change in the law, for example regarding religious discrimination, and to what extent would that change our society and the students?

The above is an outline of a significant amount of the planning for Year 9 in the CIS Key Stage 4 curriculum (Collins *et al.* 2009).

Points to note:

1  As with all planning produced according to the conceptual enquiry methodology the focus on the key concept within each cycle is paramount, and as the unit of work progresses through its five cycles so the students are encouraged to draw on learning and concepts from earlier cycles and bring those to bear in later ones. This provides continuity and threads in the learning and adds to the depth and complexity achieved.

2  A focus is also maintained on the development of students' skills, dispositions and attitudes. Students are encouraged to change their minds and give reasons for changes in their thinking and attitudes as evidence of the impact of the learning on themselves and their own progression.

3  The unit of work is clearly linked to ideas of citizenship and community cohesion and mature decision making in groups. Individuals' thinking is woven into group and class activity and decisions in a democratic way, reflecting the school's commitment to the processes that underpin being a rights-respecting school.

4  The unit of work extends students' thinking beyond themselves and into an increasingly larger picture of change and influence in societies at a national and global level, in which religion has its influence amongst other factors, within which it is interwoven and not necessarily distinct.

5  By the end of the unit of work students are expected to be able to speak with some evidenced and informed authority on the relationships between the key concepts studied: the

significance of the idea of humanity and what that entails; the significance of the idea of community and its value and larger possibilities; the significance of freedom of expression and its possible limits; the role of the media as an agent in reflecting and influencing opinions and values; the manifestation of Islamophobia and its connections to a variety of expressions of Islam and to Otherness in society.

## Example 3: Religious education and science education

This guidance on creation and evolution was originally produced for Hampshire SACRE. The innovation in the guidance was its interdisciplinary nature, the idea that science educators and Religious education specialists would jointly teach it. For a considerable time there have been options in Religious Studies GCSEs in which scientific topics have been included, such as creation and evolution. But these are taught by RE specialists within an RE syllabus. This opens up a cause for concern. In researching for the guidance I became aware of just how difficult it would be for students to grasp the intricacy of the theory of evolution unless it was taught by a science specialist. Certainly, as a religious studies specialist I would not be qualified to teach it. This begs the question of whether a serious enquiry into the creation–evolution debate could ever really be constructed on any other than an interdisciplinary basis. This suggests that when introducing students to debates of this kind interdisciplinary collaboration is essential to achieve the depth and complexity required.

## Creation and evolution: incompatible explanations?

### Introduction

The following needs to be noted:

■ It is not recommended that evolution be taught in science at Key Stage 3. Therefore this approach would most usefully be included at Key Stage 4 and above, unless used specifically for gifted and talented students.

■ The creation–evolution debate is included in some Religious Studies GCSE syllabuses already but what is proposed here is that science specialists be involved by teaching evolution and religious studies teachers teach theological responses to that.

The approach set out below is based on an interdisciplinary enquiry between RE and science. This does not mean that teaching theological views on creation should be part of the science curriculum. Rather, this presents a new model of working in an interdisciplinary fashion – across and between disciplines – as advocated by the QCDA. Using a conceptual enquiry methodology makes this possibility an easy one to achieve. At present I have only included theological arguments within a Christian context but this could be made more comprehensive by incorporating arguments from the perspective of other religions. Generally speaking it is protagonists within theistic religions that are most engaged with and, sometimes, critical of the theory of evolution because of the doctrine of creation at the heart of those religions. However, it needs to be stressed that not all proponents of monotheistic theologies are antagonistic to evolution. Nevertheless, a more comprehensive treatment would involve incorporating Muslim and Jewish responses and those of other religious traditions. You may wish to go to the DfES/DCSF and QCDA guidance on this, which does include reference to religions beyond Christianity:

- DFES and QCA National Framework for RE (2006) *How Can We Answer Questions about Creation and Origins?*, http://www.qca.org.uk/libraryAssets/media/qca-06-2728_y9_science_religion_master.pdf;

- DCSF (2007) *Guidance on the place of Creationism and Intelligent Design in Science Lessons*, http://www.teachernet.gov.uk/docbank/index.cfm?id=11890.

There are already a significant number of further resources we can employ for examining science and religion, and the creation–evolution debate. A recent one of value is *Religion and Science in the 21st Century Classroom*, by Tonie Stolberg and Geoff Teece (2008). This is published by the University of Birmingham School of Education. Copies are available from Tonie Stolberg and he can be contacted at t.l.stolberg@bham.ac.uk. This sixty-page booklet offers a pedagogical approach based on enquiry that can easily be adapted to a conceptual approach. It covers a number of aspects of fruitful engagement between science and religion, providing ideas for lessons, informative background reading and suggestions for resources. For a fuller volume there is Tonie L. Stolberg and Geoff Teece (2009) *Teaching Religion and Science: Pedagogy and Practice*. The importance of Stolberg's and Teece's approach is that it is well informed, thorough and thoughtfully worked out in terms of teaching and learning, using the idea of 'skilful means' borrowed from the Buddhist tradition as a basis for enquiry. Their Lesson 2 (pp. 46–48) focuses on the evolution debate. I have adapted that below to suit a conceptual enquiry methodology and give a more detailed focus to the enquiry activities. Also, there is the fairly recently published *Science and Religion in Schools: A Guide to the Issues for Secondary Schools* (The Science and Religion in Schools Project (2006)). This provides detailed materials and lesson plans that can be adapted to a conceptual enquiry methodology. It also includes perspectives from different religions.

## Creation–evolution debate

Summary of points:

- Evolution is a theory propounded by Charles Darwin based on empirical scientific method.
- Natural selection is the key idea that Darwin uses.
- Natural selection is in tension with any idea of design.
- Creationism, as a literal reading of the account in Genesis, is at odds with Darwin's theory.
- Metaphorical readings of Genesis have been aligned with evolution as a scientific theory by some theological responses.
- The idea of a God who created individual species does not accord with the principle of natural selection.

- Sometimes creationism (the literal reading of Genesis) and intelligent design are conflated as religious understandings that oppose evolutionary theory.

## Cycle of learning

*Key concept: evolution*

### Enquire

*Key question: What did Charles Darwin (1809–1882) mean by evolution and what issues does it raise?*

*Activity 1: Use the Darwin cartoon (Figure 9.1) to introduce students to the issues*

- Why would a cartoonist portray Darwin in this way?
- What does the cartoon suggest about the way his theory of evolution has been interpreted?
- Who would want to portray Darwin in this way and why? (Scientists/religious believers?)

Encourage students to see how his theory of evolution led to him being portrayed as a monkey-like character and why both scientists and religious believers might have found that amusing at the time.

**Figure 9.1** Anti-Darwin cartoon, 1800s

*Source:* Published in *The Hornet*, a British satirical magazine, 22 March 1871.

So far students have been speculating and relying on their prior knowledge and powers of observation and deduction. Use their responses to move on to an analysis of Darwin's evolutionary theory (below):

Darwin's theory of evolution is based on five key observations and inferences drawn from them. The biologist Ernst Mayr summarised these. From this summary the following argument can be made.

Because species have great fertility not all of their offspring can grow into adulthood. Populations remain at roughly the same size. Food resources are limited and remain relatively constant. Therefore there will be a struggle for survival.

In sexually reproducing species generally no two individuals are identical. Variation is rampant and much of this variation is heritable. Therefore those with the 'best' characteristics are likely to survive and these will be passed on to their offspring. The population that survives will evidence these advantageous characteristics and these will be passed down through generations. This is natural selection in which organisms with the most beneficial genetic traits are more likely to survive and reproduce. Because variation is ongoing in this process Darwin imagined that it was possible that all life could be descended from an original species.

*Activity 2: Students can work in pairs or groups*

Students should:

- highlight what they think are the most important statements this text makes;
- discuss and note any implications for our understanding of ourselves as a human species that this raises;
- register any disagreements in discussion in the group and feed those back to the class;
- compose a statement that they think explains what 'natural selection' means.

In using this text students need to:

- be acquainted with the meaning of some of the technical terms used;
- consider the difference between *evidence* and *inference* (evidence is empirically based but inference consists of other conclusions that may be drawn from the evidence);
- scrutinise the text to identify when it is summarising theory, when it might be hypothesising (making a statement that still needs evidential support), when it is making statements of a persuasive nature that are based on opinion.

To answer the key question students also need to consider the following questions:

- What are the key aspects of evolution as a theory; for example, what does 'evolving' mean?
- What other opinions and claims might this theory be in tension with and why?

## Contextualise

*Key question: In what ways are the following different responses to 'evolution' compatible or incompatible and why?*

Distribute the texts below amongst groups of students. Given that some of these texts are harder than others you can differentiate which group gets what text.

Ask the students in each group to discuss what significant point(s) the text is making and whether it is well made. Where more than one group has the same text, ask them to confer on their observations and judgements. For example, you could use the 'ambassador' technique here of one member of a group conferring with another group and feeding back, or put the groups together with appointed scribes.

Coming back together as a class, get feedback from the groups on the text they read, the observations it was making and the issue(s) that raises, and agree the issues and rank them. Discuss any areas of the debate that students feel require more information as a result.

### The Wilberforce–Huxley debate

Wilberforce's position: Darwin has not offered a causal theory but only a hypothesis. There is no explanation of how one species could evolve into another.

Huxley's position: Darwin's theory is an explanation of phenomena in Natural History based on an explanation of facts and the best explanation of the origin of species yet offered.

### The position of the Catholic Church

The Catholic Church distinguishes between the evolution of the body and the creation of the soul. The theory of evolution explains the origin of the human body but not the creation of the soul by God.

### Darwin's challenge to theological positions

Darwin's challenge to nineteenth-century theological positions was threefold:

- First, it refuted the idea that humans were individually designed by God.

- Second, it reinforced Lyell's geological evidence that the world was much older than the chronology of the Book of Genesis. Therefore there was no compatibility between a literal reading of Scripture and scientific evidence.

- Third, because it implied apes and humans have a common ancestor, there was no distinct act of creation and humans have no theological uniqueness in creation.

### Evolution as divine purpose?

Darwin's theory explained both the beauty of adaptations (such as the beak of the woodpecker) and the repellent examples (such as the wasps who implant their larvae in the bodies of caterpillars which then eat them alive from the inside).

Since evolution contains such cruelty how can creation be defended as the means to a divine end?

# Evaluate

*Key evaluative question: Is it possible to believe in both evolution and a creator God?*

The texts below consolidate and extend students' understanding and provide different perspectives on whether evolution and theological positions can be reconciled. You can select and amend as appropriate and use them in a similar way to the activities provided in Contextualise. The main thing is to draw out the way in which the issues in the debate over creation–evolution have been responded to.

- Creationism, creation science and intelligent design are three inter-related religious theories of creation.

- Creationism states that God created the universe and humankind according to the literal Biblical account in the Book of Genesis.

- Creation science seeks to prove the world was created by God but not through evolution and uses interpretations of scientific data to support the Genesis account.

- Intelligent design argues that the complexity and organisation of the world, based on observations in the world, leads to recognising that it can only be fully explained by an intelligent cause rather than natural selection. Therefore it must be the creation of God.

*An argument from design*

William Paley produced a particular explanation of the teleological argument (argument from design) in his *Natural Theology* (1802 [2008]: 1–13). This is its initial statement:

> In crossing a heath, suppose I pitched my foot against a *stone* and were asked how the stone came to be there, I might possibly answer that for anything I knew to the contrary it had lain there forever; nor would it, perhaps, be very easy to show the absurdity of this answer. But suppose I had found a *watch* upon the ground, and it should be inquired how the watch happened to be in that place, I should hardly think of the answer which I had before given, that for anything I knew the watch might have always been there.

The reason, he says, that he couldn't conceive of the watch having been there forever is because it is evident that the parts of the watch were put together for a *purpose*. It is inevitable that 'the watch must have had a maker', whereas the stone apparently has no purpose revealed by the complex arrangement of its parts.

*An argument against design*

> If there are any marks at all of special design in creation, one of the things most evidently designed is that a large proportion of all animals should pass their existence in tormenting and devouring other animals.

(Mill 1904)

*Evolution and God as compatible: humans as made in the image of God*

> Humans are described as made in the image and likeness of God (Genesis 1:26). How can theology understand this within an acceptance of the theory of evolution, within which human distinctiveness could be said to have evolved gradually?

The characteristics of humans that reflect being in the image of God and his likeness can be said to be:

1.  human rationality;
2.  authentic relationships involving love and compassion;
3.  creativity, which allows a deeper understanding of God, the world and human purpose.

It follows that humans had to be endowed with free will, in order to be like God, and that that presumes an indeterminacy or randomness in the world, which can be seen to be expressed in evolution, but which is necessary to both its purpose and that of humans. In the words of the Roman Catholic theologian Hans Kung, this provides a deeper understanding of God, of creation and of ourselves. Because God is Love there can be no coercion in His relationship with His creation.

### Evolution and God as incompatible

Darwinian evolution, specifically natural selection . . . shatters the illusion of design . . . and teaches us to be suspicious of any design hypothesis . . . I think the physicist Leonard Susskind had this in mind when he wrote, ' . . . modern cosmology really began with Darwin and Wallace. Unlike anyone before them they provided explanations of our existence that completely rejected supernatural agents'.

(Dawkins 2006: 118)

## Communicate

*Key question: What is your response to the idea of 'evolution'?*

Stimulus: Google Earth images can be evocative for stimulating debate. Try the accompanying question 'Can the universe be both majestic and meaningless?'

Here students are being asked to make and justify a personal response. This is different to the Evaluate part of the cycle but continuous with it. They need to decide what they can bring to the argument between evolution and the issue it raises for belief in God. Where do they stand?

This might begin by summarising the class conclusions on the Evaluate question and the differing standpoints people have taken. You want the main interaction to be students responding to the views of other students and reconsidering and justifying their own position in the light of that.

## Apply

*Key question: What are the implications of your response to the idea of evolution?*

Here Apply can focus on the consequences of the debate in Communicate. This can mirror the debate they have scrutinised in their enquiry. Thus, students need to consider how disagreement should be managed: by respecting each other's views or by seeking to focus on their illogicality, lack of sensitivity to human feeling (in the case of science) or lack of evidential reasoning (in the case of religion). Here is the point where you want them to confront whether we can tolerate different ideas and processes whereby we gain knowledge or not; whether it is the case that science and religion have two different functions (science telling us how and religion telling us why; science dealing in facts and religion in meaning) or not.

You may wish to organise a class debate at this point to finalise the enquiry.

## Further reading

Midgley, Mary (2002) *Evolution as a Religion*, London and New York: Routledge.

Poole, Michael (2008) *Creationism, Intelligent Design and Science Education*, http://www.cis.org.uk,

Poole, Michael (2009) 'What's in a Name? Creation and Creationism, Design and Intelligent Design', *Resource* 31(3): 7–10.

Stolberg, T. and Teece, G. (2008) *Religion and Science in the 21st Century Classroom*, Birmingham: University of Birmingham School of Education.

Stolberg, T. and Teece, G. (2009) *Teaching Religion and Science: Pedagogy and Practice*, London: Routledge.

The Science and Religion in Schools Project (2006) *Science and Religion in Schools: A Guide to the Issues for Secondary Schools*, Manchester: Trafford Publishing.

## Example 4: Interdisciplinary learning in the humanities, arts and beyond

Here I shall cite three different case studies, the first devised by Penny Morgan and her colleagues at Beaufort College, Winchester, the second by Simon Harrison and colleagues at Swanmore College in Hampshire and the third devised by Richard McFahn, formerly of Fernhill College in Farnborough, Hampshire and now County Adviser for Humanities in West Sussex.

## Façade: attitudes to facial disfigurement

This is an adaptation of Penny Morgan's report in *Hampshire RE Secondary News* (Morgan 2008). The project was initiated by the art department, influenced by an exhibition at the National Army Museum by the artist Paddy Hartley, artist in residence. The exhibition was a response to and interpretation of the personal and surgical stories of First World War servicemen who were treated with pioneering surgical reconstruction of facial injuries by Sir Harold Gillies.

Six subject teams were involved in the subsequent school project: humanities, English, ICT, mathematics, drama and art. The humanities contribution was a conceptual enquiry cycle based on the concept of facial disfigurement. The cycle was planned for three lessons.

### Communicate

An image of facial disfigurement was displayed. Students noted down words that came into their heads, discussed their responses and why they had made them. No value judgements were made but some students were clearly somewhat embarrassed by their initial responses.

## Apply

This related back to previous work done on the First World War and trench warfare in history. Students were then given information about facial injuries suffered and the reconstructive surgery initiated by Gillies. Students were then asked to revisit their original responses to the image shown and note down any changes they felt now they knew something about it. Responses were then discussed again.

## Enquire

A quotation from the curator of the National Army Museum is shown:

> The impact of Gillies' work cannot be underestimated. Contemporary society glorified its war dead but recoiled from its war wounded. In Sidcup, where the hospital was based, street benches were painted a different colour to warn locals that disfigured hospital patients might sit there. Yet for seven years after the Armistice was signed, Gillies rebuilt not only faces but self-esteem damaged by the war. The trauma suffered by his patients was matched only by the courage they showed. But this exhibition is about remembering, not Remembrance. Some died. But most lived.
>
> (Morgan 2008: 18)

Discussion then centred on what the different coloured benches might suggest about attitudes to facial disfigurement and the students were set the task of writing a poem entitled 'Different Coloured Benches'.

A verse of one Year 9 student stated:

> Although the colour may indicate
> The sitter's current aesthetic state
> It doesn't reflect their inner-self
> And could affect their mental health.
> (Morgan 2008: 18)

## Contextualise

Here use was made of the mathematics department's work on the golden mathematical rules for beautiful faces, to do with ratios. The context was plastic surgery today, which had developed from the pioneering techniques of Gillies but now was applied to ageing and beautification rather than the treatment of horrific injuries. An advert was devised for a website promoting the service and whose appearances it could enhance. Differences between this surgery and that discussed previously emerged and facelift pictures from the internet were explored in order to ask why people might feel the need to have this sort of surgery today.

## Evaluate

The issues raised in the Contextualise tasks led to the forming of evaluative questions:

- Who is likely to want these procedures and what makes them worthwhile?
- What does this suggest about our attitudes to facial beauty today?

Responses to these questions were also informed by the enquiries carried out in other subjects' contributions to the project.

The confidence gained by staff participation and students' responses to this project has led to other interdisciplinary projects being initiated: a two-week project on the Olympics and a Geography-led project on Antarctica.

# A Humanities and Arts Enrichment Programme

This programme is followed by all students at Swanmore College in Year 9, from January until July, covering two terms, and this acts as a foundation enrichment curriculum prior to embarking on Key Stage 4. It was introduced in 2009.

Each half-term is constructed around a theme. For each theme there are six challenges, of which the pupils choose three. Themes are constructed under broad headings that provide coherence and relevance for the pupils. These are:

- Identity: Who am I?
- Where are we going?
- Money makes the world go round?
- America, China and us.

Within each theme pupils tackle their challenges consecutively in blocks of twelve periods. The curriculum is delivered by a team of twelve staff from across the humanities and arts departments. Each challenge relates to the theme and is delivered by a pair of teachers. Each challenge also relates to a lead subject discipline or disciplines. For example, below are the six challenges offered in 2009 for the theme 'Identity: Who am I?'

1 *The mask*: pupils create masks that reflect the kind of person they aspire to be. They use stimuli from different cultures and work with a sculptor to experiment with different styles and techniques.

2 *Personal identity*: looking at the world in the twenty-first century, how it has changed and how it has and will affect me, who I am and who I will become.

3 *Social masks*: practical workshops on perception of identity from different points of view based on the work of Growotoski and his perception of social masks. Through this pupils will explore their own personal identity.

4 *What does being British mean in the twenty-first century?* The history of British migration and aspects of what makes being British special will lead pupils to explore the identities of different regions of the UK and also place Britain into its worldwide context.

5 *Past personal*: what can my family history tell me about myself? By researching their ancestry back into the nineteenth century using online resources, pupils will explore how their own identity is formed by their ancestry. They will also judge how significant past events and changes were for their ancestors.

6   *Expressing identity through music*: how can music reflect culture/background? Does the music celebrities perform reflect what type of people they are? Pupils market themselves as a brand and create music that would accurately represent them.

At the end of each theme there is an event designed to celebrate pupils' achievements and this is shared with the wider school community. This can be a performance, an exhibition or a resource such as a website.

Pupils have a 'learning log' for each challenge to enable feedback on their progress to be recorded by teachers, peers, parents and themselves. Progress is directly related to a skills and attitudes framework based on the QCDA three aims for all students to become: successful learners, confident individuals and responsible citizens.

This example of an interdisciplinary enquiry into personal identity uses identity as a connecting theme across different enquiries rather than as a key concept pursued with the same conceptual enquiry methodology across the different disciplines involved.

A fuller report on this initiative will be published in *Cross-curricular Teaching and Learning in Humanities* (Harris and Harrison forthcoming).

## Making learning meaningful: broadening the horizons of history education

This is a history-based example but is relevant to teachers of all subjects, including RE. A study carried out by Richard Harris and Terry Hayden (2006) researched pupil perceptions of why they learned history. It found that many of the reasons students thought they learned history were erroneous, such as: for employment purposes; so that we didn't make the same mistakes in the future; that there was no point in studying the past; for 'trivial pursuit' reasons; studying the past to 'pass it on'; to appreciate how lucky we are to live in the present; and some reasons that were very good ones that few students mentioned.

Although a majority of pupils reported that they regarded school history as useful, there were large numbers of pupils who could not say why it was useful, or who gave reasons which bore little relation to the stated curriculum justifications for the subject.

In relation to these findings it was suggested by Ben Walsh of the History Association, a teacher of and GCSE examiner in modern history, that 'each department should be looking at ways that they can connect the history that they teach to the lives of their pupils' (see Williams 2003: 1).

In response to this situation Richard McFahn produced an enquiry that sought to do that. It focused on Charles Calonne (1734–1802) and the key question 'Why couldn't France get out of debt?' (McFahn 2009). Calonne was the French Finance Minister prior to the French Revolution. He became a figure of hatred because of his advice to tax the first and second estates (the church and nobles). As a history enquiry this bears no relationship to students' lives, but by using the conceptual enquiry methodology the enquiry is broadened to relate it to them and the present. It begins with the income and expenditure of Mr McFahn, the teacher, in order to understand how he can balance his books. At the end it then returns to the present, at this time 'credit crunch' and the options available for the Chancellor of the Exchequer in Britain to balance his books. Both of these analyses are detailed and present hard choices, especially the latter, relating to changes in taxation, who should pay how much tax and whether payments on services (hospitals, teachers, etc.) should be reduced. Thus, it is the key concept of debt that creates the link to making the enquiry meaningful to students.

McFahn reported an increased engagement by students when he related the enquiry to the present and a willingness of students to examine the difficult financial options available and make judgements. In making this connection the enquiry was also demanding the development of skills beyond the history curriculum into economics, citizenship and related to managing personal finances.

## Conclusion

Interdisciplinary enquiry needs to enrich learning by going beyond subject disciplines but also by including them, as relevant, and building on their strengths and integrity. It also has to be relevant, or meaningful, in relation to students' lives. In this way it can offer more than the traditional subject-based curriculum can provide. In the examples presented above a number of different possibilities have been suggested, but there are many others that could be provided. In some of these RE might provide a lead role, in others it is the contribution it can make to values education or ethical dimensions of a project that matters. This is not to suggest that religious education should lose its particular distinctiveness, any more than other disciplines, but it should be prepared to look beyond itself and ask what it can offer to interdisciplinary learning. As a first step in planning an interdisciplinary enquiry it is useful to identify an RE enquiry already planned and determine how it could be enlarged or augmented to relate to a further discipline to which it is germane.

# Bibliography

Ahmad, A. (2008) 'Islam, Islamisms and the West', *Socialist Register*, London: Merlin.

Ali, A. H. (2007) *Infidel: My Life*, London: Simon & Schuster.

Astley, J., Francis, L. J. and Robbins, M. (eds) (2007) *Peace or Violence: The Ends of Religion and Education?*, Cardiff: University of Wales Press.

Atherton, J. S. (2009) *Learning and Teaching: Bloom's Taxonomy*, http://www.learningandteaching.info/learning/bloomtax.htm.

Barnard, H. C. (1961) *A History of English Education from 1760*, London: University of London Press.

Barthes, R. (1972) *Mythologies* (trans. A. Lavers), London: Paladin.

Baumfield, V. (2007) 'Editorial: Religious Education and Schwab's Four Topics of Education', *British Journal of Religious Education*, 29(2): 125.

Bell, A. (1985) 'Agreed Syllabuses of Religious Education', in I. Goodson (ed.) *Social Histories of the Secondary Curriculum: Subjects for Study*, London and Philadelphia: Falmer Press.

Berkeley, R. with Vij, S. (2008) *Right to Divide: Faith Schools and Community Cohesion*, London: The Runnymede Trust.

Bhagavad Gita (2004), London: Longman.

Blaylock, L. (2005) 'Aung San Suu Kyi', in J. Mackley (ed.) *Developing Primary RE: Special People of Faith*, Birmingham: RE Today Services.

Bourdieu, P. and Passeron, J.-C. (1990) *Reproduction in Education, Society and Culture*, 2nd edn, London and California: Sage Publications.

Bowen, J. (1981) *A History of Western Education, Volume 3: The Modern West*, London: Methuen.

Bowker, J. (1996) 'World Religions: The Boundaries of Belief and Unbelief', in B. Gates (ed.) *Freedom and Authority in Religions and Religious Education*, London: Cassell.

The British and Foreign Bible Society (1972) *The New English Bible*, Oxford: Oxford University Press.

Calhoun, C., LiPuma, E. and Postone, M. (eds) (1996) *Bourdieu: Critical Perspectives*, Cambridge: Polity Press.

Cavanagh, S. (2008) 'Is Being Good the Path to a Better Life?' (unpublished).

Cavanagh, S. (2008a) 'Is Making Mistakes Part of the Journey?' (unpublished).

Chadwick, P. (1997) *Shifting Alliances: Church and State in English Education*, London: Cassell.

Chater, M. (2006) 'The Big Curriculum, How Do RE, Citizenship and Spirituality Sit in a Changing, Diversifying Curriculum?', 7th International Conference on Children's Spirituality, Winchester, 26 July.

Collins, R. *et al.* (2009) 'Being Human' (unpublished).

Commission for Racial Equality (2007) *A Lot Done, a Lot to Do: Our Vision for an Integrated Britain*, London: Commission for Racial Equality.

Commission on Integration and Cohesion (2007) *Our Shared Future*, London: Commission on Integration and Cohesion.

Cooling, T. (1994) *Concept Cracking: Exploring Christian Beliefs in School*, Nottingham: Stapleford House.

Copley, T. (1997) *Teaching Religion: Fifty Years of Religious Education in England and Wales*, Exeter: University of Exeter Press.

Copley, T. (2000) *Spiritual Development in the State School*, Exeter: University of Exeter Press.

Copley, T. (2005) *Indoctrination, Education and God: The Struggle for the Mind*, London: SPCK.

Copley, T., Savini, H. and Walshe, K. (2003) *Biblos Secondary Teacher's Handbook*, London: RMEP.

Costambeys, R. (2006) 'One Billion People Follow Islam, So What Does It Mean to Be a Muslim?', in Hampshire, Portsmouth and Southampton Councils, *Living Difference: The Secondary Handbook*, Winchester: Hampshire County Council: 366–392.

Costambeys, R. (2007) 'Humanism', *Hampshire RE Secondary News*, Spring Term 2007, No. 47, Winchester: Hampshire County Council.

Costambeys, R. (2008) 'Freedom Cycle', *Hampshire RE Secondary News*, Summer Term, No. 50, Winchester: Hampshire County Council: 21–24.

Costambeys, R. and Timms-Blanche, P. (2006) 'What Is the Problem with the World?', in Hampshire, Portsmouth and Southampton Councils, *Living Difference: The Secondary Handbook*, Winchester: Hampshire County Council.

Dawkins, R. (2006) *The God Delusion*, London: Bantam Press.

DCSF (2003) *Every Child Matters*, London: DCSF.

DCSF (2007) *Guidance on the Place of Creationism and Intelligent Design in Science Lessons*, London: DCSF (http://www.teachernet.gov.uk/docbank/index.cfm?id=11890).

Debray, R. (2002) *L'Enseignement du fait religieux dans l'école laïque*, Paris: Odile Jacob.

Debray, R. (2004) *God: An Itinerary* (trans: J. Mehlman), London and New York: Verso.

Derrida, J. (1981) 'Plato's Pharmacy', in *Dissemination* (trans. A. Bass), London: Athlone Press.

Dewey, J. (1902) *The Child and the Curriculum*, Chicago: University of Chicago Press.

DfES (2007) *Guidance on the Duty to Promote Community Cohesion: Draft Guidance for Schools and Consultation Response Form*, London: DfES.

DfES and QCA (2006) *DfES and QCA National Framework for RE: How Can We Answer Questions about Creation and Origins?*, London: DfES/Qualifications and Curriculum Authority (http://www.qca.org.uk/libraryAssets/media/qca-06-2728_y9_science_religion_master.pdf).

Eagleton, T. (2009) *Reason, Faith and Revolution: Reflections on the God Debate*, New Haven, CT, and London: Yale University Press.

Eliade, M. (1959) *The Sacred and the Profane*, New York: Harcourt, Brace & World.

Eriksson, K. (2000) 'In Search of the Meaning of Life: A Study of the Ideas of Senior Compulsory School Pupils on Life and Its Meaning', *British Journal of Religious Education*, 22(2): 115–127.

Erricker, C. (2003) 'Viva Che!?', *Hampshire RE Secondary News*, Autumn Term, No. 38, Winchester: Hampshire County Council: 6–13.

Erricker, C. (2005) 'El Salvador: A Role Play-Contextualising in the New Methodology for Teaching and Learning,' *Hampshire RE Secondary News*, Autumn Term, No. 44, Winchester: Hampshire County Council: 10–19.

Erricker, C. (2006) 'Learning Strategies and Concept Based Cycles of Learning: Aung San Suu Kyi', *Hampshire RE Secondary News*, Spring Term 2006, No. 45, Winchester: Hampshire County Council.

Erricker, C. (2007) 'The Crucifixion in Art: A Creative Form of Assessment', *Hampshire RE Secondary News*, Spring Term 2007, No. 48, Winchester: Hampshire County Council.

Erricker, C. (2009) 'A Buddhist Approach to Alternative Schooling: The Dharma School, Brighton, UK', in P. Woods and G. Woods (eds) *Alternative Education for the 21st Century*, New York: Palgrave Macmillan.

Erricker, C. and Erricker, J. (2000) 'The Children and Worldview Project: A Narrative Pedagogy of Religious Education', in M. Grimmitt (ed.) *Pedagogies of Religious Education*, Great Wakering: McCrimmons.

Erricker, C. and Erricker, J. (2000a) *Reconstructing Religious, Spiritual and Moral Education*, London and New York: Routledge.

Erricker, C., Erricker, J., Ota, C., Sullivan, D. and Fletcher, M. (1997) *The Education of the Whole Child*, London: Cassell.

Freedland, J. (2006) *Jacob's Gift: A Journey into the Heart of Belonging*, Harmondsworth: Penguin.

Freire, P. (1980) *Pedagogy of the Oppressed*, Harmondsworth: Penguin.

Gaine, C. (2005) *We're All White, Thanks: The Persisting Myth about 'White Schools'*, Stoke on Trent: Trentham Books.

Geaves, R. (1998) 'The Borders between Religions: A Challenge to the World Religions' Approach to Religious Education', *British Journal of Religious Education*, 21(1): 20–31.

Geertz, C. (1983) *Local Knowledge*, New York: Basic Books.

Giroux, H. (2004) 'The Politics of Public Pedagogy', in J. Di Leo and W. Jacobs (eds) *If Classrooms Matter: Progressive Visions of Educational Environments*, New York: Routledge.

Gray, J. (2009) *Gray's Anatomy: Selected Writings*, London: Alan Lane.

Grimmitt, M. (1987) *Religious Education and Human Development*, Great Wakering: McCrimmons.

Grimmitt, M. (ed.) (2000) *Pedagogies of Religious Education*, Great Wakering: McCrimmons.

Hadi al-Hakim, A. (1999) *A Code of Practice for Muslims in the West* (trans. S. M. Rizvi), London: Imam Ali Foundation.

Halstead, M. (1995) 'Voluntary Apartheid? Problems of Schooling for Religious and Other Minorities in Democratic Societies', *Journal of Philosophy of Education*, 29(2): 257–272.

Hammond, J., Hay, D., Moxon, J., Netto, B., Raban, K., Straugheir, G. and Williams, C. (1990) *New Methods in RE Teaching: An Experiential Approach*, Harlow: Oliver and Boyd.

Hampshire, Portsmouth and Southampton Councils (2004) *Living Difference: The Agreed Syllabus for Hampshire, Portsmouth and Southampton*, Winchester: Hampshire County Council.

Hampshire, Portsmouth and Southampton Councils (2006) *Living Difference: The Primary Handbook*, Winchester: Hampshire County Council.

Hampshire, Portsmouth and Southampton Councils (2006a) *Living Difference: The Secondary Handbook*, Winchester: Hampshire County Council.

Hand, M. (2006) 'Answers for a Troubled World', *Hampshire RE Secondary News*, Summer Term, No. 46, Winchester: Hampshire County Council: 31–33.

Harris, R. J. and Harrison, S. (forthcoming) *Cross-curricular Teaching and Learning in Humanities*, London: Routledge.

Harris, R. J. and Hayden, T. (2006) 'Pupils' Enjoyment of History: What Lessons Can Teachers Learn from Their Pupils?', *Curriculum Journal*, 17(4): 315–333.

Hatch, B. (2006) *Diversity and Dialogue: Building Better Understanding between Young People in a Multi-faith Society*, London: Save the Children Fund.

Haught, J. F. (1995) *Science and Religion: From Conflict to Conversation*, New York: Paulist Press.

Hay, D. (1987) *Exploring Inner Space: Is God Still Possible in the Twentieth Century?*, London and Oxford: Mowbray.

Hay, D. (2000) 'The Religious Experience and Education Project: Experiential Learning in Religious Education', in M. Grimmitt (ed.) *Pedagogies of Religious Education*, Great Wakering: McCrimmons: 70–87.

Hay, D. with Nye, R. (1998) *The Spirit of the Child*, London: HarperCollins.

Hayward, J., Jones, G. and Mason, M. (2000) *Exploring Ethics*, London: Hodder Education.

Hegel, G. W. F. (1807 [1977]) *Phenomenology of Spirit* (trans. A.V. Miller), Oxford: Clarendon Press.

Hitchens, C. (2007) *God Is Not Great*, London: Atlantic Books.

Hull, J. M. (1998) *Utopian Whispers: Moral, Religious and Spiritual Values in Schools*, Norwich: Religious and Moral Education Press.

Husain, E. (2007) *The Islamist*. London: Penguin.

Jackson, R. (1997) *Religious Education: An Interpretive Approach*, London: Hodder and Stoughton.

Jackson, R. (2000) 'The Warwick Religious Education Project: The Interpretive Approach to Religious Education', in M. Grimmitt (ed.) *Pedagogies of Religious Education*, Great Wakering: McCrimmons: 130–152.

Jackson, R. (2004) *Rethinking Religious Education and Plurality: Issues in Diversity and Pedagogy*, London: RoutledgeFalmer.

Johnson, H. (2006) *Reflecting on Faith Schools*, London and New York: Routledge.

Judt, T. (2008) *Reappraisals: Reflections on the Forgotten Twentieth Century*, London: William Heinemann.

Kierkegaard, S. (1989) *The Sickness unto Death*, London: Penguin.

King, L. (2008) 'Implementing Living Difference and Conceptual Learning at KS4', *Hampshire RE Secondary News*, Spring 2008, No. 49, Winchester: Hampshire County Council.

LiPuma, E. (1993) 'Culture and the Concept of Culture in a Theory of Practice', in C. Calhoun, E. LiPuma and M. Postone (eds) *Bourdieu: Critical Perspectives,* Cambridge: Polity Press.

Lowndes, J. and Erricker, C. (2007) *Jesus Through Art*, Winchester: RE Centre.

Lowndes, J. and Erricker, C. (2007a) *Myth*, Winchester: RE Centre.

Lyotard, J.-F. (1984) *The Postmodern Condition*: *A Report on Knowledge*, Manchester: University of Manchester Press.

McFahn, R. (2009) 'Why Couldn't France Get out of Debt?' (unpublished).

Marples, R. (2006) 'Against Faith Schools: A Philosophical Argument for Children's Rights', in H. Johnson (ed.) *Reflecting on Faith Schools*, London and New York: Routledge.

Maule, J. (2006) 'Planning a Conceptual Cycle: Suffering', *Hampshire RE Secondary News*, Summer 2006, No. 46, Winchester: Hampshire County Council.

Midgley, M. (2002) *Evolution as a Religion*, London and New York: Routledge.

Mill, J. S. (1904) 'On Nature', in *Nature, the Utility of Religion and Theism*, Oxford: Watts and Co, The Rationalist Press.

Morgan, P. (2006) 'Aspects of Christianity', in Hampshire, Portsmouth and Southampton Councils, *Living Difference: The Secondary Handbook*, Winchester: Hampshire County Council.

Morgan, P. (2007) *Aspects of Christianity*, Winchester: RE Centre.

Morgan, P. (2007a) *Hats Off*, Winchester: RE Centre.

Morgan, P. (2007b) 'Introducing the Conceptual Enquiry Methodology', *Hampshire RE Secondary News*, Spring 2007, No. 47, Winchester: Hampshire County Council.

Morgan, P. (2008) 'Façade: A Cross-curricular Project at Henry Beaufort School', *Hampshire RE Secondary News*, Summer Term 2008, No. 50, Winchester: Hampshire County Council.

Morgan, P., Costambeys, R., Green, G. and Erricker, C. (2007) *Type B Concepts*, Winchester: RE Centre.

Mountbatten College RE Department (2006) 'Myth', in Hampshire, Portsmouth and Southampton Councils, *Living Difference: The Secondary Handbook*, Winchester: Hampshire County Council.

Nora, P. (1984–1992) *Les Lieux de mémoire*, 3 volumes, Paris: Gallimard; English trans. *Realms of Memory*, Chicago: University of Chicago Press.

*Observer* (2007) 'Is God Democratic?' *Review*, 30 September.

*Observer* (2007) *Television Guide*, 30 September.

O'Grady, K. (2003) 'Motivation in Religious Education: A Collaborative Investigation with Year Eight Students', *British Journal of Religious Education*, 25(3): 214–225.

Ofsted (2007) *Making Sense of Religion*, London: Crown copyright.

Ofsted (2007a) *Diversity and Citizenship Curriculum Review*, London: Crown copyright.

Omaar, R. (2007) *Only Half of Me*, London: Penguin.

Paley, W. (1802 [2008]) *Natural Theology: Or Evidence of the Existence and Attributes of the Deity, Collected from the Appearances of Nature*, Oxford: Oxford University Press.

Palmer, M. and Bisset, E. (1999) *Worlds of Difference*, London: Nelson Thornes.

Patten, B. (1985) 'Looking for Dad', in *Gargling with Jelly*, London: Puffin.

Phillips, S. (2004) *Theatre of Learning Experiential RE: Making RE Make Sense*, Bristol: SfE.

Poole, M. (2008) *Creationism, Intelligent Design and Science Education*, http://www.cis.org.uk.

Poole, M. (2009) 'What's in a Name? Creation and Creationism, Design and Intelligent Design', *Resource*, 31(3): 7–10.

Priestley, J. (2006) 'Agreed Syllabuses: Their History and Development in England and Wales, 1944–2004', in M. de Souza, G. Durka, K. Engebretson, R. Jackson and A. McGrady (eds) *International Handbook of the Religious, Moral and Spiritual Dimensions in Education*, Vol. 2, Dordrecht: Springer: 1001–1017.

Priestley, J. (2007) 'The Peace that Passes all Secular Understanding: Facing Religion and Ourselves', in J. Astley, L. J. Francis and M. Robbins (eds) *Peace or Violence: The Ends of Religion and Education?*, Cardiff: University of Wales Press: 30–45.

Pullman, P. (2004) 'The Art of Reading in Colour', in *Does God Love Democracy? Index for Free Expression*, 33(4), issue 213: 156–163.

Pullman, P. (2007) *His Dark Materials*, London: Scholastic.

QCA (2004) *The Non-statutory National Framework for Religious Education*, London: Qualifications and Curriculum Authority.

QCA (2006) *A Big Picture of the Curriculum*, London: Qualifications and Curriculum Authority (http://www.qca.org.uk/qca_13575.aspx).

QCDA (2007) *Religious Education: Programmes of Study (Non-statutory) for Key Stage 3*. London: Qualifications and Curriculum Development Agency (http://www.qcda.org.uk/curriculum).

QCDA (2009) *Religious Education: Non-statutory Programme of Learning for a Statutory Subject*, London: Qualifications and Curriculum Development Agency (http://www.qcda.gov.uk/libraryAssets/media/095654_QCA_PCR_Rel_Educ_SSS.pdf)

Ramsey, I. (ed.) (1970) *The Fourth R*, London: SPCK.

Rodinson, M. (1971) *Mohammed*, Harmondsworth: Penguin.

Rodinson, M. (1974) *Islam and Capitalism*, Harmondsworth: Penguin.

Rowling, J. K. (2007) *Harry Potter* Boxed Set, London: Bloomsburg.

Rushdie, S. (1988) *The Satanic Verses*, Harmondsworth: Penguin.

Sambrook, T. *et al.* (2006) 'Jewish Identity', in Hampshire, Portsmouth and Southampton Councils, *Living Difference: The Secondary Handbook*, Winchester: Hampshire County Council.

Sarhan, A. and Davies, C. (2008) 'My Daughter Deserved to Die for Falling in Love', *Observer*, 11 May.

Sartre, J.-P. (1971) *Nausea*, Harmondsworth: Penguin.

The Science and Religion in Schools Project (2006) *Science and Religion in Schools: A Guide to the Issues for Secondary Schools*, Manchester: Trafford Publishing.

Smart, N. (1971) *The Religious Experience of Mankind*, London: Fontana.

Smart, N. (1998) 'Foreword', in P. Connolly (ed.) *Approaches to the Study of Religion*, London: Cassell.

Southgate, C., Deane-Drummond, C., Murray, P. D., Negus, M. R., Osborn, L., Poole, M., Stewart, J. and Watts, F. (1999) *God, Humanity and the Cosmos*. Edinburgh: T&T Clark Ltd

Spencer, R. (2006) *The Truth about Muhammad*, Washington, DC: Regnery Publishing.

Spens, W. (1938) *Report of the Consultation Committee on Secondary Education*, London: HMSO.

Stern, J. (2006) *Teaching Religious Education*, London: Continuum.

Stokes, P. (2006) *Philosophy: 100 Essential Thinkers*, Foulsham: Acturus.

Stolberg, T. and Teece, G. (2008) *Religion and Science in the 21st Century Classroom*, Birmingham: University of Birmingham School of Education.

Stolberg, T. and Teece, G. (2009) *Teaching Religion and Science: Pedagogy and Practice*, London: Routledge.

Sumathi, S., Hampsapriya, T. and Surekha, P. (2008) *Evolutionary Intelligence*, Berlin and Heidelberg: Springer.

Suri, S. (2007) *Brideless in Wembley: In Search of Indian England*, Chichester: Summersdale Publishers Ltd.

Suzuki, S. (1982) *Zen Mind, Beginner's Mind*, New York and Tokyo: Weatherhill.

Swan, Lord (1985) *The Swan Report: Education for All* (Report of the Committee of Enquiry into the Education of Children from Ethnic Minority Groups), London: Her Majesty's Stationery Office.

Von Glasersfeld, E. (1995) *Radical Constructivism: A Way of Knowing and Learning*, London: Falmer Press.

Walshe, K. (2003) *Troubled People*, London: RMEP.

Webster, R. S. (2009) 'The Educative Value of Dewey's Religious Attitude for Spirituality', *International Journal of Children's Spirituality*, 14(2): 93–103.

Wedell, K. (2009) 'The Living Difference Evaluation Project Report', http://hias.hants.gov.uk/re/course/view.php?id=42.

Williams, S. (2003) 'Archives Unlimited', *TES Magazine*, 14 November, London: TSL Education Ltd (http://www.tes.co.uk/article.aspx?storycode=386792).

Wright, A. (2000) 'The Spiritual Education Project: Cultivating Spiritual and Religious Literacy through a Critical Pedagogy of Religious Education', in M. Grimmitt (ed.) *Pedagogies of Religious Education*, Great Wakering: McCrimmons: 170–187.

Wright, A. (2007) *Critical Religious Education, Multiculturalism and the Pursuit of Truth*, Cardiff: University of Wales Press.

Wright, A. (2007a) 'Hospitality and the Voice of the Other: Confronting the Economy of Violence through Religious Education', in J. Astley, L. J. Francis and M. Robbins (eds) *Peace or Violence; The Ends of Religion and Education?*, Cardiff: University of Wales Press: 64–80.

Wright, A and Brandom, A.-M. (eds) (2000) *Learning to Teach Religious Education in the Secondary School*, London: RoutledgeFalmer.

# Websites

http://www.areiac.org.uk

http://en.arocha.org/bible/index7.html

http://www.fenwicklawson.co.uk

http://www.judges.co.uk
http://www.marcusreichert.com
http://members.tripod.com/siekman
http://www.odu.edu/educ/roverbau/Bloom/blooms_taxonomy.htm
http://www.voy.com
http://en.wikipedia.org/wiki/Bhavacakra

# Index